CIRCULATING WITH THE LISTED PROBLEMS(S):

Circled page numbers and print mistakes

MPCGLB 1-2918

LITTLE HOUSE
in the Hollywood Hills

A Bad Girl's Guide
to Becoming Miss Beadle,
Mary X, and Me

*By Charlotte Stewart
and Andy Demsky*

BearManor
Media

Albany, Georgia

Published in the USA by

BearManor Media

P.O. Box 71426

Albany, GA 31708

www.BearManorMedia.com

Cover photos: (top) used by permission of Friendly Family Productions, LLC (bottom) courtesy Jeanne Field

Cover design by Michael Kavish, Kavish + Kavish
Edited by Annette Lloyd

Softcover Edition
ISBN-10: 159393906X
ISBN-13: 978-1-59393-906-9

Printed in the United States of America

Table of Contents

For Mom and Honey

Introduction

Beadle Mania

IT'S THE SUMMER OF 2014 and I'm on a getaway in sunny France, my first visit to Toulon, a serene, ancient seaside town where outdoor cafes and little shops line crooked, medieval streets. Here you find the kind of blue-sky, boats-bobbing harbor scene where you might picture Ernest Hemingway wiling away a few hours over martinis with a dark-haired mistress.

As afternoon turns into evening a beefy middle-aged guy takes notice of me, a flash of recognition in his eye. He approaches and without warning pulls me into a crushing bear hug. Then he begins to sob. Huge, whole-body sobs.

He's not hurting me, other than making it a little hard to breathe, and he doesn't seem intent on anything other than producing convulsive, big-man, French tears.

Out of the corner of my eye, I see a woman, presumably his wife, beginning to cry too and two teenage girls (daughters?) are standing nearby looking somewhat embarrassed yet surprisingly empathetic.

Finally this big guy is able to get enough breath to say in his very heavily accented voice, "You were such a... big part ... of my childhood."

So why have I found myself on the coast of France bringing a guy the size of a polar bear to near emotional collapse?

It's about a television series I was part of 40 years ago – a show about hard work, friendship, loyalty, and family, that touched the hearts of millions of viewers (and still does) each week, moved by the timeless power of community, forgiveness, and love.

Like other fans, he likely associates me with things that are authentic, traditional, simple, and good. And what a thrill to be part of that. Hollywood is bursting with actors and there are many, many others who could have been cast in the role that became mine. I feel so fortunate to know that so many people – something like three generations now – have looked to that show for some glimpse of humanity and goodness, for an idea of who parents, teachers, and mentors can be.

When I talk to fans, pose for pictures, exchange emails and, yes, receive bear hugs, I have a sense for who they'd like me to be and I try my best not to disappoint. But it doesn't always feel honest. It's something I've wrestled with. And on that very day in Toulon I'd been giving serious thought to writing a memoir – this book – that for the first time talks candidly about how I only barely survived a lot of my own mistakes, mental and moral lapses, and stupidity, and how extremely fortunate I am to have lived past the age of 40 much less to reach the age I am today.

The show I'm talking about dates to 1974. And it came to me as a gift after I'd appeared in dozens of guest roles on prime time programs such as

Gunsmoke, Hawaii Five-O, The Waltons, Mannix, My Three Sons, and as many commercials as there are stars in the sky.

My agent called one day and told me about a project Michael Landon had gotten the green light on called *Little House on the Prairie.* Would I be interested in reading for the part of a 19th century schoolmarm?

Well, this raised two questions. First, what the hell is a marm? I'd always wondered. It sounded like a combination of harm and mime. Second – and it was less a question and more a concern – I knew very little about the book series by Laura Ingalls Wilder. So while I was no expert, nothing about a nice family in Minnesota in the 1870s exactly shouted "hit TV series."

In 1974 America was in the middle of a huge cultural changing-of-the-guard that saw the era of *My Three Sons* and *Petticoat Junction* being replaced by hippies, Black Panthers, the Vietnam War (which was winding down), school busing, Old Hollywood being replaced by New Hollywood, and sex, drugs, and rock-n-roll. The world was moving in a new direction. Was there still a market for rugged, frontier stories? Yes, there was still *Gunsmoke* on Mondays at 8 pm, like a force of nature, hanging in there for its 20th season. The only other thing like *Little House* was *The Waltons,* in which I'd already filmed an appearance in the pilot episode, but no one yet knew where that one was going.

The top shows at the time were edgy and contemporary – *All in the Family, Sanford and Son,* and *Maude.* They were challenging audiences while entertaining them and were driving the network censors to their whiskey cabinets.

Any doubts I had though were offset (mostly) by Michael Landon, whom I was acquainted with from a couple of appearances on *Bonanza.* I knew him more from his work than I did personally but was well aware that he was an unusually talented guy, who could write, act, produce, direct – and – look great on a horse. Serious skills.

The other name attached to this endeavor was producer Ed Friendly, who had created the iconic *Rowan & Martin's Laugh-In,* a rapid-fire sex and politics comedy show that absolutely nailed the sensibility of the time, which had launched the careers of Lily Tomlin and Goldie Hawn, among others. Everyone wanted to be on *Laugh-In,* saints and sinners alike, including John Wayne, Billy Graham, Gore Vidal, Oral Roberts, Hugh Hefner, Ringo Starr and even Richard Nixon. How you went from Sock-It-To-Me to Walnut Grove, I wasn't sure, but Ed apparently had a plan.

I walked into Michael's and Ed's production office at Paramount Studios wearing my usual around-town outfit – bell-bottom jeans and a light, floaty top with my blonde hair long and loose. I probably looked more like I was trying out for a part on *The Partridge Family.*

In an earlier phase of my career I probably would have found a dress from the period and neatly pinned my hair up, so the producers could picture me in the part. I was confident, probably too confident, but I had a resume that stretched back to the early black-and-white days of television, when I appeared on shows such as *The Loretta Young Show* and *Bachelor Father.* I'd done drama and comedy, played teenage ditzes, saloon girls, prostitutes, girly-girls, and yes, teachers, and all sorts of other character types.

In the audition I chatted with Michael and Ed and the other producers in the room. They told me a little about the show and talked about the part of the prairie schoolteacher. As I read the script pages, I realized pretty quickly the kind of persona that was required. I asked Michael if we could trade places – if I could sit behind his desk and he could move around to the front where I was. He seemed surprised by this request but was totally game. Once behind his desk I now had all the power and arranged Michael and everyone else in the room into rows as I would with a room full of schoolchildren. At this point Michael was giggling (just like you've seen him do on the show) and there was a lot of goofing among the others and I berated them like the brats they were being, commanding them to behave and listen to their teacher.

When the audition wrapped up, I was unsure how it had gone. We'd had a lot of fun and the tone in the room was friendly but I'd been around long enough not to take that to mean anything in particular.

I drove the hour to my house in Topanga Canyon and by the time I got to my kitchen and poured myself a post-audition drink, I was stunned to get a call from my agent saying that they had officially offered me the part. Whoa. These guys didn't mess around. I would discover that Mike Landon kept everything and everyone around him moving at an explosive pace.

The one thing that distinguished this part from all others, I learned, is that it came with a four-year contract.

The life of an actor is basically uncertainty gaffer-taped to chaos, and most of the time we welcome the roller-coaster-ness of it all. But every now and then a dose of financial stability is just the thing. I was 32 and newly single – no one was paying my bills but me. Steady paychecks start to sound pretty cool in such circumstances. Besides, I thought I looked kind of hot in a prairie dress.

I happily signed on to play patient, considerate, and stable Miss Beadle and began to think through the idea of spending the next four years in a make-believe version of Walnut Grove, Minnesota circa 1870s. Damn, if all went as planned I'd be doing this role until 1978 – that sounded so far away.

I did wonder how it would go working with all those child actors. Unlike the other adults in the cast, I would be interacting almost exclusively with the cast members who were under five-feet-tall. And in the case of Melissa Gilbert well under, making the nickname "Half Pint" especially apt.

I liked kids though I'd never spent much time with them, professionally or otherwise, beyond visits with my sister's wonderful brood of seven, whom I absolutely adored. But working day to day with child actors is much different than spending Christmas with nieces and nephews you love. There's a reason there is an old adage in Hollywood that if at all possible avoid playing opposite children or animals. Kids have a reputation for being scene-stealers and their parents, always lurking just off camera, tend to be a pain. I'd just have to work hard and hope for the best.

One thing I already loved about the role, before even taking my first step onto a sound stage, was that as part of this ensemble cast, I would not be appearing in every episode and would have time to do other things I enjoyed such as playing around with my hippie clothing store on Santa Monica Boulevard called The Liquid Butterfly. This is where I made and sold tie-dye dresses, cowboy shirts, and even costumes for TV and film productions. It was also a great place to hang out with friends in the music business such as Joni Mitchell, Miles Davis, Neil Young, and my drinking buddy Jim Morrison of The Doors, along with actors, artists and weirdoes of every stripe.

Besides that, I also had a little time to play other roles. In fact I'd recently been shooting (at night) the most intriguing, surreal film I'd ever been involved in written and directed by a student filmmaker named David Lynch, who could be pretty surreal all on his own. The film had the unlikely name of *Eraserhead* and I had agreed to play the role of Mary X opposite a wild Texas genius by the name of Jack Nance. We were to have one of the most hideous and disturbing babies in film history.

From the start of *Little House*, I threw myself into the role (and blonde wig) of Miss Eva Beadle, though in the days before YouTube or even VCRs, I didn't give any thought to it having any more longevity than last month's issue of *People* magazine. Today *Little House on the Prairie* is widely considered a blockbuster, a television icon, but at the time, I don't think those of us in the cast had any idea of the impact it was making out in the wider world.

We shot at the same studio as *Happy Days*, the Ron Howard and Henry Winkler sitcom that was massively popular and was indeed having a big impact – I'm pretty sure they sold more lunch boxes and t-shirts than we did. *Little House,* by contrast, was a stable though not quite razzle-dazzle performer in the television world (neither Ringo Starr nor Hugh Hefner was vying to make an appearance), at least in terms of ratings or awards; the first season it ended in 13th place, behind shows such as *Chico and The Man, Maude* and *Rhoda.*

We were all very happy for Michael and later Melissa Gilbert when they were eventually nominated for Golden Globes but no one working in front of the camera ever walked off with a statuette. The show won four Emmys, two each for musical composition and cinematography in various years. (Tellingly, we were rather popular with *The People's Choice Awards.*) But in the fishbowl of the L.A. entertainment community, our show was considered pretty beige and benign stuff. We were corny. We were as sincere as a county fair quilt. The people who ran Hollywood weren't interested.

Cut to 40 years later. Unlike nearly all of those shows that were beating us in the ratings and the awards tally, *Little House* has never been out of syndication. It is still seen in more than 100 countries around the world and, as you read this, is on television somewhere in the U.S. or abroad, in countries like Spain where it's called *La Casa de la Pradera* or in France where it goes by the lovely name *La Petite Maison dans la Prairie* and has an unbelievably huge following. Thus, explaining the mystery of my French bear-hugger in Toulon – this was a French fan expressing his deep feelings about the show and its connection to the very foundations of his life. (He was a very sweet guy!)

The enduring popularity of the show really hit home with me in July 2014 in the actual Walnut Grove, Minnesota, where thousands of fans showed up for the show's 40th anniversary.

I was there with 11 other actors from the series and for two days remained astounded by the intense fandom and love of the people who were there from all over the country. Many stood in line for hours – in the rain – to get an autograph or a photo with a favorite cast member. These were grown people who were too nervous to speak when they met us, whose hands where too shaky to hold their own cameras for a selfie.

Never in my wildest dreams would I have imagined in the 1970s – in the waning days of the Nixon administration, when many families still had black and white TVs – that in the year 2014, I would be attending *Little House on the Prairie* conventions across the U.S. and Europe every year, meeting thousands of fans of this TV show about simple, homespun values such as friendship, patience, and love.

Like many characters on the show, Miss Beadle lived simply and worked hard.

Eventually she fell in love with a sturdy, slightly poetic frontier gentleman, a pig farmer, and she moved away from Walnut Grove to help him follow his ambitions. While not the star of the ensemble, Miss Beadle has made her mark and certainly found her way into the hearts of millions of viewers around the world.

I get a lot of weird and wonderful questions about playing the part such as which is my favorite episode? ("Troublemaker," in which Miss Beadle gets fired.) What was it like to work with Alison Arngrim, who played Nellie Oleson? (Fantastic – I adore Alison. She is a total brat!) What was it like to work with Michael Landon? (He was hard working, whip-smart, talented, drank throughout the day, never wore underwear, liked to play jokes on people and was always, definitely, in charge.) I've even been asked if I slept with Michael. The assumption being, I guess, that in Hollywood everyone sleeps with everyone else. And the answer is, I did not sleep with him; though the invitation was once made, I pretended not to notice. Or hear, or whatever. I probably handled it badly. Point is, while I was not always as picky as I should have been about whom I slept with, as you'll see, in this case, having a quickie with the boss just seemed like a bad idea.

What lots of fans ask is how much my life mirrors that of the gracious, solid Miss Beadle. And I suppose the answer is that my life has been a great deal like hers, well, except for that time I starred in a movie about venereal disease ... demonstrated my amazing talent for putting my foot in my mouth such as when I tried to bum some weed off Henry Fonda – the wrong Fonda as it turned out ... enjoyed a made-in-Hollywood love life that included a lot of flings and two marriages and divorces ... worked with artists like Gene Kelly, Elvis Presley, Rock Hudson, Peter Falk, Kyle MacLachlan, and Kevin Bacon ... drank too much, got cancer, survived the death of a spouse ... oh, and was cast as the first walk-around Alice in Wonderland at Disneyland.

Hmmm. Okay...so maybe I wasn't always much like Miss Beadle on the outside; but I do love her and find a great deal in her to admire (I'll tell you later who I based her on). And I hope that over the course of this book you'll see that somewhere inside of me were – and are, I think – some of those qualities that you saw on screen.

When my contract was up on *Little House* in 1977, I had money. More money than I'd ever known. I had a gorgeous house in the Hollywood Hills. I bought an apartment building, made lots of other investments, had a business manager to handle my finances and pay my bills, and for the first time I felt like I really didn't need to work. I stopped going to auditions and let cocaine and alcohol do their magic.

By 1984 thanks to addiction I'd lost everything, absolutely everything, including my house. I'd cut off contact with most of my friends and my family. I had to beg Jack Nance, from *Eraserhead*, to let me live with him in a building I had once owned and was among the many things I'd lost.

His place was a hoarder's paradise, filled with piles of magazines, weird knick-knacks, old books, garbage and overflowing ashtrays. Jack and I didn't do anything. We stayed in the apartment and stayed drunk and watched the Summer Olympics on TV. This might have gone on until my liver gave out except that one day Jack woke up at 7 a.m. with wild hair and a dangerous, deranged look and said to me, "You better leave, Charlotte, or we're going to go out into the desert and kill each other." I knew Jack. He meant it.

The darkness was so thick around me it felt like I could hardly breathe. And I knew I had to only two options left: change or die.

So, yes, this is a story about playing Miss Beadle in one of the most successful TV franchises ever made. And frankly I'm surprised none of the other adult cast members has written about the *Little House* experience. Fortunately there've been books by some of the kids – Alison Arngrim and her delightful *Confessions of a Prairie Bitch* as well as books by Melissa Gilbert (Laura Ingalls), and Melissa Sue Anderson (Mary Ingalls). But nothing from Katherine MacGregor (Mrs. Oleson), Victor French (Mr. Edwards) or Karen Grassle (Caroline Ingalls) all of whom have had amazing stories to tell. Even Michael Landon never wrote a book – I'm not sure why.

Likewise, no one involved in David Lynch's brilliant and ethereal *Eraserhead* or the cast of *Twin Peaks* has, to my knowledge, written a word about that experience. I hope they do.

But beyond the stories of playing Miss Beadle, this is a memoir about failures, collapses, trying to be good while enjoying being bad, aiming high and missing, and some of the general silliness of my life. It's also a backstage look at Hollywood in the 1960s, 70s, 80s, and beyond with a pretty wild cast of characters.

If I were to pitch the heart and soul of this story to a movie producer I'd say it's more than anything the story of a girl who grows up out in the country with good but damaged parents. A girl with few obvious talents yet who manages to make a success of it in the treacherous, glorious, sexed-out, drugged-up, faster pussycat wonderland of Hollywood in the 1960s and 1970s until addiction takes everything she's earned, everything she's built, and very nearly kills her. Then without missing a beat life deals her another blow – she's diagnosed with breast cancer. And with mortality shoved in her face like never before, she turns 50, starts going through menopause. And that – *that* – is when she finds love.

Any good story, as my Shakespeare teacher used to tell us at the Pasadena Playhouse, begins in a kind of paradise, descends into hell, and through tragedy and life-or-death struggle our heroine emerges transformed. Is that the shape of my story too?

I guess we'll find out.

It all begins in a peach orchard.

Chapter 1

Smoking on the Jungle Ride

MY EARLIEST MEMORIES are mostly cocktails and television.

Willis and Alice Stewart, my parents, were part of that era we now call the "Greatest Generation," who defeated the Nazis, worked very hard, raised families, went to church, subscribed to *National Geographic*, ate red meat, smoked unfiltered cigarettes, and drank like there was no tomorrow. Life for these guys seemed to have two modes. You worked stoically. You raised kids stoically. You didn't talk about bad memories or emotional turmoil. But on Friday and Saturday nights, you drank, danced, laughed, sang, told dirty jokes, made trouble, and painted the town red.

1

I was born in 1941 and so don't remember wartime itself, the rationing, the black-out curtains, Walter Winchell, and all the rest. The world I recall most vividly begins on those Friday and Saturday nights in the late 1940s and early 1950s with my mother in pearls and a shiny cocktail dress hosting a houseful of boisterous adult friends and family. The men wore dark suits and white short-sleeved shirts (the jackets came off and ended up on the back of the sofa fairly early in the evening), with their hair brilled back just so and the ladies wearing stylish figure-hugging dresses with smart jewelry and their eyebrows penciled in.

They drank hi-balls and lo-balls with names like the Sidecar, White Lady, Colorado Bulldog, Tom and Jerry, Staten Island Ferry, and Gin Rickey. If you drank whiskey it was on the rocks or straight up and you got two fingers or three fingers. Or more.

You needed a special cabinet to house your cocktail essentials – low squat glasses for brown spirits and taller, narrow glasses for clear. You needed martini glasses, little bottles of bitters, cocktail olives, pickled pearl onions, and maraschino cherries. You needed ice tongs. You had your own secret recipe for Bloody Marys.

And you had proven ways of making it through the next day. My dad's "hair of the dog" was bourbon, which he drank every morning at breakfast time. He kept cases of Jim Beam in the barn to make sure he'd never get caught short.

Alcohol was part of the secret club of adulthood along with gambling, politics, sex, and swearing. To me, alcohol was glamor. It was sophistication. It was laughter and celebration on ice. Except when it wasn't and descended into anger and chaos. Such as when my parents, who were normally good and decent to each other, would end these long party nights behind their closed bedroom door shouting and arguing drunkenly.

Years later I found out that my older sister Barbara Jean couldn't wait to go to college to escape these kinds of scenes. I had no idea they tore her up too.

I would take a pillow off my bed and lie down outside their door whispering, "Please stop … please stop …" over and over until I fell into a troubled sleep. When they fought it was my fault – so went my nine-year-old logic. If I was smarter, more obedient, or, I don't know, just a better girl, they wouldn't go at each other like this. This was partly the bewildered view a child has of the grown-up world and partly the fact that everything that happened in the world centered around me. (Yes, if you've been looking for the center of the universe, you've found it at last. Right here.)

I grew up on a 320-acre peach orchard in Yuba City, California, about 40 miles north of Sacramento, the state capitol. It was a place that hadn't been much until after the war, when the population began to boom with the building of Beale Air Force Base. My dad sold one of our three orchards for a housing development, which was called Stewart Gardens and featured street after street of identical one-bedroom stucco houses that marched away into the distance in a repeating pattern of green, yellow, pink and blue. The town continues to grow and change as all things do and today there's a Starbucks where our house once stood. You can order a Frappuccino in the space once occupied by my bedroom.

In my childhood years, I was surrounded by family of all kinds. My grandmother had a house on the same ranch as ours. Her grand old home was situated on a nearby knoll, which was fortunate because the Christmas of 1955 the levy broke on the Feather River and our area experienced massive flooding. All kinds of people came swarming over to stay in her house and I remember over the course of a couple of days eating all the food in her walk-in freezer – mostly venison from various hunting trips – while watching people in boats float past our property.

It was the kind of life where I played outdoors, rode tractors, helped feed and raise chickens, took care of our hunting dogs, climbed trees, and enjoyed big adventures in our orchards and on other neighboring farms. I had a rooster at one point, who each morning attacked my mother's prized stockings. One day the rooster was gone under mysterious circumstances and we had chicken for dinner.

For a girl who would one day play roles on outdoorsy shows like *Gunsmoke*, *The Waltons*, *Bonanza*, and *Little House on the Prairie*, it was the perfect setting in which to grow up. Of course like most kids I also liked to lose myself in television (and was part of the first generation in all of humanity to do so). My daily ritual for years was to run home from school and watch *The Mickey Mouse Club*, which featured a series called *Spin & Marty*, about two kids like me who lived on a ranch. I had a huge crush on Tim Considine who played Spin. Later he appeared on another Mickey Mouse Club Series, *The Hardy Boys*. What a dreamy dreamboat.

My parents were successful and they expected their children to excel at something in life. As it turns out my brother, Lewis, who was seven years older than me, thrived in school and eventually graduated from University of the Pacific. He would go on to be the mayor of a small town here in California later in life. My older sister, Barbara Jean, nine years my senior, similarly, was a straight-A student who was accepted into UC Berkeley. She later worked for Senator Barbara Boxer.

And me? Well .... I liked to roller-skate. And I wasn't terribly good at it.

When I was in the third grade at Sisters of Notre Dame Elementary School, my dad had taken me roller-skating at the College View Roller Rink and I fell in love with it hard and fast – the rush of speed, the camaraderie with friends, the cacophony of the wheels on the smooth wooden floor, and the raw joy a kid takes in discovering all the things that arms and legs and bodies can do. My dad was at the rink with me for every class and team practice. During open skate, he'd lace on a pair of skates too and was very graceful for such a large man. Mom tried skating but fell, bumped her knee, and that was it for her – she called it quits. But Dad was always there. When I'd look up from practice I would see my dad, the only man sitting with all the moms. I didn't think a thing about it then but I realize now how unusual it was then for a father to spend time with his daughter that way. My dad, I need to tell you, was always called Honey by my sister, brother, and me. When my sister was very young she had realized that that's the name my mom always used for him so she started calling him by that name too. My whole life he was always Honey. So there was Honey night after night watching and encouraging me.

Our roller-skate team competed around the region in events much like you see today in ice skating – singles, pairs, doubles, etc. – which required a lot of practice. Essentially it was dance on wheels. A few times we traveled to competitions in Southern California and once even in Denver.

To help pay for our travel, the team put on fund-raising exhibitions and Honey was always ready to build sets or to help out in any way. In one case the show was themed around "The Old Woman Who Lived in a Shoe." My dad built the set – a huge granny boot, which the other girls and I were able to enter and exit on our skates – and perhaps because my dad built the set, I was cast in the starring role as The Old Woman.

Honey was also responsible for my first brush with honest-to-God celebrity, which intertwined with my love of roller-skating. He owned a duck blind down in the Sacramento Delta where he and his buddies would go during the season to drink and swap stories and once in a while they'd shoot a duck. Well, apparently in the world of duck blinds this was a pretty good one because people would rent it from him; one weekend one of those renters was the famous singing cowboy Roy Rogers.

One day after roller-skating practice my dad told me that Roy Rogers was at our farmhouse. Wait – what? Roy Rogers? In Yuba City?! At our house?!?

It felt like 85 million volts of electricity shot through me.

Honey drove the car up the driveway and there was he was, Roy Rogers, an actual movie star standing in our front yard, and I was too excited to take my skates off. I burst out of the car and did an instant face-plant in our gravel driveway. I was so humiliated that I clomped tearfully into the house, refusing to come out and thus never met my idol (and more-or-less setting a lifelong pattern with me and celebrities).

Other than roller-skating I found that I was pretty good at, of all things, radio. During my high school years my best friends were nearly all guys who, like me, loved *Mad* magazine, and sports and goofing off. Two of these guys, Dick Catlett and Ben Price, hosted a Saturday radio show called "Teen Time"

on the local ABC affiliate. One summer the guys called and asked if I'd like
to take over the show as they were moving on to college. Are you kidding?
Me and a microphone? Of course I said yes and while it was a ton of work, it
was also lots of fun. I had an hour and a half to fill each week, plus had to find
sponsors for the show. The part I loved most is that it offered the chance to
meet and interview musicians in town for a day or two, directors and actors,
who were traveling with a show, local entertainers, and others who gave me a
glimpse of the gypsy-like world of performers.

Unfortunately none of this really seemed to solve the looming problem of
my future. I wasn't academic, as they say. The parts of school in which I excelled
were spending time with friends and being in clubs. Reading, remembering
the dates of battles, doing math, taking notes, and paying attention – those
were the elements of education that didn't go so well. As I got older I learned
to dread revealing my report card to my mom and dad.

I wasn't stupid, was I?

It would have been nice to know then that one day I would play a kind,
empathetic school teacher on television and this all would be great emotional
material to draw from. I knew intimately what it felt like to flounder hopelessly
in reading, writing and arithmetic – and to so desperately not want to feel like
the village idiot.

The sense of not being good enough that emerged in my teenage years
would become the tape that would play in my head, forming my worst
decisions, and shaping my unhealthiest relationships for decades.

As my high school years neared their end, I didn't have the grades to go to
college – not a good college anyway, certainly nothing like UC Berkeley. And
yet I knew I wouldn't, shouldn't, couldn't stay in Yuba City.

I felt embarrassed and thought I'd let my parents down. Both my siblings
had distinguished themselves in so many ways. What was I going to do?

I flummoxed around for all sorts of ideas and possibilities and kept
coming up dry until eventually my eyes fell on an advertisement in the back
of *Seventeen* magazine for the College of Theater Arts at Pasadena Playhouse.
I looked on a map and realized that Pasadena was basically Los Angeles and

Los Angeles was, as far as I was concerned, Hollywood. Well, that sounded promising. And I liked the term "theater arts." I'd been on-stage (sort of) with my roller-skating team and on radio with some, though not unbridled, success. People had said I was good. Not great. But good. But, come on, surely learning to act was something I could do. Right? God I hoped so.

Without a word to anyone – especially my parents – I sent off for an application and when it arrived, I filled it out, and mailed it back.

Then I asked permission.

Pretending it was something I'd just found, I showed the advertisement to my mother, who had a very different reaction. She thought a theater school sounded like a den of iniquity. (This happened to be among its top selling points as far as I was concerned, though kept that to myself.) I begged to go. I brought up the subject in a thousand ways. I worked on Honey, who, in his quiet fashion indicated that I needed to be working on my mom instead. Somehow I talked her into at least looking into it.

We flew down to Burbank, rented a car, and drove to the Playhouse, which still sits in the heart of old town Pasadena, a large, lovely Spanish mission style fortress on a quiet side street. I wonder now if that first impression helped soften my mother's heart. We were Catholic and it really did look like at any moment a saintly Father Don Francisco would emerge out the front door with a white dove in one hand and a chastity belt in the other.

I'm guessing Mom was a bit stunned then to be met by Bea Hassell, one of the teachers, a short woman half of whom was made of a poof of wild red-dyed hair tied up in colorful scarves and who completed this look with lots of bling-y, jangly bracelets and bangles. She was cheerful, brightly-lipsticked, tirelessly theatrical and knew how to wear a pair of wedges. The whole of Yuba City contained not one single such person. But for all her eccentricities, Bea must have read my mom. She showed us the classrooms, theater spaces, and dormitory. The curriculum, it turned out, was intensive. Students were in classes all day in dance, movement, acting, fencing, diction, Shakespeare studies, theater history, and more. It was the first school on the West Coast to integrate theater-in-the-round and to offer classes in television production, both in front of and behind the camera. In the end my mother was impressed. It was a terrific program and seemed exceedingly well run.

Once the Playhouse passed the "mom test," the dad test was easy. The dad test was basically passing the mom test.

When my parents asked about filling out an application, I let them know that that was already taken care of, fudging the timeline in such a way that I appeared to have been proactive rather than devious.

So I was in. At long last I had a plan for my future. I was going to be an actress.

Going public with this information in Yuba City, in the late 1950s, was a bit like announcing that you're going to strap on a pair of homemade wings and flap your way to Mars. What I got was a lot of very polite skepticism. People from our town went to movies, they weren't in them. Nor were they empty-headed and ridiculous enough to ever wish to be. I could almost hear the eye-rolls.

I suppose too this reflected poorly on my parents. As the baby of the family, they'd always treated me with a far looser approach than my older brother and sister. When I was sixteen I took our Mercury station wagon filled with high school friends out to, what I told my parents, was a night at the movies. Instead we drove out to Burris Ranch, a shit-kicking cowboy bar, for an evening of music and dancing. On the way home I missed a curve, shot across the highway, smashed through a billboard and sailed down an embankment. Everyone was fine – miraculously – but the car was totaled and I was in big trouble. My dad blustered and fumed that I'd never drive a family car again. Well, when they bought their new Country Squire station wagon, guess who was the first behind the wheel? Yep. Miss Charlotte.

So the fact that they were going to now fund their indulged, air-head daughter – the roller-skater who could barely roller skate – the one with no prospects and a C-average – to follow her little theater pipe dream? That could not have looked good. I don't doubt that there was a fair amount of incredulous head shaking and tongue clucking at my mom's bridge games or among my dad's drinking buddies.

In early September I packed up, said *hasta la vista* to Yuba City, made the eight-hour drive down Hwy 99 through California's Central Valley, and with the help of my parents moved into the women's dormitory at the Pasadena Playhouse.

My first stint on a school stage was for an audition scene in which I was assigned a role in the ancient Greek play, *Lysistrata* (which I thought was a tragedy; later I learned it's a comedy). I knew nothing about Greek theater; the only acting I'd ever seen was on TV and in movies; it was people like Danny Kaye cavorting for the camera or Cyd Charisse looking cool and amazing. It was TV shows like *Spin and Marty* with kids who looked and sounded like me and my friends, where people used a normal speaking voice, along with gestures and body language that felt natural and familiar. Not so with the Greeks apparently. There I was on stage in a breezy toga shouting lines that meant nothing to me (I might as well have been doing it in the original language) and making what I thought were the requisite stiff, stage-y, statue-like gestures.

Afterwards, a teacher, Ruth Lane, took me aside and said gently but with alarming conviction, "I don't think this is for you."

"This" did not mean "this scene" or "this role" or "or this toga" or "this particular audition."

"This" meant "acting."

I don't think acting is for you.

You know that thing around which you have based your entire future? Well – you don't have it.

Her words were the piano that falls on an unsuspecting cartoon character. I was crushed under their weight. Here I was in my first weeks at a school for acting being told I didn't have the basic tools. I didn't have any clay they could mold something into. What was I going to do? The idea of returning to Yuba City having learned a lesson in aiming too high was not going to happen.

I lay in bed that night feeling alone, inadequate, stupid, and desperate; there came wave after wave of the thought 'I'm not good enough.' I cried and railed about the unfairness of it all – as kids do. I was furious and humiliated.

More than anything I was in a panic; I had no alternatives, nothing to fall back on.

As it happens, having no Plan B can be very motivating.

By morning I had a strategy: I would refuse to go. My parents had already paid for the first semester, I reasoned, and the school surely wouldn't throw me to the sidewalk. Would they?

We'd find out.

As though nothing had happened, I kept attending classes, learning and absorbing as much as I could, throwing myself into life at the Playhouse and a month later I had another audition scene, this time for a play called *Street Scene*. In contrast to *Lysistrata*, this was a modern play in which I read the part of a girl my age. She sounded like me; she felt things I felt. I knew how to wear her clothes, I knew how flirt like she did, how to react with anger, to cry, and to fall in love. And guess what? I didn't suck.

This time no one spoke of my leaving the program. In fact at an assembly a few days afterward I was announced as the student who had shown "Most Improvement." I could have viewed this as a back-handed compliment, I suppose, but I was just so filled with relief, I could only see it as the lifting of a dark cloud.

The Pasadena Playhouse became a place I truly and completely loved. Looking back I feel so fortunate to have been part of this legendary place where some of the best actors, dancers, models, directors, and other entertainment business people emerged in this era. If you love TV and film from the 1970s and 1980s, this is where a lot of it came from. Rue McClanahan, who would later be known for her role on *The Golden Girls*, was a year ahead of me. Gene Hackman and Dustin Hoffman had just left prior to my arrival to pursue their careers. I became lifelong friends with scads of classmates including Stuart Margolin, who later played Angel on *The Rockford Files* and has more than 100 credits acting in TV and film roles and more than 50 credits behind the camera as a director. There's Bill McKinney, a nice southern boy who drank hot sauce like Pepsi and who one day became widely known as the most psychotic redneck in film history in *Deliverance*. Bill also appeared in a lot of Clint Eastwood's films. Another friend, and one of Bill's roommates, was a guy who eventually went by just one name, Mako, and won an Academy Award for his role in *The Sand Pebbles*. Sid Haig was part of this group. If you love horror movies you've seen Sid in *The Devil's Rejects*, *Halloween*, one of the *Night of the Living Dead* movies and lots of TV appearances. And there's Josh Bryant, whose list of acting credits is as long as a phone book including several appearances on *Little House on the Prairie* that are close to my heart.

The alumni includes world-class talent such as Leonard Nimoy, Nick Nolte, Sally Struthers, Charles Bronson and Raymond Burr. In my second year I also befriended a guy named David Banks, who realized that acting wasn't his thing but went on be the tour manager for *The Rocky Horror Picture Show*, the pop group The Manhattan Transfer, and so on. He started dating my roommate, Lydia, and shows up later in this book. (Tuck that name away.)

Because of the rich pool of talent at the school (willing to work for next to nothing), entertainment companies would come to the Playhouse with all kinds of job offers. In the fall of that first year, a gentleman from Disneyland showed up to hire students to play characters in the park – Minnie and Mickey Mouse, Pluto, Chip and Dale and, most exciting of all to me, Alice in Wonderland. This was an idea they were trying out for the first time – having live walk-around film characters who would interact with park visitors.

I lobbied him for the part of Alice in Wonderland, following him around the school, not leaving him alone. Not only was I a former Mickey Mouse Club fan who had dreamed of going to Disneyland since the day it opened, I knew what made Alice special – she was one of the few female bad-asses in the world of Disney. She was a girl who made her way through a wild, dangerous adventure – went on her own, made her own mistakes, solved her own problems, and wasn't rescued by anybody. I wanted this part!

The problem with my playing Alice, as the man from Disney patiently pointed out, was that I had a short blond shag that looked nothing like the character. No problem. I swore I'd get a hairpiece and make it work. Finally, he relented. I had the job of Alice and needed to report to the Anaheim headquarters on December 20 for a two-week holiday stint along with several other students playing the other roles.

Most of the characters were to wear the Ice Capades costumes, except for me. I would dress in the Alice uniform already made for the staffers on the new Alice in Wonderland ride.

But first, I needed hair. A trip to Woolworths in Pasadena provided an almost matching ponytail that would do by pinning my very short hair back and hiding the pins with a large black bow.

Off to Anaheim.

We arrived at an employee parking lot on the appointed day and found our way into a building that housed wardrobe, employee lockers, lounges and so forth. Once I was in my Alice pinafore I got the full details of the job.

As a walk-around character of the fairytale variety my strict instructions were to stay within the boundaries of Fantasyland, which kept me near things like the recently unveiled Alice in Wonderland ride (naturally), Dumbo Flying Elephant, and Midget Autopia, as it was then known. What a dream gig – greeting visitors from all over the world, making friendly conversation, waving, and posing for pictures with many, many children. By the end of the first day my face ached from smiling. I spent the ride back to Pasadena massaging my lips and cheeks along with facial muscles I didn't know existed. Second day the same thing; however, I began to realize it all came with the added bonus that I was allowed to go on all the rides and could take whomever I wanted along with me. This may not sound like much of a superpower today, but in the late 1950s it was like being a fairy godmother. Disneyland charged an admission fee of $1.50 per person and then you bought a booklet with A, B, C, and D tickets, which allowed you onto various rides and attractions. Once you'd used your tickets – especially the D ticket, which was the hot one – your options were A) buy more tickets or B) wander around the park looking sad wishing you could. I learned by that second day to recognize the forlorn expression of children whose parents couldn't afford more tickets. I would see a family gazing wistfully at, say the Mad Hatters Tea Cups and I would scoop up the kids and take them with me. Man, Alice was a hero.

(For you die-heard Disneyland fans I should mention that the D-ticket was indeed the hot one until the legendary E-ticket made its debut in 1959.)

This went on day after day. I loved it. Occasionally after my shift was over, I changed back into my street clothes and walked over to Main Street to check out the bakery for goodies to take home to my roommates. Forgetting I was "out of uniform" I would continue to wave and smile at visitors – as I had all day as Alice – and of course people would look at me as if I were bonkers.

Once during my shift I took a smoke break with my Playhouse friends and other employees behind the firehouse, the front of which faces Main Street. There were strict rules about smoking for employees, designed to keep it well away from the eyes of guests. As I stood there making small talk, up drove a black limousine, and out of the back stepped the man himself Walt Disney. He was smoking too and gave us a smile, heading inside. I learned that he had an apartment inside the firehouse and stayed there often as he liked to personally keep an eye on things. In fact, word was that at night after the park closed Walt Disney would walk around and enjoy the place all to himself. I pictured him in his pajamas wandering through Fantasyland like an overgrown kid turning on the carousel and taking a ride caught up in the fun of his personal magical kingdom. I think the fact that he took personal pleasure in the park is what made Disneyland Disneyland. It wasn't a corporate product. It was the dream-come-true of one man who chose to share it with the world.

Every December, Walt Disney hosted the fabulous Christmas Parade live on national television. I traveled through the park with the parade arm in arm with "The White Rabbit" (played by another Pasadena Playhouse friend) and as we waved to the TV cameras – and thus my first appearance in front of millions of home viewers – my carefully pinned Woolworths ponytail fell to the street. I artfully scooped it up and danced away reattaching it as best I could. "Nice move," muttered the rabbit.

Just before New Year's, the Iowa Hawkeyes football team was in Pasadena for the Rose Bowl game. I was asked to escort a few players, including the star running back Ray Jauch, around Fantasyland, which I happily did and, daringly, took them on the Jungle Ride, which, being Adventureland, was totally off limits to the animated characters. And not satisfied with breaking just one rule, and feeling like a show-off, once the ride starting chugging away, I decided it was perfect time for a smoke. I kicked up my Alice shoes and lit up a Winston as we steamed past the elephants.

I realized the gravity of my mistake when I saw a child staring with big, bewildered eyes at Alice puffing away like a Teamster.

Afterward I had New Year's Eve off and was invited to a big Hollywood party by a student who was a year ahead of me. Malcolm Cassel was already a "working actor," having appeared as one of the children in *Cheaper by the Dozen*, the Clifton Webb classic. I was dolled up in high heels, a borrowed cocktail dress, and dripping with rhinestones.

We stopped on the way at DuPars Café to grab a bite before the party and as I made my way across the restaurant I heard a voice call out, "ALICIA!" There sat a family who had seen and remembered me from Disneyland a week previous. I had taken the children on a Fantasyland ride a few days before. The father took my hand and in broken English said, "You made Christmas for my family." I felt tears starting to loosen my false eyelashes.

Wow. So, I'd traumatized one kid on the Jungle Ride and had brought Christmas joy to others. Hopefully it all balanced out.

It was a wonderful two weeks as Disneyland's first walk-around Alice. At a big $1.75 an hour I'd earned my Social Security card and was moving up in the world of entertainment!

Not long after Disneyland, I was contacted by the people running the Miss USA organization, as they needed a "Miss Yuba City" to take part in the Miss California portion of the competition. We were all just going to pretend that I had somehow earned the title, obviously a much vied-for position of prominence.

Even though I'd been asked to participate, it came with a catch – I still had to be "sponsored," ideally by the city my face and figure would be representing. My parents went to the Yuba City Council to secure the $150 sponsorship and were turned down flat. I learned years later that my dad finally just wrote the check himself.

To pull off this charade I would need an intensive course in "charm," learning how to sit, stand, and speak – it's as much like dog training as it sounds. I signed up for a fast-track session at a Hollywood charm school and quickly learned the finer points of how to walk down stairs in high heels without looking (scary) and how to pose on stage with shoulders sideways, hips turned, left shoe pointed just so.

To make it all look legitimate I had to drive to the Burbank airport for my arrival photo – the official narrative being that girls from all over the state were just landing for the big event. The jet was parked and the stairway to the tarmac was in place. I had to dash up the stairs into the plane and then turn back around and be photographed "arriving" in Los Angeles fresh from Yuba City for the competition, hat box in hand.

Next I had to move into a dormitory where the 50 contestants were staying – and could be protected from scandal – until the night of the official competition on June 27, 1959 in Burbank's Starlight Bowl.

Even though the whole set-up was as phony as a padded bra, I took it seriously, parading about in my modest, low-hipped bathing suit and then striking poses in the evening gown competition, cheered on by my boys from the Playhouse. I was actually really proud to make it to the semi-finals – not bad for a girl who'd never even *been* to a beauty pageant in her whole life.

All in all it was a bit like the Alice role in that I wore a costume and did lots of smiling and waving. Ultimately, while I was more than happy to play the role of Yuba City's most alluring beauty, it wasn't quite what I had in mind for my career.

The day after the competition, I took one look at my over-sprayed, horribly teased and combed hair and had it all chopped off, ending up with a smart, little Pixie cut. Meanwhile I'd gotten a call from Maxine Anderson, a casting director specializing in advertising; she'd seen me at the Miss California event and wanted to discuss some possible work. When I walked into her office she took one look and said, "What did you do to your hair?" She shook her head and said come back in a year – which I did. Maxine was as good as her word and set me up for a photo shoot for Toni Home Permanent, to appear in a booklet that came with the product's packaging featuring a number of trendy hairstyles. Not only did I make it into the book, but without my knowing, the book was used in a TV commercial where it was opened to the page that bore my photo. As a result one day I picked up my mail and found a residual check – my first ever – and I had no idea what it was for.

It felt as though I was inching toward my dream of being a working actor – dancing at the outer edges of the entertainment universe. At school I was always checking notices for work opportunities and finally read about an audition for a female lead in a low-budget film called *Damaged Goods*, about teenagers and the danger of venereal disease. I cast my Miss Yuba City tiara aside and went for it.

If sexually transmitted disease was my way into Hollywood, so be it.

Chapter 2
Damaged Goods

THE AUDITION FOR THE ROLE of Judy Jackson was in a motel room in West Hollywood, where producer Sid Davis had set up an office. I went in, read the lines and got the part. Sid told me that I needed to secure an agent and could likely get one just a couple of doors down. I took his suggestion and indeed found a small talent agency, where they also signed me up on the spot. In a single day I had landed a film role and an agent. I thought I'd explode with excitement.

The three weeks I spent making *Damaged Goods* (also released under the charming name "VD") was a huge learning curve. At the Pasadena Playhouse our on-camera training was in front of a single, stationary television camera, like the ones used at that time on a broadcast of the evening news. Shooting in a small studio with a stationary camera is completely different than shooting on, say, a rollercoaster – which we did – or in a speeding car or at a high school track. I had to simultaneously remember lines, hit my mark, not bump into things, keep in mind where the camera was, and know where my light was, all at the same time. Oh, and act.

The opening scene in the film has my character and her boyfriend, played by Mory Schoolhouse, blazing around Los Angeles in a cream-colored 1958 Triumph convertible. The camera shoots behind us, beside us, in front, and we're even chased by the police because we're teenagers and obviously a menace to civilized society. Finally we're parked at a lover's lane, making out – acting can be such fun. (Spoiler alert: I'm not the one who gets venereal disease.) I had a tremendous crush on Mory during filming. I'd flirt with him, sit beside him during lighting set-ups, and try to coax him down a conversational path that would lead to him inviting me over to his place. But I was 18 and he was about 22 or 23. In real life he was all motorcycles, leather jackets, drugs and alcohol. He finally said, "You need to stay away from me, I'll only get you in trouble." Well, trouble is exactly what I was looking for but Mory refused to help. Looking back it was fortunate that he was adamant about keeping me at arm's length. A few years later I heard that he'd died of an overdose.

Filming *Damaged Goods* was also my introduction to something that would happen many times afterward. You work on a film like this together for three weeks – three intense weeks – the actors, director, producers and crew. The days are long; the work can be difficult, especially if things are going wrong with lights or equipment. It's that phenomenon of having a shared mission, a common purpose; it's that small band of pirates against all the forces that would kill this project off. It's one for all and all for one. You bond, friendships are formed, romances spark – and then the film wraps and everyone moves on to their next project and you lose touch.

I liked everyone, both personally and professionally, on *Damaged Goods* and when we finished I thought we'd all stay in touch and get together often and be great friends. It didn't happen. And such is the life of an actor. There can be tears but there's also a lot of joy in it. You get the best (and occasionally worst) of people – very open, creative, electrifying people. Making a film can be a close, passionate interaction—and then it's over.

I didn't hear much from anyone back home in Yuba City about my first foray into the movie business. But I learned years later from a friend of my dad's that *Damaged Goods* had a weeklong run at the Yuba City drive-in and my dad was there every night watching in his pick-up.

While Mory Schoolhouse had turned me away, back at school I found others perfectly willing to help me get in trouble. A group of guys who studied at the Pasadena Playhouse lived in a house together that acquired the name Heartbreak Hotel. This was Bill McKinney and Mako, who I mentioned earlier, and a third guy, Carl Munson. Oh my, I thought Carl Munson was so hot. My roommate Lydia and I and other kids would party frequently at the Heartbreak Hotel. And one night after a lot of drinking Carl pulled me upstairs, we flopped on a bed, and about 30 seconds later I'd officially lost my virginity.

"What the hell?" I thought, "That was *it*? That's all there is?"

Sex had come with such a long, huge, myth-sized build-up – all the late night talks with other girls, all the years of wondering what it was like, and all the scheming to make it happen. I'd always figured it to be like skydiving while eating a birthday cake and painting the Mona Lisa.

In fact it all came down to a few seconds of being wrestled around on some college guy's stale, unmade bed.

"So now I'm a woman," I thought.

I soon learned though that sex is like playing the tuba – to get really good it's practice, practice, practice. And as with most things I had a highly developed worth ethic.

Likewise by my second year at the Playhouse, all the work I'd put in was paying off, securing lead roles in plays, including performances for the paying public. (A lot of the work up to that point had been part of the school curriculum and was seen only by teachers and fellow students.)

Even better, as *Damaged Good* wrapped, I started reading for parts on television and was being sent out for advertising work.

I was thrilled beyond words when my agent called and said I'd nailed down a role on an episode of *The Loretta Young Show*. While not a show you hear much about today, it was a big hit at the time. NBC aired episodes twice, first in its evening primetime slot and again in the afternoon, when it could be enjoyed by its core female audience.

Each episode started with Loretta Young, a film star from Hollywood's golden age, making a glamorous entrance in a swirling gown and introducing that week's story —always an inspirational tale in which a woman learned an important life lesson. Loretta was a strict Catholic and a renowned tight-ass, who would fine crew members for swearing. (It was also pretty well known in Hollywood that during the shooting of the 1935 film *Call of the Wild* Clark Gable had sired her daughter, Judy Lewis, whom Loretta had claimed for years was adopted. The rest of America would not learn this until 2000, when Young allowed her authorized biography to be published after her death.)

The show was produced at Samuel Goldwyn Studios on the corner of Formosa Avenue and Santa Monica Blvd in West Hollywood, on a lot originally owned by Mary Pickford and Douglas Fairbanks as United Artists, where countless great old movies had been shot.

My call time was 6 a.m. for hair and makeup and we started shooting at 8 a.m. The director walked us through our blocking, the crew lit the scene, and we were off and running.

My character on that first episode was a girl who attends Alateen (Alcoholics Anonymous for teenagers) for support because her mother is an alcoholic. As such the first lines I ever spoke on television were:

God grant me the serenity to accept the things I cannot change,
The courage to change the things I can,
And the wisdom to know the difference.

It's the "Serenity Prayer," an important mantra in addiction recovery, and the fact that these were my first lines on television was something that would seem supremely ironic years later.

The actress playing my mother, Audrey Totter, who in real life didn't touch alcohol at all, was brilliant at playing drunk. I watched her as we filmed, so impressed at the subtle touches she brought to her performance. Playing drunk convincingly is often under-playing it, and she was one of the best.

As a young actor I had a lot to learn. The three weeks on *Damaged Goods* had taught me a few basics such as hitting my mark, which can be a bit of a trick. Before a scene is filmed you typically first block it – meaning the director has you physically walk or go through the movements. This gets the actors and the cinematographer (camera operator) on the same page in terms of what's going to happen while the camera's rolling. The cinematographer needs to make sure the lighting and camera set-up throughout the scene are going to work and the actor needs to make sure not to wander out of camera range or to lose their light. If you're just standing or sitting in one place then that's pretty simple. But a lot of scenes ask the actor to walk a few feet and then stop at some point. Where you stop needs to be a fixed distance from the camera lens so that you'll be in focus. Where you're supposed to stop is marked on the floor with an X of something, like black electrical tape. The trick to hitting your mark is that you need to be able to get there without looking at it, although I see actors all the time who to my eye are pretty obviously searching the floor for that X.

I got pretty good at hitting my mark and throughout the years I'd show others who were new to it how it was done. On the movie *Tremors*, in the late 1980s, I taught country music singer Reba McEntire how to hit her mark – she was a quick study. The trick is to keep it in your peripheral vision without betraying that to the all-seeing eye of the camera.

Beyond these kinds of basics came a whole other level of understanding of how a scene is shot. Among my first scenes on that episode was at the family dinner table, in which we were served a beef stew prepared by one of the prop guys. It smelled unbearably delicious and I was starved. The director said "Action" and I dug in with gusto not realizing that I'd have to match those actions (shoveling food into my mouth) while we continued to shoot and re-shoot the scene, meaning that the prop guy kept refilling my bowl and I had to keep eating and eating and eating – for four hours. I thought I was going to explode. You'll notice that when experienced actors are sitting around a dinner table they move their forks around, they cut their meat, they might even lift a spoon as though about to take a bite but in most cases they eat next to nothing. Of course there are exceptions. Once on a TV commercial I was directed to give the featured burger a big chomp and just off camera there sat a bucket that let me spit out each bite over the hours of filming.

While I was doing that episode, shooting at the same time on the Goldwyn lot on a different sound stage was the glorious, sprawling musical *West Side Story*. Every day at lunchtime the commissary (the studio cafeteria) was packed with sexy young singers, dancers, and actors. In the lunch line I made sure to strike up a conversation with a lean, dark-haired guy who was so insanely good looking I thought I'd die, an actor I recognized from a couple of previous films. His name was Richard Beymer, one of the *West Side Story* leads, and a guy I would know, as it turns out, for a long, long time – eventually working together 30 years down the road on *Twin Peaks*, where he played Benjamin Horne. He was another one who was brilliant at getting me into trouble – but that would come later.

My agent found loads of advertising work for me – everything from Olympia beer to Head & Shoulders shampoo to one of my favorites, a magazine ad for a product called "Wate-On," a diet supplement that gave skinny girls the womanly curves they so urgently yearn for.

To get my face and name out there, I hired a publicity agent who landed me in magazines such as *Teen Screen, Teen World, Celebrity Hairdos*, and *Teen Life*. I'd go on PR-engineered dates for the cameras with other young performers and we'd have a great time. These fake romantic outings – such as one I had with heartthrob singer Bobby Vinton – would grace the magazines of various teen magazines and make young hearts across the country dream of Hollywood. The name of the game was getting your name and photo in print as often as possible. To that end there were countless rounds of publicity appearances, such as being a cigarette girl at this or that charity ball. I was at the same events with girls such as Stefanie Powers, later of the show *Hart to Hart*, and Linda Evans, who went on to star in *The Big Valley* and in *Dynasty*. We were all out there hoofing it to get our careers off the ground. For a while I was doing ten times more publicity for my acting career than I was actually acting, my face showing up in everything from *TV Guide* to *Mechanix Illustrated*.

About this time, my agent gave me news that rocked my world – I'd been hired for a guest role on the hugely popular show on ABC, *My Three* Sons (it later moved to CBS in 1965 when the show went from black and white to color). Not only would a part like this give me great exposure, it'd give me the chance to work with actors I'd long idolized. Growing up watching *I Love Lucy* I was thrilled at the chance to work with William Frawley, who had been Lucy and Ricky's neighbor Fred Mertz and was now in the cast of *My Three Sons*. The other was one I'd had a crush on for such a long time – since the days I'd rush home from elementary school and plop down in front of the TV to watch *The Adventures of Spin and Marty* – I'm talking about the dreamy Tim Considine.

A few days before my gig on *My Three Sons* a friend invited me along to a big birthday party in the Hollywood Hills for the singer Dinah Washington, who unfortunately died far too young. If you don't know her music, do yourself a favor and find it online. You can thank me later. The party was pure magic – there I was listening to Sam Cook and Ella Fitzgerald sing happy birthday to Dinah. And as I looked across the huge, grand piano, there on the far side stood Tim Considine. With his date. He was looking straight at me. Like he was burning laser beams through me with his eyes. Well, how could I miss this opportunity? I edged around the piano, politely elbowing and excusing myself, until I was next to him and introduced myself and said we'd be working together in a few days. He seemed delighted and we chatted for a few minutes in a completely normal, sociable way while inside my head I was screaming, "I'm talking to Tim Considine!"

Getting the chance to work on *My Three Sons* would do more than give me a career boost and a chance to meet a couple of my idols. It would upend my entire world.

Chapter 3

Tim and Elvis

MY THREE SONS FILMED AT DESILU STUDIOS, a production facility that had originally been the legendary RKO studios until Lucille Ball and Desi Arnaz purchased it in 1957. The husband and wife team, whom I'd grown up revering on *I Love Lucy*, turned it into the biggest independent studio in Hollywood, pioneering a lot of what we know today as standard practice in television such as use of multi cameras, filming in front of a live audience, and the idea of syndication. Desilu produced some of the biggest hits of the time: *The Andy Griffith Show*, *Mission: Impossible*, *Hogan's Heroes*, *The Lucy Show*, and *The Dick Van Dyke Show*. When Lucy and Desi divorced in 1960, she ended up with the studio and proved that not only was she one of Hollywood's most gifted comediennes, but was also a savvy producer and business person. Here's some great Lucy trivia – against a lot of advice to the contrary, she gave Gene Roddenberry the green light for *Star Trek*. And she produced its first season.

Eventually Desilu was purchased by Paramount Studios – which it neighbored – and was swallowed up in its sprawling campus. A decade later I'd be back on the former Desilu grounds in sound stages 30 and 31 filming *Little House on the Prairie*.

On that first day on *My Three Sons*, at 6 am I drove into the Gower Street entrance and went into hair and make-up. I'd memorized my lines and was ready to go. Before filming started that day though there was a lull and I went outside into a courtyard where I saw an extremely nervous young actor. He told me it was his first TV role, his first day on a sound stage, and he looked like he was going to throw up. I told him he'd be fine and offered to run lines. You'd never know today that Beau Bridges had ever experienced a moment of anxiety in his life, he's so often cast as a loveable laid-back guy. But we're all young and terrified once.

Back on the set it was a real treat to work with the cast and crew of the show, especially, as I'd anticipated, with William Frawley, who played the show's grandfather Bub O'Casey. Bill was a grouchy, foul-mouthed old son of a bitch, whom I came to adore. We didn't have any scenes together but there's a lot of down time on a set and you get to know the other actors. During filming on this and other episodes I was later on, we'd go to lunch together at Nicodell on Melrose, where everyone from Paramount had eaten since the 1930s. He always entered through the kitchen and there was perpetually a red-leather booth waiting for him. He'd glare at the waitress over the menu and shoot his mouth off with stuff like, "What kinda goddamn slop are you gonna poison me with today?" Under all that he was a sweetheart. My parents visited the set once while we were filming an episode a year or two later and Bill was so kind to them. I have a black and white photograph of Bill with my mom, dad, and me. It's one of my most treasured mementos.

Then, of course, there was Tim Considine. Tim had grown up in Beverly Hills, an enclave of wealth and privilege that made Yuba City feel like the Ozarks, and had been famous most of his life. Before showing up on millions of TV sets around the country on *My Three Sons* each week, he'd come though the Disney star-making machine, appearing in a couple of Disney films including *The Shaggy Dog* in which he played opposite Fred MacMurray (as he did on *My Three Sons)*. Of course before that he starred in two long-running serials on *The Mickey Mouse Club.*

For the world's first generation of kids who grew up on television, Tim was a big deal. He had the honest face of American boyhood, straight out of a Norman Rockwell painting. He played decency, tenacity, and friendship with a touch of twinkly mischievousness that every kid growing up in the '50s hoped to embody. There wasn't a mother in the country who wouldn't die to have their daughter on the arm of Tim Considine.

One of the first scenes I shot on that episode of *My Three Sons* was with Beau Bridges and Tim. I played Agnes, a dreamy girl who had landed in the sports department of the high school newspaper and hoped to write her stories in the form of poems. Beau was a kid who was trying to get out of doing any work at all and Tim's Mike Douglas character was attempting to organize our efforts as sports editor. It was fun, goofy material and I had a wonderful time. (You can find this episode, called "Deadline," on YouTube.)

I really liked Tim. Well, I more than liked him. I had a huge crush on him and tried to figure out how to get his attention. I was only going to be on set for about three days so I didn't have a lot of time to make an impression.

The set for the Douglas home was all in one area of the sound stage and at one point during a break I went into one of the bedrooms and laid down on one of the beds. (I could have just as easily relaxed by plopping down in one of the living room chairs or in one of the chairs provided off the set.) This was – let's just be honest – a total girl move. I spread myself out alluringly (or so I imagined) on the bed cover and pretended to take a nap, knowing that Tim and another guy were nearby. As I'd hoped, they wandered into the bedroom, where I'd laid my trap. Thinking I was asleep they stood at the end of the bed whispering to each other about me – apparently they liked what they saw. I continued to snooze, sweetly oblivious to their admiration.

This was truly acting.

Okay, as amateur-hour as this may have been, something worked because not long after I shot that episode, the telephone rang at my little one-bedroom apartment in Burbank. It was Tim calling to ask if I wanted to go out. I don't remember what we did or where we went on that first date or even of the ones that followed soon after, I can only remember the feeling of it all, which was totally thrilling. Even though I was now 21, had done some film and TV work, had met a lot of celebrities by now, I was still a teenage fan-girl when it came to Tim.

Fortunately, things clicked between us. We started seeing each other pretty regularly at that point. He introduced me to his mother, Carmen, and I began to be included in family dinners and events.

At the time we met, Tim and his mom lived in a two-apartment building – she had the lower story, he had the upper – between Sunset Boulevard and Fountain. In some cases this kind of proximity to a guy's mom might have stopped a pair of 21-year-olds from getting sexually active or from smoking pot. But while not ideal, it didn't slow us down. The situation improved when not long afterward, Carmen moved to a pretty house in Beverly Hills and Tim rented his own house in Laurel Canyon where our privacy was complete.

Not that we were living together. That still wasn't widely done at the time and I don't think either of us was really ready for that level of commitment. With my first drizzle of money, I had secured a little one-bedroom, $125-a-month apartment near Warner Brothers Studios. It sat on a quiet residential street in Burbank where I'd occasionally see the singing cowboy, Gene Autry, park his huge Cadillac under my window and visit a Chinese woman who was my neighbor and his mistress.

Usually I'd spend time at Tim's place, though every now and then we'd find ourselves holed up at mine.

Dating Tim had dimensions I hadn't anticipated. We were having a ridiculously good time going to movie premieres, charity events, and parties of all sorts. His mom would take me aside and insist I wear her ermine stole or chinchilla coat for a big night – in an era when such things were acceptable. What I hadn't foreseen were all the logistics that went into an evening out. Tim had a publicity rep and so did I. They were always on the lookout for ways to get our faces into newspapers and magazines, which wasn't a huge uphill climb really, we were a popular couple for a while, but our reps had to work together, coordinating our arrival and movements with event planners and with writers, editors, and photographers.

Because Tim had grown up appearing on television and in film – he landed his first onscreen role at the age of 11 – I realized that he was a little weary of acting and the whole mechanics of fame; none of it was new and exotic, as it was for me. Besides his own acting career, he'd grown up in a legendary show business family.

In the early 1900s his maternal grandfather, Alexander Pantages, had been a powerhouse impresario based in Seattle, who owned a chain of some 50 Vaudeville houses throughout the Western states while Tim's grandfather on his dad's side, John Considine, had been one of Pantages' bitterest rivals in the theater world, owning his own string of Vaudeville houses. When Tim's parents, John W. Considine, Jr., and Carmen Pantages married it was truly the joining of two great, warring households, in near Romeo and Juliet fashion.

After the death of Vaudeville Tim's family was able to convert some of the old song-and-dance halls into movie theaters. His uncle Rodney Pantages managed the Hollywood Pantages Theater until he sold it to RKO in 1949.

Tim's father cut his own path as a prolific film producer beginning in the silent era. Working from the 1920s up through the mid-1940s he produced more than 50 movies, among them were hits like *Boys Town* and *Puttin' on the Ritz*, working with a who's-who list of the legends who forged the film industry – DW Griffin, Buster Keaton, Rudolph Valentino, John Barrymore, Mary Astor, Ernst Lubitsch, Samuel Goldwyn, and Louis B. Mayer.

There had been a great deal of money in the family at one point though by the time I came along, I think Carmen was to some degree living off the largess of Tim's Uncle Lloyd, a deeply tanned and fashionably flamboyant soul.

Because acting had lost some of its glitter, Tim had started to explore other interests such as writing, directing, photography, and, easily his favorite, getting behind the wheel of a race car, specifically Go Cart racing. During our dating life more and more of his life was centered around the track hanging out with drivers and mechanics. I'd go with him and it was fun at first – what woman doesn't enjoy being with a funny, popular guy. Over time, Tim taught me a lot of driving secrets. We'd race each other down Mulholland Drive – Tim in the Mini Cooper, me in the Mercedes – he'd give me hand signals for when to brake and when to accelerate.

At one point he recruited me to drive a Go Cart in a 150-mile race. He was impressed when, while speeding down the track, he saw me reach back behind my head and, without needing to turn and look, adjust the carburetor.

Afterward he said, "How'd you know how to do that?"

"I had to adjust," I said matter-of-factly. "The engine was running too rich."

Sometimes those farm girl skills gained me an extra point or two in his favor.

Even though we spent a lot of time together and I'd become close to his family throughout this time Tim was still seeing other women, which I only knew about in the vaguest way. I didn't ask about any of it and didn't want to know. It was just easier. Likewise I was still seeing other men though no one I really cared about.

Tim and I were floating along in a sunny bubble, going out on the town, partying with friends. It was all pretty easy. I was having a good time, overall, and it seemed like he was too. I figured at some point we'd get married. He'd see me as his one and only and would surprise me with an engagement ring, we'd stand up in a church and pledge ourselves to be faithful, and things would change. I'd be important to him.

None of this passed between us out loud. I wonder how many 22-year-olds are able to put words to such half-felt, vague sensations of the heart.

I was passively thinking that things would just work themselves out. I didn't have enough life experience to believe otherwise. And my own sense of self-worth was pretty shaky. I was still, in my mind (and I believed in his mind too), Charlotte from Yuba City, while he was Tim from Beverly Hills. I was the country mouse, the wannabe.

Whatever Tim wasn't giving me emotionally in reality was amplified by my own sense that I really didn't deserve much and anything nice that came my way was probably some sort of accident. Those old waves of "I'm not good enough" that I'd felt so early on at the Pasadena Playhouse and in high school were always there in the background.

One day while shopping for a few things, I came out of a department store on Hollywood Boulevard and staggered, feeling like I was going to pass out. I caught myself and hung on until I could get to my car and start feeling more stable. I wasn't a hypochondriac but it was such an unnerving, out-of-the-blue moment I visited my doctor to see if everything was okay. Then came the shock – I was pregnant.

Yes, Tim and I had been having sex but I'd faithfully used birth control and thought I'd eliminated pregnancy as a possibility.

As the news sunk in, my most immediate thought was that I didn't feel ready for motherhood, but then again who does? I remember sitting in my car after the doctor's appointment trying to think this through and the only thing that came to mind was that this was it – this was when Tim and I would get married. This is what would set things in motion. I'd tell him about the pregnancy. He'd probably freak out a bit but then he'd calm down, think it over, and say we should tie the knot.

When I drove over to Laurel Canyon and broke the news to Tim though, where I had been confused, he had clarity – he wasn't ready for marriage, wasn't ready to become a parent, and I should get an abortion.

It was a lot to take in.

I felt Tim was right that a pregnancy wasn't a sound basis for a wedding. I think that's what he meant. Though what he'd actually said was that he didn't want to get married. To me. The inner voice that constantly whispered,

"You're not good enough" had once again been proven right. This was more evidence that I didn't hit a high enough standard for Tim.

Would I ever? What would I need to do to earn a place in his world?

The other consideration was career-related. How could our PR reps ever spin this one to the America of the early 1960s? An era so obsessed with sexual purity that Dick Van Dyke and Mary Tyler Moore, who played married people on *The Dick Van Dyke* show, couldn't been seen in the same bed together. An era in which Lucille Ball had fought the network censors to use the word "pregnant" on her show – and had lost.

The idea of clean-cut TV star Tim Considine marrying his pregnant girlfriend would not play well. It would damage both of our careers – his more – and it could even hurt *My Three Sons* – meanings the careers and incomes of everyone on the show, cast and crew – people we both cared deeply for.

Within a few days I came around to the idea that if we weren't going to get married then, ending the pregnancy would be the best of bad options. Could I have raised a baby on my own? Of course. There are always ways to make that happen. But it would've been nearly unheard of then. I couldn't go back to Yuba City – the embarrassment and pain for my parents would've been off the charts. I couldn't do that to them. I didn't have the wherewithal financially or emotionally to raise a child on my own. I was 22 and single and oh, yeah, I partied a lot. If Tim didn't want me enough to marry me, if he didn't want the child, then I couldn't see moving forward with it on my own.

Abortion wasn't legal in the U.S. so not knowing of any options in Los Angeles, I flew down to San Diego, then rented a car and drove to Tijuana, Mexico, with Tim's brother John. Tim felt like it was too risky career-wise to be spotted going into an abortion clinic – it would have been juicy fodder for the tabloids, which even then could be pretty awful.

It took a while to find the clinic, which was above a dentist's office. Once inside, the physician was all business. There was no "How're you feeling?" or "Are you comfortable?" There was no one to talk me through the procedure or hold my hand. I wasn't sure exactly what was going to happen but I knew it wasn't going to be good.

I was instructed to get my legs into the metal stirrups and after a quick exam, out came the terrifying-looking equipment. Since I was in my first trimester, it probably took about ten minutes but an abortion without anesthesia seems like forever. It felt like the doctor was ripping my insides out. The pain was brutal and petrifying, like something from a medieval dungeon. I tried to hold it together but the pain and fear was overwhelming. I lost control, pleading with the physician to stop, trying to pull myself out of the stirrups and two nurses had to hold me down.

When it was over, I felt as torn up in soul as I did in body. Once I got my clothes on I stumbled down the stairs where John was waiting for me. I was nauseated and crying. In the car I was throwing up. At the U.S.-Mexican Border, the officer asked where home was and I was so out of it I said Yuba City. By the time we got to the airport in San Diego blood had soaked through my pants so John had me wait in the ladies room and he went to buy me a new pair of jeans.

On the plane back to L.A., I was shaking and sick, praying the bleeding would stop.

I had difficulty forgiving Tim for not going with me. One part of me understood it – protecting your career was important. At the same time, I kept thinking, when two people are really together, you shared messy, painful, frightening ordeals like this. Getting pregnant takes two – it's not as if I'd done this to myself. If I were really important, he'd have insisted on being there. He'd have held me. He'd have made me feel loved.

Looking back now, I realize that after the abortion, my drinking picked up, which is saying a lot. Going all the way back to my Pasadena Playhouse days, I'd enjoyed cocktails, beer, and wine as part of a night out. (Or, really, a night in. Any night would do.) But even then I was drinking three times more than most of my friends, which I didn't see at the time. I thought I was just being a normal kid.

Now I found that night after night instead of a glass or two of wine, I might have most of a bottle on my own and then switch to vodka. Alcohol stepped in where my relationship with Tim let me down, making me feel attractive and special. At least temporarily.

If this is going to be an honest portrait of my life at this point, I don't want to give the impression that it was all darkness. Far from it. There was always a lot going on and much of it was really fun. Friends came over a lot to Tim's Laurel Canyon house – actors, musicians, and people we knew in the industry. We'd get high, talk and laugh a lot, play board games, dance and listen to music. In a way, we'd recreated those Friday and Saturday nights I'd grown up with in Yuba City. We made it our own, of course, but it felt like I had entered that secret club of adulthood that had seemed so distant and inscrutable – and exciting – as a child.

And life went on. Tim kept going to the studio filming *My Three Sons*. He was not only acting but was more and more often directing episodes. I kept up a busy schedule too with TV parts and advertising gigs. In March 1964 I was at The Cellar Theater in a well-received revival of the play "The Front Page" directed by Ken Rose, one of my teachers from the Pasadena Playhouse. Among the cast was Sid Haig, another buddy from the Playhouse (who would go on to Comic-Con fame as the evil clown figure, Captain Spaulding, in Rob Zombie's *House of a Thousand Corpses* and *The Devil's Rejects*.)

Tim and I dated for four years until, in the spring of 1965, talk of marriage started up between us. I don't remember who said what but the idea began to grow seemingly on its own. He didn't propose to me on a bended knee or any of that. We just slowly started to talk about it and then it became a reality. We were engaged.

News of our engagement made all the entertainment press. *TV Picture Life* wrote breathlessly that Tim had presented me with a diamond-shaped wristwatch, which made me "the first girl in Hollywood to have a diamond too large to wear any place but the wrist." Meanwhile, *Teen World* magazine, claimed that Tim had slipped a huge diamond ring on my finger. Uh-huh. Pure La-La-Land stuff.

What actually happened is that early in our relationship we'd spent the day at Disneyland and at a shop on Main Street USA he purchased an enamel ring with two Siamese Dancers engraved on it, which I slipped onto the ring finger of my right hand. A few years later when we made the decision to become engaged, Tim simply took my hands and switched the ring from my right hand to the left.

In one sense it seemed kind of sweet and goofy, in another I knew if he'd chosen to he could have given me something really elegant from a jeweler in Beverly Hills. I tried not to interpret this gesture too closely but you can guess what that voice of "you're not good enough" was whispering to me.

Photos of Tim and me applying for our marriage license appeared in the *Los Angeles Times* and other LA media outlets – in many cases on the front page. A friend in England sent a clipping from London's *Evening News* in which news of our imminent nuptials appeared in a news box above the main headline

Tim and I married at 3 pm on October 23, 1965, at Bel Air Presbyterian. John was Tim's best man and several close friends such as Liz Baron and Lydia Banks were my maids of honor. Lydia was my roommate at the Pasadena Playhouse and had married fellow student – and great friend – David Banks. I had been a maid of honor in their wedding. Among the guests were Fred MacMurray (the only time I met him) and the other cast members from *My Three Sons* such as Don Grady, Stanley Livingston, William Demarest, and Bill Frawley, who'd recently lost his spot on the show. The studio had replaced Bill earlier that year because they could no longer insure him due to declining health. He didn't take it well and I heard that he would still drop by the set now and again and wasn't terribly nice to William Demarest, who was a really sweet guy who did a terrific job on the show as Bill's replacement, Uncle Charley. At the wedding though everyone was on their best behavior. Bill gave Tim and me a very funny letter saying he couldn't decide what to get for us. And even though it was possible we needed a bird cage he was giving us $100; he exhorted us not to spend it all at once. Bill died about four months later of a heart attack and we missed him terribly.

After the wedding, I found Tim's mom and sister packing my bags for our honeymoon. Which was odd to me. We had tickets for New York with a later stopover in Nassau. And while I was thrilled at the prospect, since I'd never been east of Denver, packing is something I thought of myself as qualified to do. I tried to think of it as a nice gesture but that voice of inadequacy inside of me strongly suspected it had something to do with Charlotte from Yuba City not being up to the task, not really knowing what to wear in front of the press or East Coast society types. The family had a reputation to keep up and it was going to take an extra boost to get this country girl to look the part.

Or – wait – was it their way of showing some kindness and generosity? Was I unfairly misjudging them through the filter of my crappy self-worth?

When we arrived at the airport with a group of family and friends, Tim handed me a document titled "Itinerary for Mr. and Mrs. Tim Considine" provided by our travel agent. I scanned the top of the thrice-folded sheet. Okay, as expected, Los Angeles to Chicago, then Chicago to …wait, what? Chicago to PARIS…? Paris to ROME! Rome to VENICE! Venice to MADRID! Madrid to LONDON! Oh my God.

We were going to Europe – everywhere in Europe – for six weeks!

What a wonderful surprise my darling had arranged and what a doofus I felt like for not suspecting a thing – having my bags packed for me all became clear. I have a great picture of us with our friends as we boarded the steps up to the plane. No elevated boarding structure in those days. Tim and I are in suits, me with a hat and gloves. So proper. So young.

As we traveled, our honeymoon received a lot of press coverage thanks to our hard-working PR agents. Fortunately though in this era before rabid paparazzi we had plenty of time to ourselves and enjoyed many under-the-radar adventures.

In London I realized immediately that all the girls were wearing miniskirts and I folded the top of my skirt over a few times to keep up.

Rome was everything it promised to be. Our hotel stood at the top of the Spanish Steps with easy access to the Western Union office frequented by all the local American students. We took side trips as suggested by our Fielding Guidebook and wandered the Trevi gardens and the Coliseum. After about a week of pasta I was dying for some good old American food. Mr. Fielding's book listed a hamburger spot so we consulted the map and soon we were chowing down on burgers, like those from home, along with *patatine fritte*.

In the booth next to us we noticed an older American couple, who we figured were probably satisfying a craving for food from home as well. I watched as Tim picked up our guidebook and looked at the couple then glanced back at the book. It was Temple Fielding, our guidebook's author. What a cool opportunity.

We introduced ourselves and they congratulated us on our wedding. We were pleased to tell him how wonderful his book had made our first European trip. As we chatted Mr. Fielding asked about our next stop and we said we'd been invited to spend several days on the west coast of Italy in a little town called Porto Santo Stefano. He knew it well and said that not only was it a lovely seaside town but in fact they had a friend there, the Contessa Lily Gerini.

"That's who we're staying with!" Tim answered.

The Contessa was a friend of Tim's mother and had arranged a visit. They wished us well as we left for our hotel.

Our train trip to Porto Santo Stephano was confusing. We didn't speak Italian making all the station announcements indecipherable. Holding our tickets and our train change instructions, we were at the mercy of the conductor who occasionally walked through our car. Lots of hand signals finally got through to us that we must change at the next station. With papers, passports, and tickets waving we managed to get on the right car at last.

Waiting for us at the station was the Contessa's driver in a beautiful Mustang convertible. He told us that Lily Gerini was an American woman from Chicago who married a titled Italian and owned half of the Appian Way. She had built a villa on top of Nero's birthplace and was renowned for her entertaining. A short and lively ride brought us to the villa and Lily.

"My darlings at last! Forgive us for not waiting," she said, urging us inside.

We walked into a large room with about 20 people already into their meal. Snatches of Italian, Spanish, and French conversation floated back and forth across the table. We were ushered to our seats, Tim way down and across from me as they always do at such dinner parties. Once seated I surveyed my place setting and found an alarming fan of cutlery. Some of the utensils were as foreign as the food before me. I hadn't learned any of this in my fast-track charm school.

The dinner mate on my left was a handsome young man, barely older than me. He registered my confusion and leaned over and whispered in a polished Spanish accent, "It's easy. You only have to start from the outside and work your way in." We both laughed and I was grateful he didn't treat me like an American rube. He inquired about our trip and I told him that after a brief train ride to Modena, Italy, where Tim wanted to tour the Ferrari factory, we were on our way to Madrid. He seemed familiar with both places and assured me that we would have a memorable time.

As it turned out my dinner companion knew more about silverware and expensive cars than I'd imagined. Ten years later when he, Juan Carlos, was crowned King of Spain, I realized I'd learned a lesson in table manners from European royalty.

And as Spain's future monarch had predicted, Tim did indeed enjoy the time we spent in Modena. He loved the Ferrari he tried out so much that he ordered one to be shipped to Los Angeles, where he planned to pay for it at the Beverly Hills dealership. Gulp. Though I had little knowledge of Tim's finances I wasn't at all sure he (or we) could afford that. But he was thinking like a TV and film star. The money would show up. The future was golden.

After we returned Tim and I were the "It Couple" for a while and we had lots of adventures that were documented in gossip columns and industry papers.

One night in Hollywood we were at a restaurant waiting for our table when in walked Charlton Heston, whom Tim knew from a film they'd worked on together with Julie Andrews in 1955, *Private War of Major Benson*. Heston in gregarious style came over with that radiant "Ben Hur" smile and greeted Tim by name. It was then Tim's turn to greet him back and to introduce me. I could tell that even though he knew Heston, Tim was a pretty star struck. He looked at Heston. Heston looked back and then looked at me. I smiled at Heston and then at Tim. This went on for a long awkward moment until finally Charlton Heston gave Tim a "Good to see you" nod and walked away. I laughed and said to Tim, "Did you forget his name?" And he said, "No, I forgot yours!"

While I was still working like crazy to ramp-up my career – auditions, business lunches, parties, the chase for parts – Tim was pulling away from acting. While on our honeymoon, Tim's agent had engineered a career-crippling disaster. Tim had expressed the desire to direct more episodes of *My Three Sons* and his agent had gone to the producers – while we were in Europe – and tried playing hard-ball, demanding that Tim direct half of the next season's episodes. It was an all-or-nothing proposition. The producers went for nothing and promptly cut Tim from the show.

It wouldn't be his only post-honeymoon disappointment.

Thinking it was time for the Ferrari he ordered to arrive, Tim stopped by the dealership in Beverly Hills where it was to be delivered. When he asked about the car he learned that, yes, it had arrived but actor Steve McQueen had been at the dealership that day, seen it, and wanting to throw some of his *The Great Escape* money around bought it on the spot.

Tim was furious but the truth is it was the best thing that could've happened. Neither of us had a Ferrari income at that point.

Tim spun into a funk, started spending more and more time in his dark room working on photography projects, and didn't leave the house much. He stopped going to auditions and let his hair grow, which he stubbornly refused to cut and as a result started losing out on new roles. His mother and his agent begged him to get a haircut – nope. He wasn't going to do it. He spent more and more time with his racecars and other interests. He and his brother John were working on scripts for a TV show they planned to pitch to the networks.

He was also settling into marriage, partying less, and becoming a homebody. In fact one night he said we should stop drinking and smoking pot altogether. Looking back I think this must have come, as least in part, from my own drinking. Not long before this, we'd invited some neighbors over for dinner and before they'd arrived, while cooking I'd downed an entire bottle of wine and had passed out. Tim was stuck with the job of a very awkward last minute cancellation.

While Tim did indeed stop drinking and smoking weed, I couldn't imagine life without alcohol. Our entire social life centered on hanging out and having drinks or getting high. Rather than do as he suggested, I not only continued but almost certainly drank more. And since I couldn't do this at home – or at least didn't find it fun anymore under Tim's sober gaze – we started spending less and less time together. He'd be at home or off behind the wheel of a racecar and I'd be out drinking with friends, and in many cases making new friends he knew nothing about.

He was in the Air Force Reserves, which meant he was gone for a training weekend once a month and I took advantage of those absences to pack in some extra fun.

On the acting front I was pursing every opportunity – TV, film, special appearances, and advertising. At one point I was so busy my agent started being contacted for "a Charlotte Stewart type but not Charlotte because she's in everything." Call it a farm girl's work ethic.

In October 1966, I was back at The Cellar Theater in a production of *La Ronde*, a farce set in Vienna in the late 1800s, again directed by Ken Rose. The *Los Angeles Times* reviewer found a lot to dislike in the production though I was one of two performers she found some merit in saying that I "had my moments." Seriously. That's as good as the review got.

In 1968, I landed a part in *Speedway,* which starred Elvis Presley, toward the end of the run of bubble gum films he appeared in in the 1960s. It was such a treat to play a couple of scenes with him at MGM. In real life Elvis was as startlingly handsome and gracious as I'd always imagined. One afternoon, while waiting out a lengthy set-up for a scene he caught my eye, called me over, and set me up with a chair next to his. My stomach did a flip-flop because, well, he was Elvis – hands-down the most famous person on the planet – and I had no idea what he wanted. When I settled in he took my hand and apologized for the movie.

"It's a terrible film," he said and gave a deep sigh. "I get the girl, I get the car …"

Beyond the predictable script he thought the music written for him to perform was thin, uninspired, and forgettable.

This put me in a weird spot. How to respond? "Yes, Elvis, your movie is crap."

I just wanted him to keep talking in the silky, smooth, Southern voice. And to keep holding my hand. The fact that I wasn't visibly freaking out is probably the best acting of my life.

Whatever I said in response did the trick because he did keep talking about how he'd dreamed of being in movies, like any regular boy or girl, and how that had turned into making B-grade romps like *Girl Happy* and *Clambake*. One topic led to another and before I realized it an hour sailed by as he told me about his life, his music, and his mama – the whole time holding my hand. He was by turns funny, intense, and thoughtful. It was very sweet and it was the first time I saw him as a person, not as an icon or a star but as a very nice, vulnerable guy – almost a kid – who was caught up in a career like a typhoon. It was one of my first experiences meeting a music legend, only to discover a kind, thoughtful, shy, and uncertain artist behind all the fame and tabloid stories. It was not to be my last such experience. His conversation with me ended abruptly, when his manager, Col. Tom Parker, walked into the sound stage. Elvis was up and out of his chair like a shot and nearly standing at attention in Parker's presence, confirming a lot of what I'd heard about the hold Parker had over him.

My next film, back at Goldwyn Studio, was *The Cheyenne Social Club* with Jimmy Stewart and Henry Fonda, directed by the great Gene Kelly. I played a saloon girl and in my first scene was to enter through the swing-doors with food on a tray for Stewart and Fonda. When I heard Gene Kelly say "Action," I swung through the doors and all the food on the tray sailed halfway across the set, which got a big laugh, especially from all the barflies. The scenes I was in were all with the guys in the saloon, a bunch of old time cowboy actors from the early days. Between set ups they'd sit around and swap stories about shooting Westerns all the way back to the days of silent flickers. What a hoot to hang out with those guys. Gene was a joy to work with too. One day at lunchtime a group of us were heading out to the Formosa Cafe up on the corner and I asked him if he'd dance with me. He said, "Sure, what would you like to do?" I asked him if he'd do the scissor-step and he seemed surprised that I'd know it. So Gene Kelly and I did the scissor-step together down the middle of Formosa Avenue.

or knew

It was a kick to work with legends like Jimmy Stewart and Henry Fonda, though beyond shooting our scenes together we didn't exactly hang out and practice our dance moves. In the long periods of downtime on the set Jimmy Stewart, who had recently lost his stepson in Vietnam, would sit on the steps of his dressing trailer playing the accordion to himself. Jimmy had been a heroic figure in World War II as a wing commander for a bomber squadron based in Southern England. His courage and commitment had inspired a whole generation. But that was a different war and a different time. I wondered what his thoughts were now but he kept them to himself. Henry Fonda was a pretty keep-to-himself guy too. I always called him Mr. Fonda, which he preferred to anything less formal. I did try to warm up to him at the cast party when I pulled him into a stairwell and asked if he had any weed. This made him grumpier than usual and he stalked off saying, "I think it's my son you want to talk to."

I had a great deal more success in this regard – in the weed-scoring department – when I appeared on a western series on NBC called *The Virginian*, as the ditz wife of actor Dennis Weaver. What a foul mood Dennis was in on that shoot. Took himself very seriously and took an almost instant and long-lasting dislike to me; I was never sure why.

An

The episode was called "The Dark Train" in which the cast spent six days on small set built to look like the interior of a passenger train from the late 1800s. To give the sense of movement over tracks and terrain, the entire set was jiggled this way and that throughout the six-day shoot.

By the end of it the entire cast was pretty exhausted from all the jostling and to celebrate the end of our travails, most of us (minus Dennis) gathered in one of the dressing trailers to share the comforts of weed. When we were all feeling pretty fantastic, there was a sudden, loud knock at the door. We got busy inside the trailer opening windows and fanning smoke and arranging ourselves in such a way as to not look stoned.

When we opened the door, an assistant director was there to inform us that noise on the set had ruined the sound and that we all needed to come back to loop (meaning re-record) our dialogue. They hadn't taught us at the Pasadena Playhouse how not to sound high when you are. It's just one of those skills you pick up on the job.

***

Leaving the old west behind for a while, I got to fly to Hawaii and play a drug addict on an episode of *Hawaii Five-O*. The thing is I actually had a lot of weed in my luggage – we'll call this method acting. The driver who picked me up at the airport in Hawaii was a big Samoan guy who was really easy to talk to and likeable. He helped get all my bags into the hotel and as a thank-you I gave him a couple of joints, which he appreciated. Out on my balcony I saw him crossing the courtyard below. He'd already lit one up and when he saw me he gave me the "OK" sign. Apparently my L.A. pot measured up to his Maui-Wowie standards. So far so good.

In one of my first scenes I was running down the street toward the camera, which was mounted on a car and moving away from me. I tripped and fell and wound up in the hospital with a broken kneecap. For the remainder of the shoot they had to find ways of shooting me from the waist up to avoid the cast on my leg. In the long shots, like where you'd see me walking away, they had to find a body double, who also had my long blonde hair.

And yes, in this episode, I worked with *Hawaii Five-0* star Jack Lord. Jack was a big shot on the island. He owned a huge house in Honolulu and was the resident star in those parts – you got the sense just from the way he moved through the world that he was very much lord of the manor, no pun intended. He seemed unusually aware of his status and his appearance, even by TV standards. Though we were shooting an episode in the first season of the show, already the joke among the crew was that they could only shoot outdoors if the wind was coming from the right direction and didn't mess up Jack's hair.

In this episode Jack and I had an emotional scene in which I'm lying in a hospital bed – a fake one this time versus the real one I'd recently been in. And while we were shooting, he was holding my hand and nearly crushing it to a pulp. Did he think this was going to improve my acting? I don't think I've ever been happier to end a scene with anyone.

Of course, did I say anything to him in between takes? Did I ask the big deal TV star to stop mangling my hand?

Nope. Speaking up for myself was not on my list of skills.

Back home I auditioned relentlessly and got guest roles on shows that have sunk into pop-culture oblivion such as *The F.B.I.*, *The Young Lawyers*, and *The Interns*.

But good things come to those who audition, and a great career boost came with getting parts on *Bonanza*, an iconic show even at the time, during which I got to see the young Michael Landon at work. Even though Lorne Greene was billed as the star of the show, really it was Mike, who played "Little Joe." Even then he was Mr. Charisma. What woman wouldn't melt at least a little at that smile? But Mike was more than a pretty face and a pair of suspenders. He was ambitious and driven. He was a good writer, who had a dead-on understanding of story and character. He knew how to make an audience care. Sounds easy, I guess, but nothing could be more difficult.

On *Bonanza*, like lots of Westerns, we filmed interior scenes at Paramount Studios and the exteriors at sprawling Big Sky Movie Ranch, located outside of Los Angeles in Simi Valley. (This is exactly what we'd do a few years down the road, when Michael was the boss of his own show, *Little House on the Prairie*.) In one sequence, the script called for me to escape from a bad guy who was inside my cabin, a scene that we shot on a Paramount sound stage. A week or so later they needed to film me bursting out of the front door of the cabin at that same level of distress. At Big Sky I was inside the ramshackle house set waiting to hear the director call "Action." I prepped myself on the other side of the door, breathing heavily and getting myself into the right mindset. When I heard "Action," I flew through the door and thanks to hyperventilation promptly blacked out, landing in the huge arms of Dan Blocker, who played "Hoss."

There are worse places to end up.

On the set of *Ben Casey* in an episode called "For Jimmy, The Best of Everything," I had a scene with Peter Falk – this was just before he played his career-defining role of *Columbo*. I was a medical student and Peter was a doctor who asked a question of me. The line I had in response to his question was pretty complicated, full of medical jargon, and I "went up," meaning the line just vanished from my mind while the cameras were rolling. Instead of stopping and waiting for me to pull it together, Peter, who got his start in off-Broadway theater, just kept going, goading me for the answer like a real doctor would until the line just tumbled out of me. And I loved him for it. It made the scene feel real, provoking the very reaction a flustered student might give.

Also for Paramount I was briefly in *The Slender Thread*, a film directed by Sydney Pollack – it was his first feature though he'd acted and directed in TV for a long time. I played a telephone operator receiving a desperate call from Sidney Poitier at a suicide crisis center. Poitier was trying to track down the location of a suicidal caller (played by Anne Bancroft). We filmed the scene in an actual telephone company, in which there was a long bank of switching panels where operators would move plugs around a grid to connect calls. My scene was pretty simple. I was to take the call, recognize the gravity of the situation and ask my supervisor over to deal with it.

In the first couple of takes I really laid on the shock and explosiveness of the situation – throwing as much movement and "acting" into my few seconds of screen time as possible. Finally Sydney called "Cut" and came over, put his hand on my shoulder and said gently, "She's just a telephone operator." We shot the scene again and this time I took my performance down about ten notches, which worked. But it was at times like this when I wondered how much more I had to learn. Since the days of mastering the art of hitting my mark on *Damaged Goods* or eating so much I nearly burst on *The Loretta Young Show*, I hoped that I was getting better. Hoped I was learning my craft. But was I?

While jobs were coming in – TV, film and advertising – the thing I still lacked was confidence. Every time I was in front of a camera, I felt like a screw-up. Cast members were usually very supportive – though I could always find a Dennis Weaver who'd treat me like dirt. My career felt fragile like I was just one blown line away from seeing it all end. I couldn't shake that feeling of being in a sound stage filled with crew and cast all waiting for me to cross a room or deliver a line and looking around thinking "I wonder if they know I don't know what I'm doing." Still, just as at the Pasadena Playhouse when I'd been invited to leave the program, I kept going to auditions, kept working at it. I still had no Plan B.

The fact is I had learned a lot about both the craft and logistics of acting since my first on-screen roles. By logistics I mean things like which gate you enter at Warner Brothers, where hair and makeup is located at CBS, where you'll find stage 13 at Paramount (there is no stage 13 – ha!). And as far as craft goes, I mean what can you deliver emotionally, what kind of authenticity can you bring to a character when the director says "Action" and the crew goes silent and 150 lights in the rigging overhead are warming your skin.

Something was working because I was getting parts. But I'd often find myself on set preparing for a scene and feel my breath coming more quickly and a rising sense of panic like "I don't know if I can do this." Or I'd feel as though the people who'd hired me hadn't done their homework and didn't realize their mistake.

The truth is I was well liked. A number of directors hired me for multiple projects. Part of that may have been because I was never any trouble – always showed up prepared, didn't question anything, simply did my lines and got out of the way.

Peter Tewksbury, whose career went back to the early days of television, directed all the episodes that I was in on *My Three Sons* and later asked me to come play a role on another show he was directing called *It's a Man's World*. And then again, when he moved into features and was directing the Sandra Dee and George Hamilton big-screen comedy, *Doctor, You Must Be Kidding*, he again asked me to come play a role.

The sense of inadequacy I felt with Tim was mirrored in my lack of confidence on set. And like anyone would, I looked for ways to bolster my feelings about myself. Alcohol was an obvious crutch but with Tim's self-imposed sobriety, I could really only indulge in that away from him.

Drinking was only part of the picture though. I was hungry for something deeper. Something bigger than myself. Something spiritual. Growing up, our family had been more or less Catholic. My dad never went to any sort of church but my mom was sort of a holiday Catholic, going to Mass on Christmas Eve. My sister Barbara Jean, however, was big into it, in part perhaps because it offered an escape from our home. She nearly always took me to Mass with her. When I moved away and went to the Pasadena Playhouse I attended Mass regularly there. Not entirely because I was a serious believer but because it was a connection to home.

While dating Tim, a friend had invited me to check out the Hollywood Christian Group. There were a lot of familiar industry faces at these once-a-week meetings. And it wasn't heavy-duty stuff. I just found it inspirational. One night the speaker was Dale Evans, who was well-known for appearing on TV and film alongside her husband, Roy Rogers, whom I'd almost met as a child. I don't remember the specifics of what Dale talked about that night – probably things that had happened in her life and ways that her beliefs had seen her through hard times.

On the way home in the car, I came to a stop light on Vine Street when suddenly I had the feeling that my dad needed something. He needed it urgently. I didn't know what it was but I felt his presence right there with me. I'd never felt such a powerful sense of someone being with me like that.

I knew my parents were on a little getaway together in Calistoga, up in Napa Valley, spending a few days at one of their favorite hot springs spas. I couldn't imagine what this feeling meant but right then and there, I did the only thing I could. I prayed for my dad – asking God that Honey get whatever it was he needed.

Back at my apartment, about an hour later I got a telephone call from my brother Lewis – Dad had died. My sweet, quiet, loving father was suddenly gone.

Earlier that day at the spa, he'd walked from their room out to the truck to retrieve something and he'd had a sudden, incapacitating spasm of pain in his abdomen. The agony was so intense he couldn't move. He could only honk the horn until help came.

My mom followed the ambulance as it took him to St. Helena Hospital, which was only a few miles away. There they stabilized him and it looked like he was going to be okay. The truth is things weren't good for him health-wise. He was 80 lbs. overweight or more and ten years prior had been diagnosed with cirrhosis of the liver from years of alcoholism. But that night, they'd knocked the pain in his liver and he was feeling better, though they'd need to keep him for a few days. My mom asked the physician if she should remain there or if she could run back to Yuba City to get the things they'd need for a longer stay. Because all signs were good, the physician said it'd be fine for her to go.

On her way back home that night, dad's temperature spiked, and with very little warning he died, slipping from this world in an unfamiliar hospital room surrounded by strangers. For a guy who had always loved being around his family it must have been an awful and disorienting way to go. At the very moment of his passing I was on Vine St., sensing him calling out to me.

He was just 56 years old.

Even now, more than 50 years later, I still feel the loss of a girl losing her daddy. And tears still blur my eyes when I think of that night.

***

Tim had no interest in the Hollywood Christian Center nor in organized religion in general. He didn't give me a hard time about going, it just wasn't his thing. What he did have interest in was transcendental meditation and so on our second anniversary we went to the Westwood Meditation Center where we studied meditation techniques and were given our mantra – the multi-vowel word that you repeat as you descend into a meditative state. Typically each student is given their own mantra but since we were a couple we were given the same word, which I found annoying. I wanted my own.

We threw ourselves into mediation. Practicing at home, continuing to go to the center, and even going to a retreat in Tahoe where we worked with Maharishi Mahesh Yogi, who founded the Transcendental Meditation movement, videotaping his hours-long talks. Honestly, meditation didn't do a lot for me. I was trying to find something that Tim and I could do together as a couple. That's what couples do, right? Couple things. By now his Go Cart racing had become boring to me. Hanging out with the other drivers and mechanics and their wives was drudgery. His photography was interesting. He was really good. We'd become friends with Joni Mitchell, a Laurel Canyon neighbor and we'd go down to the Troubadour to watch her perform. Tim took a gazillion pictures of her. In fact one of his best is on the cover of her iconic *Blue* album.

The problem with photography is that he spent a lot of time in the dark room.

I kept up the mediation, at some point, simply for the social side of it. But I could feel things changing in our relationship … we were drifting from each other. Hollywood was old news to Tim but it was still a very shiny new object to me. I was in my twenties and living in a town of limitless possibilities – for work, for parties, for friends, for sex, for drugs, for everything that made being alive exhilarating.

It killed me to stay home at night. How could you possibly spend an evening at home when you were young and good-looking and in movies and in the heart of Tinseltown? Someone somewhere was having more fun than I was and I wanted that someone to be me.

At a meditation retreat I met Richard Beymer again – whom I'd first run into at the commissary at Goldwyn Studios while I was shooting *The Loretta*

Young Show and he was filming *West Side Story*. I still thought Richard was one of the yummiest men alive and soon we were meeting up for drinks and seeing each other and all the rest.

Meanwhile, back in Laurel Canyon Tim and I lived next door to a well-known architect, Jon Jerde and his wife Gail. Jon was an intense, fascinating, brooding kind of guy. The sort who would tear through the Hollywood Hills on his motorcycle at three in the morning when he couldn't sleep. When the timing was right, Jon or I would sneak through the opening in our back fence for a quickie.

Also, my old friend from the Pasadena Playhouse days, Stuart Margolin, lived around the corner. There was some long-standing attraction between us that had been the inspiration for his 1965 two-person one-act play called *Involution*, which Stuart directed and I performed at The Cellar Door Theater with Smokey Roberds. Coleman Andrews wrote a terrific review in the *Free Press* saying that the play was at times painful "because one has to constantly remind oneself that it is only a play, and not a nightmare repetition of something that took place in one's own life not too long before." He added that "Smokey Roberds and Charlotte Stewart live the play, as though it were written for them." Funny Coleman should say that.

By now my relationship with Stuart had progressed a great deal past the stage of *Involution* in which we'd been dancing around the idea of mutual attraction. We were now getting together at his house or at mine whenever possible. There were other men too, like Johnny Mandel, the composer who wrote "Shadow of Your Smile" and "Suicide is Painless" and still others in situations best described as dressing-room flings.

There's no way to dress any of this up as quirky, romantic, or adventurous. By our second year of marriage I was cheating on Tim.

Why did I sleep around? At the time, I told myself it was fun and it felt good. On a deeper level though, and in hindsight, I realize that an unsettling portrait of our relationship had emerged for me. The house we lived in was Tim's house. My name wasn't on it. We never had a joint bank account. He never visited my parents in Yuba City; they always had to come south. And then there was the business of the cheap Disneyland engagement ring. Yes, Tim married me, but underneath it all, I wasn't sure why – I didn't seem important to him. I didn't feel like I measured up. This was never going to be a partnership. I was never going to have a say. He'd made that clear to me yet again when, as a wedding present he had bought me a 1966 Mustang, which I absolutely loved. Then one day I came home and it was gone. He informed me that he thought it was junk and – without any prior discussion – sold it to a friend of his. With no offer of a replacement car, my parents gave me their Country Squire Station Wagon, which I drove around Hollywood, while Tim drove his Mercedes.

By contrast, the men I slept with wanted me. I ranked high in their priorities. They risked a lot to be with me. I felt desired. I felt good enough. To them I wasn't Charlotte from Yuba City. I was just Charlotte, an actress from Laurel Canyon – I was pretty, confident, sexy, and great in bed. That's the Charlotte I wanted to be. But being her *and* being married to Tim meant telling a lot of lies about where I'd been, who I'd been with, how I'd spent my day, how I felt about our lives together. Lies that built up and up and up requiring more sex and more alcohol to make each day livable. Like drinking one poison as an antidote to another.

Chapter 4

Meltdown

BY 1969 IT WAS CLEAR I couldn't keep this up. I was living an entire life apart from Tim – a life I had to work harder and harder to conceal. I had to conceal my restlessness, discontent, anger, sadness, recklessness, and self-loathing. It's hard to be "the bad guy." In a situation like this the most comforting thing you can do is concoct an alternate narrative in which everything you've done is someone else's fault. Blame your spouse. Blame your upbringing. Blame Hollywood. Blame the '60s. Fault anything but yourself. Delusion can be very cheering. But I couldn't pull that off. I knew what I had promised at the altar, knew what Tim believed about us, and what he imagined our future to look like.

I also understood that while I had loved the sparkly swirl of our dating life, our honeymoon, and the early romantic days, I clearly, clearly, clearly wasn't ready to spend the rest of my life being Mrs. Tim Considine.

I cared deeply for Tim and I didn't think of myself as a quitter but I didn't know what to do. I was in more pain than I'd ever known: greater than the abortion, greater than my dad's death. Pain that was becoming more impossible to keep inside.

Then I was just done.

I reached a breaking point where I couldn't lie anymore and I couldn't tell the truth. The constant, grinding inner turmoil, the fear, the churning in my stomach, the unbearable self-hate – I just wanted it to stop.

Tim was going to be away for the weekend for his Air Force Reservist training and it seemed like the best moment to resolve everything.

I was in a play at the time and I drove into town and informed the director that I couldn't be in the show any longer.

He responded, understandably, by losing his mind.

"I'm sorry," I told him. "I'm sick. I can't be in the play."

I'd never done anything like this before. My whole career had been all about never missing an audition, an appointment, a day of shooting or a performance, never calling in sick, never questioning a director, never knowingly being a disappointment. In my professional life, being five minutes early was being late. I always knew my lines, tried to have amicable relationships with everyone in the cast and crew, did my best to please.

But the truth is, I *was* sick. Down to my very core.

After leaving the theater, I was driving home along Highway 1 with the Pacific stretched out to the horizon and I thought, "This is the last time I'll see the ocean ... this is my last day ..."

I got back to the house and wrote a note that simply said, "I'm sorry." I sat on the bed and poured a bunch of Miltown tablets into my hand – Miltown was a popular relaxant, a precursor to Valium and Xanax. I swallowed enough to do the job and just as I was lying down I heard a knock at our gate. I'm not sure why but I got up and looked outside. It was a neighbor who saw me peek through the blinds. He waved and I stuck my head out the door. Turns out he'd brought his mother over to meet me. I smiled, excused myself, and went into the bathroom, stuck my finger down my throat and brought up the Miltown. It would be terribly rude to pass out in front of company.

The three of us visited for a while and when they left, with that final farce over, I began again – swallowing the remaining Miltown tablets, lying down next to the suicide note, closing my eyes, and feeling darkness wash over me.

To a queasy mix of surprise, disappointment, and relief, I realized I was waking up. How long I was asleep, my body dutifully metabolizing all that Miltown, I don't know. It may have been hours, a day, perhaps longer.

Tim was lying next to me.

He'd read the note and wanted to know what it meant.

I started crying. This was it.

I had no way out.

I told him I had another life, that I'd been going out, that I'd been sleeping around.

He listened with a kind of palpable intensity emanating from him. He told me in a quiet, steady voice that he wanted to know everything and I didn't hold back.

Maybe I should have kept some of it to myself. Maybe I went too far. Was I giving him the honesty he was asking for or was I just vomiting up all the toxins that were inside of me? My suicide attempt hadn't been a cry for help. I thought I was beyond help. I couldn't imagine what else would make the pain go away. Everything had gotten so complicated. I couldn't justify my behavior. I was seeing so many men while trying to please so many people. I couldn't say no and felt completely out of control.

Tim didn't yell, didn't cry, didn't make a scene, didn't demand that I leave. He absorbed it all and then called my mother, calmly told her that I was very sick, and asked if she would come down for a few days.

Other than that, his reaction was numbness. Silence.

Mom flew down right away and he was polite and nice to her and he seemed to tolerate my presence reasonably but it was a very tense week. I don't know what Tim told her. Perhaps not much. The only details I gave her was that I had attempted suicide – though told her nothing about all the reasons for it – which I knew that, especially after losing my dad, would be devastating to her. When she left she said to me, "We will never speak of this again." And she didn't. Not a word, not a hint. That's how she dealt with things like this, with pure stoicism.

Now it was just the two of us again in a very quiet house. Tim had shut down. He literally sat on the couch and stared at the wall for what seemed like weeks.

I apologized in every possible way. I tried to get him to talk, tried to break through. But he simply wouldn't – or couldn't – respond. He was completely traumatized.

I remember sitting in the living room watching him sit in silence. And I knew that I would never be able to say "I'm sorry" enough. It was over. There were no pieces to pick up.

With enormous, choking sadness, I told Tim that I was moving out and wanted a divorce.

In the meantime, Gail Jerde from next door had gotten wind of what happened and she and Jon were in the process of splitting up. She'd moved in with her parents for the time being. She knew I was looking for a place and asked if I wanted to move in too.

You had to know Gail to understand this. She didn't hold anything against me – as far as she was concerned, Jon was a lousy human being. She loved to tell people when we went out together that I'd slept with her ex-husband. She even dragged me along with her to one of their divorce sessions in court. She was very entertained by this.

When it came time to deal with lawyers in our divorce, I made it clear that I didn't want any of Tim's money and being lawyers of course they suspected that I was up to something. They actually required me to undergo a psychological evaluation because they thought I was either crazy or was feigning mental instability for some cunning purpose.

In fact, I didn't want Tim's money. I knew how hard he'd worked for it. But the biggest reason was simple – I didn't deserve any. Again, I'd stood in a church and vowed to Tim to be faithful and I'd broken that promise and in doing so had broken his heart and had damaged his spirit.

His family was angry with me, which I didn't like but completely understood. I was angry with myself.

At the same time, I knew I needed to live my own life. I didn't want to be tied to anyone else. I was young and wanted to have fun.

I had tried the conventional route of dating and marriage and it hadn't worked. When I looked around me, in the era of the late 1960s, I saw that male-female relationships were all rapidly changing. The traditional roles, the pathways to companionship, to emotional fulfillment were all being thrown out the window. Words like friend, boyfriend, and husband did not have the same sharp boundaries around them that they once had, and we would need to come up with a whole new vocabulary to describe who we were to each other. What our responsibilities and commitments looked like.

Men and women my age were living together and foregoing the step of marriage. One-night stands were more and more commonplace both in Hollywood and beyond. People were living on communes and raising children together.

I left my marriage with Tim with a very heavy heart filled with the sense that I was taking my first steps into the unknown, unsure if I was feeling anxiety or anticipation. Or both.

***

After moving out of the Laurel Canyon house, my first job was a guest spot on *Gunsmoke* in an episode called "Lyle's Kid" with Robert Pine (father of actor Chris Pine).

I played Iris Wesley, a saloon girl who'd fallen on hard times.

On the set, I remember facing a particularly challenging set-up. It was a long, continuous shot with Robert in which we were walking and talking across the "Main Street of Dodge" set for about two minutes, which in television is so long it's practically avant-garde.

I remember going through the blocking and trying to keep it all straight. Robert was a great scene partner with a lot of subtlety and focus to his approach.

When the director said "Action," Robert and I talked for a while at a hitching post on one side of the street and then walked slowly across the set doing dialogue and reactions, keeping the camera in sight of the corner of my eye, and finally hitting our marks on the far side. Meanwhile all around us extras were milling about, horses pulled wagons and all kinds of activity. And the whole thing worked in one take.

When the director said "Cut," a new, beautiful, potent realization poured through me. For the first time in my professional life I thought, "I can do this."

Not: "Holy shit, what am I doing?"

Not: "Good God, if they only knew I have no idea that I'm totally lost."

All those questioning, belittling voices had, for that one moment at least, gone silent.

I could handle this. Performing complicated scenes was something I did for a living – something I had been doing successfully for 10 years.

It was the first time I remember feeling confident, grasping that I actually had what it took.

Not that this feeling of adequacy cascaded into my personal life. Nor was it always present when I was on set. No. This was not the moment I was transformed from caterpillar to butterfly; but it's fair to say that it felt like I'd turned a corner.

It wasn't until years later that I put the pieces together that this moment only came after leaving a marriage in which I'd been plagued by a sense of inadequacy and second-rate importance.

Coincidence? Hard to say.

Chapter 5

The Liquid Butterfly

A CULTURAL CHANGE IS EASY TO SEE in hindsight but not terribly obvious when you're swimming around in the middle of it. Like a lot of people my age I had been undergoing a transformation – in my case from the sunny pixie blonde of the early 1960s to a long-haired, braless hippie chick. The last time I'd worn a suit with a knee-length skirt was in 1965 on my honeymoon. After that Tim and I had both became what you might call city hippies, letting our hair grow and being a lot more informal in how we dressed.

I moved out of Gail's parents' house into a bungalow her sister had just vacated, a one-bedroom guesthouse on Lexington Avenue in Hollywood. An artist named Delana Bettoli would room with me on and off. She was funny, having various obsessions, the biggest was with Jim Morrison; she produced countless drawings of him as the alluring Lizard King, with full pouty lips and perfect cheekbones, which we had fun putting up throughout the house.

I didn't necessarily share the obsession but I saw it all around me and understood it. Music was changing. New voices were speaking directly to those of my generation – those of us born during or just after World War II. The music that our parents had listened to spoke of overly sweetened, idealized takes on love and life. Think of popular songs like "Polka Dots and Moonbeams" or "Paper Moon." The music icons of the 50s and early 60s like Louis Prima and Frank Sinatra were sounding dated; the swing-inspired sound of that era was being superseded by music that was raw and defiant and spoke to the uncertainty of a world in flux. Many of the new voices in music, as it turns out, lived just up the street from me. The neighborhood included Frank Zappa, Mama Cass from the Mamas and the Papas, David Crosby, Steven Stills, and Graham Nash.

Joni Mitchell, who'd become a friend, didn't drive so I often gave her a lift to recording sessions or gigs at the Troubadour and other clubs in Hollywood. It was a pretty incredible time in her life. When she was younger Joni had thought she was going to be a painter but started singing in Canada where she was from. She found some success as a folksinger and ended up in Los Angeles performing around town and making records. When I first met her she was working on her *Blue* album, which *Rolling Stone* would rate as one of the best albums of all time. The song "River" on *Blue* offers lines like:

"I made my baby cry ... he tried hard to help me, put me at ease, and he loved me so naughty made me weak in the knees ... I wish I had a river I could skate away on ... so hard to handle, I'm selfish and I'm sad, now I gone and lost the best baby I ever had ... Oh I wish I had a river I could skate away on ..."

It's like she'd pulled the mish-mash of longing and self-loathing right out of my heart and set them to music. Me and many other 20-year-olds at the time.

Her music and lyrics emerged out of Joni's life – her ups and downs, relationship and break up with Graham Nash and other guys – and people gravitated toward that kind of authenticity. She, her voice, and her music had a mix of tenderness and grit, girlish dreaminess and emotional toughness, which certainly appealed to me as it did to many others my age.

In her house she had a bulletin board on which she'd pin words and phrases as they came to her. Once I remember seeing "The bed's too big and the frying pan's too wide." And I thought what a beautiful way to talk about loneliness. These words later showed up in her song "My Old Man."

To be able to write and perform something so personal and so universal was nothing short of brilliance. It was more than just pop music. It seemed revolutionary and important. It seemed like the music of people my age had the power to change the world.

Because of this, it was an era when a group of friends would put on a record – the needle hitting the vinyl with a lovely hiss – dim the lights, sprawl on the furniture and the floor, pass a joint and listen to the whole album. Maybe more than once. I'm so glad that was part of my life. I see people going through their lives now plugged into ear buds and it makes me wish they could have that experience of communal listening.

From hanging out with Joni Mitchell, I met her manager Elliot Roberts, who I fell pretty madly in love with. We saw each other on and off unofficially for a long time. While Elliot was a guy of average looks he had eyes that locked onto you, absorbed you, and shut out everything that was going on. He could create an orbit of two no matter where you were, no matter what else was going on, no matter who else was in the room. I loved that about him. Also, Elliot was the kind of guy who seemed to move through the world in the middle of his own personal hurricane. Wherever he was, things of noisy significance were happening. When I went out with him, I never sat in the audience. I was always backstage or in the wings. I remember once at the stage door of the Troubadour, someone from the club asked who I was and Elliot blustered, "She's my old lady," and I was shown right through along with all the other cool kids. The Troubadour on Santa Monica Boulevard was tiny, maybe 150 seats, but it was the epicenter of everything happening in music at the moment. On a given night you might see performances by Bonnie Raitt, Neil Young, Elton John, Neil Diamond, Jackson Browne, James Taylor, Carole King, Kris Kristofferson, or Judy Collins.

Besides managing Joni, Elliot also managed Neil Young, David Crosby, Stephen Stills, and Graham Nash and between him and his business partner David Geffen, he turned those guys into long-haired millionaires in their mid-20s. Which was a little odd. The whole hippie vibe was about not being into material things, living on communes, bombing around in VW buses, living off the land, setting up food co-ops, keeping things simple.

But here these guys were, icons of the hippie age, sitting on big old-fashioned piles of money. And ultimately they did what anyone else would do – they bought a lot of stuff. Neil Young split off from Crosby, Stills and Nash, started his solo career and bought a big ranch just south of San Francisco, where he built a barn and filled it with his beloved Lionel trains. Graham Nash bought a big place up there too. David Crosby bought boats. A lot of them bought expensive cars, homes, and various pricey toys though, of course, they didn't advertise any of this.

The thing that kept a lot of these guys on an even, semi-normal footing was their wives. They didn't marry actresses or super models. They married really smart, grounded women, who sewed their own clothes, made sound decisions about money, and were really great moms. In the case of Neil Young's wife Susan, I think she even sparked a fashion trend. She used to patch all of Neil's jeans and when he appeared in a heavily patched pair on the cover of his album *After the Gold Rush*, it sparked the big-time '70s trend of patched jeans. Patched jackets. Patches on everything.

Friendships like this take lots of forms. I often found myself backstage at the Troubadour with Elliot learning my lines for a show like *Mannix* or *Gunsmoke*, hanging out with Neil Young and his band while Joni or some other great act was on stage.

At one point Stephen Stills borrowed my Country Squire Station Wagon and no one knew where he was for two days.

In other cases, we went through some pretty dark moments together. One night in August 1969 I was with Joni and Graham Nash at Dallas Taylor's house in Benedict Canyon. Dallas was a drummer for Crosby, Stills and Nash. As I was about to head home for the night, David Crosby burst through the door with a gun shouting that killers were loose murdering people in Benedict Canyon and no one could leave. He wanted us to hole up there and protect ourselves.

The reason David was freaking out was because a pregnant Sharon Tate, Jay Sebring and others had been brutally murdered two nights before in Benedict Canyon on Cielo Drive – a killing eventually tied to Charles Manson and his followers. The barbarity of the killings had sent shockwaves through Hollywood. Now two days later the bodies of Leno and Rosemary LaBianca had been discovered also stabbed to death in their home with similar messages scrawled in blood on the walls. Later I would realize that those murders had taken place in Silver Lake, not Benedict Canyon, but still it was horrific and jarring.

The thing I had to deal with is that I did in fact have to leave. I had a 6 a.m. call at Warner Brothers to film an episode of crime show *The F.B.I.* Against David's strong wishes I drove myself home feeling panicky and more alone than usual in my bungalow.

Just as the Troubadour and new friends' houses became a big part of my life, Elliot's office also became a favorite hangout. He was in the second story of The Clear Thoughts Building (so named by its 90-year-old owner who lived behind the building) at 947 La Cienega Blvd, about a block south of Santa Monica Blvd.

Electra Records was located across the street, where Elliot's clients had contracts. It made his office a hub for some of the most exciting names in music at the time.

Next door to Elliot's office, I struck up a friendship with a model-beautiful blonde name Dani Senator, who ran an incense- and ganga-scented clothing shop called The Liquid Butterfly. She made gorgeous tie-dye dresses and shirts and she also restored antique clothing, which was all the rage.

Miles Davis was a fan of her clothes and would drop by the shop for a shirt or two – or just to hang out. The more I talked to Dani, the more I realized we'd have a great time going into business together.

I'd loved to sew since I was a kid. My sister, Barbara Jean, had taught me the basics and by the age of nine I was making my own roller skating costumes. Later in my 20s I made some of my own dresses and I sewed Tim probably a dozen collar-less tunics that he loved, a style popularized by the Beatles.

I showed Dani a couple of my patchwork peasant dresses and cowboy shirts and proposed the idea that we partner up, each sell our own clothes, split the $100 monthly rent and all the more mundane tasks of running a business. We shook on it and started working together to make a success of our store.

Everything post-marriage seemed to explode beautifully around me. I was surrounded by exotic and boundary-pushing artists, musicians, drugged-out visionaries, models, filmmakers, and hangers on. People camped out at my house; I crashed at theirs. It was like Hollywood was one big college dorm. I was getting a lot of work in TV and commercials, studying acting at The L.A. Actors Studio with Lee Strasberg, sitting in on history-making recording sessions, and learning to use cocaine as an aid to help me drink more.

In the midst of finding my feet, I was cast as a young woman who'd just gotten engaged in an episode of *Medical Center* called "The Crooked Circle." *Medical Center* was a hospital show starring Chad Everett – I'm not sure anyone remembers the show or Chad now, but it was a big deal at the time.

What really sent me into a spin, though, was when I got on set and learned that my character's husband-to-be was being played by Tim Considine. A true WTF moment if there ever was one.

I'm guessing the producers thought it'd be a great promotional idea for the show to cast the two of us. No one knew that we were in the early stages of divorce. To keep the atmosphere on the set as relaxed and convivial as possible Tim and I quietly agreed not to tell anyone. Which meant we were not only acting in front of the camera but behind it as well. It was painfully awkward for both of us and a relief that it only lasted a few days.

Around that same time I landed a role back at Desilu on the crime drama *Mannix* and loved getting to know its handsome star Mike Connors, whom I liked a great deal. His real name was Krekor Ohanian, from an Armenian family, born in the Central Valley, so like me had arrived in Hollywood as a complete newbie and had to make his way. Mike was a sweetie, we had a dressing room fling, and he wanted to see me again. I said of course – he could find me anytime at The Liquid Butterfly.

Within a day or two I was having breakfast on my own at a café on Santa Monica Blvd and reading the newspaper. A good-looking blond guy at the next table leaned over to say something like how impressed he was to see a pretty girl reading the business section. Well, I'd actually been reading the comics and told him so, which he thought was pretty funny. He turned out to be Jon Voight, the star of *Midnight Cowboy*, a film that also starred Pasadena Playhouse alum Dustin Hoffman.

Jon was having a moment in the sun with the release of *Midnight Cowboy*, a dark, risk-taking, beautiful film, which the previous April had earned the distinction of being the first and only X-rated movie to win the Best Picture Oscar (the X-rating had stupidly been given due to its references to homosexuality, and was changed to R in 1971). It also won best director and best screenplay. Jon was nominated for best actor, but wound up losing to John Wayne for *True Grit*.

And here he was talking to me.

Jon was sweet, flirty, chatty, and I was over the moon. I was only too happy to tell him – when he asked – that he could find me at The Liquid Butterfly if interested.

Assuming that was the last I'd see of him, I said good-bye and went on with my day.

Later on though both Mike Connors and Jon Voight walked through the door of The Liquid Butterfly one right after the other.

Both looking to hook up.

Gulp.

I plastered on a smile, having no idea how to make this work.

Mike glanced at Jon and then at my frozen smile and sized up the situation. He grinned at me conspiratorially and ducked out. I ended up going out with Jon and spent the night at his place. We saw each other on and off for about three months but by January or February of 1971 our friendship came to a sudden halt when a gossip columnist wrote about one of our dates – a date that had taken place out in public, anyone could have tipped the writer off. As soon as the column appeared, I never heard from Jon again. Though I can only speculate, I'm guessing he thought that I, or my PR rep, had contacted the columnist as a way of promoting my career by attempting to tie my wagon to his. It had certainly been done before (and still happens today) though not by me. I never slept with anyone to get a part; I didn't date anyone to get my name in the papers. I didn't play that game. I hadn't used Jon and was sorry to see things end in the way they did. But I understood. In Hollywood, "staying hot" is a big part of long-term success. Most people who are famous are not famous by accident. It's a lot of work and requires a team of PR people, assistants, and so on, who assume a take-no-prisoners position when it comes to image.

Before the year was out I heard Jon had gotten married and a few years after that I happened to walk by a restaurant in the San Fernando Valley and saw him sitting at a table near the window making sweet, funny faces to a baby in his arms. I tapped on the glass and smiled and waved. He gave me a great smile in response and waved Angelina Jolie's tiny hand back at me.

***

Back at The Clear Thoughts Building on the first floor there was another clothing store called Themis, owned by Pamela Courson, who was Jim Morrison's girlfriend. Probably "official girlfriend" is the term I should use as he was usually seeing several women at once. I rarely saw Pamela except for the time she drove her car through the front window of her store.

Themis was a hot spot. When the Rolling Stones were in town Mick Jagger stopped by and bought some clothes there.

One day I noticed a heavily bearded, bushy-haired guy in dark glasses in The Liquid Butterfly peering out our front window in the direction of Electra Records, watching people arrive in limos for some kind of swanky event. I thought he was a private investigator or a member of the paparazzi staking out the building. This was my introduction to Jim Morrison – the legendary "Lizard King," the object of insane desire for millions of girls across the world.

Where he had once looked like the statue of a Greek god come to life, he was now scruffy, massively bearded, with a bit of a gut and rounded cheeks when he smiled, looking more like a cherubic lumberjack than any kind of rock icon. He had no interest in being recognized. No desire for fame. If anything, he struck me as a kind of fugitive. I don't think he was writing or recording any music just then. Like Joni Mitchell who saw herself as a painter who'd somehow become a singer/songwriter, Jim saw himself as a poet who'd lost his way in the music world, lost his way in lots of ways I suppose. Jim reminded me of Elvis. He wasn't all sex and sizzle up close. He was quiet, on the shy side, and really funny once you got to know him. His stream of wry observations about the people and situations all around made him a lot of fun to hang out with. We discovered pretty quickly that we had a couple of things in common – we both liked to drink and play pool.

Fortunately there was no shortage of dives nearby where you could find a dark corner, down a few beers, and shoot the breeze. Which we did often. I really liked Jim and I think he liked me – possibly because I didn't want anything from him. His bullshit meter had become pretty finely tuned after years in the music business and he could spot a genuine from a fake without a lot of effort.

One night not too long after we started hanging out, Jim was dead drunk. I couldn't leave him in the bar and wasn't sure what else to do so I got his arm around me, hefted his bulk into my station wagon and drove him over to my bungalow. There I tried to lug him out of the car without any success. I honked the horn and shouted "Delana, I need your help!" Moments later she appeared silhouetted in the front door. You have to get the full effect here. This was, in fact, a dark and stormy night. She comes out in the rain where I'm trying to haul a large hairy stranger more or less over my shoulder. She's got to be wondering "What the hell? Has Charlotte killed somebody? Is she reenacting a scene from *Gunsmoke*?" But in good roommate fashion she helps cart this person inside and in the light realizes who it is. Her eyes nearly pop out of her head.

For a while I thought if she didn't take a breath I'd have two semiconscious people on my hands.

"Oh. My. God! That's really him!" she silently screamed.

Jim opened a pair of barely functional eyeballs just then and took in the Jim shrine in our entryway – Delana's collection of drawings of him with horns and skulls, wings and reptiles that filled this part of the house.

I heard him gasp, "What is this place?"

With Delana's help, I poured him into bed.

At the age of 27, Jim was as famous – or infamous – as anyone in the Beatles or the Rolling Stones. His music projected power, sex, and a kind of psychedelic mysticism that frightened a lot of older America. When he screamed, "Break on through to the other side," it inspired a lot of kids to try doing exactly that with LSD, mushrooms, weed, whatever they could lay their hands on.

I got the idea that he felt so beaten up and bewildered by fame that the added weight and the mountain-man beard were ways of shielding himself. Not only was it a kind of disguise but being less physically attractive was its own kind of protection. The less you looked like Jim Morrison, the less attention you attracted – unwanted and even threatening attention. I remember reading later that during the time I knew him there were two or three paternity suits pending against him. And I know he very much wanted to avoid photographers, reporters, fans – anyone who wanted a piece of Jim Morrison the idol, rather than Jim Morrison the person.

Beyond the paternity suits Jim was in serious legal trouble. At a concert in Miami, Florida on March 2, 1969, he had allegedly screamed obscenities and displayed his manhood to the audience, which included young girls, and was arrested for indecent exposure and one or two other related charges. I asked him once if he'd done it. He said he didn't know. He'd been drinking for about three days prior and had no memory of the concert. "I probably did," he said, resigned to it.

He had rejected a plea deal and was appealing a fine and three-year jail sentence – all of which meant he'd have to go back to Florida to face the nightmare of a hostile criminal justice system and a salivating and just as hostile media circus.

A week or two after crashing at my bungalow, he mentioned that he wanted to get away and asked if I wanted to get out of town with him for a few days. In the days before cell phones you could simply get in your car and drive out of town and you were away. No one knew where you were. No one could reach you. It could be pretty therapeutic. I said sure. Why not? He picked me up at The Liquid Butterfly in a rental car on a Friday and we drove up Highway 1. As we were leaving Santa Monica, I noticed a marquee on the Nuart Theater advertising *Midnight Cowboy*, which promoted a thought-message to Jon Voight, "And no, I'm not going to call any columnists about my outing with this guy either."

We didn't get very far that first day, stopping off at a bar in Malibu that I don't think is there any more. It had individual booths that opened out onto the beach and offered privacy while giving us a spectacular view of the sun disappearing slowly into the ocean. I ordered a vodka, he a Jack Daniels and we sat together mostly just watching the colors of the sky bleed into the water.

I really don't know why Jim asked me to go on this getaway. All these years later I think back on it and realize that we didn't know each other that well, though at the time I'm not sure that mattered much. We enjoyed each other's company and somehow, maybe, he knew that I'd be comfortable with the silences he seemed to want, perhaps to crave. Maybe he sensed that whatever happened it would be simple and laid-back and lacking any kind of expectation.

After a few more rounds of drinks we checked into a hotel next to the bar and in the morning we headed out again, toodling up the coast stopping at bars and drinking and playing pool. We had no schedule, no agenda, no goals. We were just hanging out and it was glorious. That second night we made it as far as the Madonna Inn in San Luis Obispo, staying in one of their themed rooms, though I can't remember now which it was.

At the little seaside town of Cambria the next day we visited Peter Fels, a friend of mine who was a metal sculptor, who actually looked a lot like Jim if Jim had reddish hair – the same big beard and wild hair. Funny thing is Peter lived so completely with his art he had no idea who Jim was, much less what a superstar he was to the world outside of his artist's studio. I made an introduction like, "Hi Peter, this is Jim." And these two big-bearded artists padded off into Peter's barn to look at metal sculptures together.

Afterward Jim wanted to see Hearst Castle, so we parked and took the shuttle bus that takes you up there. Throughout the trip I'd been shooting with my little 8 mm film camera and got normal goofy stuff like Jim driving or eating an ice cream cone at Hearst Castle.

Not surprisingly, he loved being out of Los Angeles, away from the music industry, away from lawyers, and all the associated pressures. He could breathe, could let go of all the tension built up inside. Not surprisingly after a taste of this, he started talking about wanting to really get away. Like out of the country, maybe going to Europe.

Jim and I were friends, drinking buddies, and we slept together and that was it. Everyone else in his life wanted something from him, which made me all the more determined to let him know that I wanted nothing. We were never going to have a relationship. I couldn't picture myself going out on the road with him, being Jim Morrison's girlfriend. It just wasn't that kind of thing. This book is the first time I've ever spoken of our friendship. After letting 40 years lapse, hopefully, I can speak of it now without cheapening the easy friendship we had together.

Our last night was at a hotel in Solvang and finally we had to head back south to the real world. I had a TV show to do and I know he had plenty to occupy his time. Among other things he was trying to decide what to do about the house he owned in Topanga Canyon, which I think he rarely used.

Back at The Liquid Butterfly I realized that a whole new group of people had moved into Elliot's extra office space. Being the nice, welcoming person I am, I bounced in and asked if anyone wanted coffee. I was met with a roomful of suspicious stares and a dishwater-blonde hippie chick a couple of years younger than me said, "What do you want?"

This fun bunch had moved over from Warner Brothers, where they'd just finished up the sound and editing on *Woodstock*, the documentary that would define the early 1970s. Elliot had invited them to house themselves at his office building as they were working together on their next project, a documentary about Crosby, Stills, Nash and Young.

They were East Coast intellectuals – snobby, suspicious, and prone to peg a freckled, blonde, easy-breezy California babe as someone who might be hiding an agenda behind that smile.

The young woman who'd questioned my motives was named Jeanne Field. And unbeknownst to either of us, this was the beginning of a friendship that would last through terrible ups-and-downs for the rest of our lives.

I responded to her skeptical question by saying simply, "I just wondered if anyone wanted some coffee."

I'm really not that complicated. When I ask if you want coffee and serve up my brightest smile, there's really no subtext.

Maybe they weren't just being East Coast snobs; they were also a bit down in the dumps. While working on *Woodstock*, Warner Brothers had given them a house to live in rent-free and now they were casting about for a place to stay.

I shocked them by offering my little bungalow. I was going to be away shooting an episode of *Then Came Bronson* in Jackson Hole, Wyoming, and said they could have the place while I was gone. They still weren't quite sure of what to make of my flower-child generosity but the temperature in the room warmed up.

A day or two later Jeanne met Jim Morrison and their need to find a place came up again. He said they could move into his house in Topanga Canyon. He wouldn't be needing it for a while because he and Pamela Courson were going to Paris.

He was happy to be getting away, really getting away this time.

***

On the evening of July 3, 1971, I was with a bunch of friends at a music studio with Johnny Rivers as he recorded an album. Someone came in with the news that Jim had been found dead in a bathtub in Paris.

There were some gasps and for a moment the room got really quiet. I just went numb. I don't recall feeling anything. In the space of 11 months we'd lost Jimi Hendrix, Janis Joplin, and now Jim Morrison. All dead at the age of 27.

I'd never met Janis and Jimi but their music had been a force that defined this new world that our generation was creating. They were role models. Celebrities. Leaders. Artists. But Jim was different to me. He certainly occupied that same rarified space – his music had also given expression to who we were, how we felt, how we saw the world around us. But Jim had been my drinking buddy. We'd played pool from here to Cambria. We'd laughed and eaten ice cream together. We'd sung Elvis songs in the car. We'd been drunk, goofy, naked, and stupid together. He wasn't a photo on an album cover.

I didn't believe the stories that he'd died of a heroin overdose. I'd never seen Jim do drugs, never even saw him light up a joint. His vices were smoking and drinking. From having rheumatic fever as a child he had high blood pressure and his face was often beet red – none of which was helped by the booze and cigarettes plus the stress of his legal troubles. The long-term effect of rheumatic fever is often serious damage to the valves of the heart. My guess is he died of a heart attack although I wasn't in Paris and there's a lot I don't know about medicine.

There's nothing deep about death for me. Nothing grand. Nothing operatic. I'd learned that when my dad died. Death happens and it's horrible, it sucks, and there's emptiness. That's what Jim's death was. It was horrible and it sucked and the world felt changed and yet unchanged. And it was hard to know which was worse.

Chapter 6

Sex, Death,
and the Rolling Stones

IF YOU LEAVE SANTA MONICA heading more or less north on Hwy 1 you'll enjoy the sparkling Pacific Ocean sprawled out to your left. Waves come crashing in on delighted children in their bathing suits while couples walk or jog along the bright sand. You'll see a few palm trees, kites, and wheeled ice cream carts. To the right you'll see the base of an embankment of rugged, arid mountains covered in scrub brush and cactus. At intervals this is broken up with beach houses, taco stands, and surf shops. You'll eventually come to a junction in the roadway that offers the chance to continue north into the tiny town of Malibu or you can take a right heading inland into Topanga Canyon.

If you head up this road, to the right, you'll find yourself traveling between the dry walls of a fairly narrow canyon for a few winding miles until reaching not so much a town but an enclave. In 1971 you'd see the handiwork of Boxcar Bruce, who had wedged an old boxcar between the banks of a stream creating a bridge from the road to his house. Everywhere there are odd-looking patched-together houses, horses, rednecks, and hippies.

I rented a two-story, four-bedroom house on Observation Drive in Topanga Canyon. You couldn't feel farther from Hollywood though the neighborhood included actors such as Dennis Hopper, Dean Stockwell and Russ Tamblyn (who all eventually worked with David Lynch either in *Blue Velvet* or *Twin Peaks*). Neil Young and Jim Morrison both owned houses there as well. A young Oliver Sacks lived somewhere in Topanga's crooked streets in the 1960s, where – surprise, surprise – he experimented with mind-altering drugs, which he wrote about in his 2012 book *Hallucinations*.

Will Geer, who would play Grandpa on *The Waltons* lived here and ran Theatricum Botanicum, a little playhouse that put on various shows. Will, whose film career went back to the 1930s, was a great old beatnik and a much-loved Topanga guy.

Daniel Ellsberg, the former military analyst who'd given the famous Pentagon Papers to *The New York Times*, was holed up nearby. I visited him twice. Once with my friend Peter Butterfield who give Ellsberg guitar lessons, and on another occasion when someone handed me a package of papers to deliver to him. Without a thought in my head about what I was transporting, I showed up at his house and he plucked the fat envelope from me, opened it up, and seemed very pleased with its contents, showing no interest in revealing what they were.

What had I delivered? State secrets? God knows.

We also had a nightclub of sorts called The Topanga Corral, where you could hear some incredible music. And we had The Elysium Institute, our very own nudist colony, though tromping around outdoors in my birthday suit never held much appeal.

If I remember right, I got the idea to move to Topanga because Jeanne Field was now living there on a commune with what she called "The Gang from Rome." This was a group of actors and crew who'd worked together on *Fellini Satyricon*, the film by director Federico Fellini. One of the actresses, the wonderful and zaftig Mickey Fox, also became a dear friend of mine.

As I mentioned earlier, Jeanne, her boyfriend Larry Johnson, and others from the Woodstock film had taken up temporary residence in Jim Morrison's house. After Jim died one of his attorneys called Jeanne and offered her the house for a ridiculously low $17,000. She said to him, "You know, I'm a hippie. I'm not even sure I believe in owning things." And with that she went to live on the commune. When commune life lost its shine, she claimed one of my bedrooms for a while.

I had a real kaleidoscope of people moving in and out of the house, mostly friends who crashed on a couch for a few days. My official roommate was Doreen Small. Jeanne liked to say that you could not find two more opposite people – I, the "farm-bred, blonde, California girl" and Doreen "the Brooklyn intellectual with lots of dietary restrictions."

Even with the always-changing cast who slept on my floors, couches, and spare bedrooms, I still managed to see a fair share of interesting guys.

I'd met the phantasmagorically good-looking Gardner McKay in the early 1960s – pre-Tim – when he was the massively popular star of a show you've probably never heard of called *Adventures in Paradise*. From about 1959 to 1962, it seemed like this guy was going to be Cary Grant-fabulous and Brad Pitt-famous. The opinion that I formed of Gardner at the time, which was based on not much, was that he was a bimbo. How could anyone that porcelain-gorgeous be anything but a hairstyle in tight jeans?

After *Adventures in Paradise* ended Gardner left town. He hated being famous – the stress, the loss of privacy, the constant unwanted attention – and he moved to Paris for a while until he started being recognized there too.

He came back to Hollywood, bought a house in Beverly Hills on a huge lot and installed a Jaguar in the front and back of his house – not the car, the actual exotic South American cat. He also started writing plays.

My friend from the Playhouse, Josh Bryant, was cast in one of his plays called *Sea Marks*, which went up at The Actors Studio in Hollywood. I went as a favor to Josh not anticipating much, only to be blown away; it was haunting and beautiful. When the play was over and the applause was over-the-top, I turned around and saw Gardner sitting by himself and thought, "I have seriously underestimated this guy." One of his plays called *Me* was eventually turned into a TV movie, which Josh also appeared in along with his buddy Richard Dreyfuss.

Josh introduced me and Gardner and we started seeing each other quite a bit. He loved Topanga, especially in the morning when the sun was just cresting the rim of the canyon and all you could hear were the sounds of nature.

He wrote a series of five poems for me called "Topanga," which he composed in longhand on my deck and later typed up and presented as a gift. Here's one of them:

Topanga Sunrise

The patchwork curtain
Paisley, tweed and rose
A luminous stained glass
Made by you

A rooster crows
And a mule off, away
Cats walking out to see

And there they are!
The hills
The sun between them
Coming up to me

> A face behind me
> Looking through a screen
> And there you are
> Bringing me my day
> In a cup.

He was soulful and sweet but could have a temper. One day I drove over to visit Gardner in Beverly Hills and to introduce Doreen. As we walked in here came one of his Jaguars and I bent down and was stroking him and basically showing off. The beast grabbed my neck in its jaws. He wouldn't let go and Doreen panicked, ran inside, grabbed Gardner, and guess who Gardner was mad at? Me! I had disrespected his cat. I had crossed some kind of human/animal line. I had violated its, I don't know, cat-ness. He eventually cooled off and I was allowed back on the property, which was good because Gardner had great parties. One Christmas I remember Will Geer was there dressed as Santa and Gardner's jaguars were silently padding through the house among the guests. I kept my distance.

Will Geer wasn't to be the only cast member from *The Waltons* whom I got know. I ended up being cast in the show's pilot episode, where I met Ralph Waite, the actor who played John Walton, Sr.

Like all sets, there was a great deal of downtime between takes and I learned what an unusual background he had for an actor. He had earned a theology degree from Yale and was an ordained Presbyterian minister, who in the early 1960s had been drawn to theater. He'd played on and off Broadway for years and came out to California for *The Waltons* a little reluctantly I think. He certainly wasn't the guy you saw on TV. He had a brain like a freight train and lived life to its fullest (decades later he ran against Mary Bono for a congressional seat) and we had a great time together.

Once when Ralph spent the night at my house in Topanga he realized the next day he'd left his wallet. He called me from the set with this tale of woe so I drove it over to the Warner Brothers and dropped it off – to the amusement of a few people on the show who realized what had happened.

I did not, I would like to point out, go to bed with every famous or semi-famous guy who came along. An example: One day I got a phone call at home. A very formal older man on the other end asked, "Is this Charlotte Stewart?" and I said that indeed it was. The caller then announced, "This is Mr. Ford." (It was like Jane Austen was writing this phone call.) By "Mr. Ford" he meant he was the esteemed actor Glenn Ford, with whom I had filmed an episode of *Cade County* and who was 30 years my senior. Mr. Ford, as he apparently preferred to be called, was inviting me to spend the weekend with him at a vacation home at a seaside resort in Mexico. I was so dismayed at the thought that I sort of lurched away from the phone and knocked a painting by Joni Mitchell (a gift) off the wall and watched it tumble down a set of stairs, an accident which this poor work of art bears to this day. I politely declined Mr. Ford's offer.

Another time, someone thought I should go out with Don Knotts, the actor who played Andy Griffith's sidekick. Now, look, who doesn't love Don Knotts – a terrific comedic performer – but he took me to dinner at the Beverly Wilshire Hotel, which was pretty old-school for my tastes. It'd be like going to The Brown Derby, which had been the happening spot in the '40s. Don was 20 years older, of a different era, and we just didn't click. I could barely make it through dinner.

In another, weirder case, the producer of a TV show I was on came over on some pretext. We had some drinks and were talking about this and that. Then I stepped out to go to the bathroom and when I came back like a minute later there he was completely, 100% naked, sitting on the floor of my kitchen with his back against my cabinets with his big, old, gut sticking out.

I wondered if this smooth move had worked on anyone else. Ever.

I asked him to leave.

Eew.

The guys I had flings with were ones I found sexy, cool, or just fun to hang out with – smart, fascinating, sometimes challenging. For example, on set Chad Everett, who was the star of *Medical Center*, could at times be a pain – kind of a big shot, told jokes that were usually in really bad taste or annoying, but he could be a lot of fun. Did I want a relationship with the guy? No. Did I want to be Mrs. Chad Everett and wake up beside him for the rest of my life? Shoot me. But he could be entertaining to play with.

At other times I just developed a mad crush. While shooting that episode of *Then Came Bronson* in Jackson Hole, Wyoming, I followed the star, Michael Parks, everywhere, totally enamored with his bad-boy-ness. He ignored me as long as possible until I just wouldn't relent and finally he deigned to speak to me. It was at that point he invited me into his trailer. Magical things happen in trailers. And then my obsession with Michael Parks was done and the world moved on. (It's funny that he ended up with a role on *Twin Peaks* years later as Jean Renault, though our paths never crossed on set.)

The thing I didn't even think to do was any sort of strategic sleeping-around, which can (I'm told) bolster your career. Think of it as naked networking. In spite of various offers, I didn't have sex with anyone on "the casting couch" in exchange for a role, perhaps to my IMDb detriment. Sex was never a kind of currency for me. I didn't obtain things with it. I didn't try to pin anyone down with it. It wasn't about control or gain. It was simply recreational, personal, and sometimes hot, sometimes it was just okay. But more often than not, if you were selective with the men you slept with – avoided the psychos, the control freaks, the users, or simply run-of-the-mill assholes – there was a lot to like.

One time a girlfriend asked me how I could be so promiscuous. Her word choice – promiscuous – not mine. And I said, "Men sleep around like crazy and no one thinks twice. I think I should be able to sleep with whomever I want whenever I want."

I believed that if you were both adults and agreed it was for fun, there was no reason not to have a good time together.

And in a sense I still believe that. However, at the time my sexual decisions were being made within the ecstatic blur of alcohol, weed, and cocaine. Add to this the fact that I was a 20-something who loved adventure, that it was Hollywood in the 70s, that everyone else was doing precisely the same, and it becomes difficult to really sort out whether I was sleeping around in defiance of social norms or if I was just doing what all my dope-smoking free-loving hippie friends were doing while still – yes still – assuaging that gnawing and usually present sense of inadequacy that I had lugged around like a dirty backpack since high school.

Oh life. So complicated.

Anyway, the guys raining down on me weren't just actors. In the summer of 1972 I was living with Robert Greenfield, a contributor and editor with *Rolling Stone* magazine.

My roommate, Doreen, had introduced us initially. They'd known each other back in Sheepshead Bay, Brooklyn. What was it with me and East Coast intellectuals? Robert had stopped by the house to say hi to her and we ended up talking and it was pretty clear right off that liking each other was in our immediate future. He was in Topanga on a magazine assignment and asked if I wanted to tag along. He explained he was writing a feature on what at first sounded like a nudist colony, except it wasn't exactly a nudist colony because not everyone was nude and mostly the reason people were there was for various kinds of hooking up.

"So it's a sex club," I said.

"Essentially, yes."

I hadn't known until that very moment Topanga had such a place among its many natural wonders.

I accepted his offer with the understanding that I was not interested in a) taking off my clothes in public or b) making the beast with two backs at this joint simply to give his story a little added color.

We drove over to this big, bulk of a house that had lots of rooms spreading out all over the place. Once inside it was quite a scene. I ended up perched in a defensive position with my arms around my knees on the shag-carpeted floor of a large but tightly crowded living room. All around me were men and women, some partially dressed, some naked, some fully dressed, mingling, flirting, or in the early-to-late stages of intercourse. It was all being taken pretty seriously. There wasn't lots of laughter or goofiness, which made it all kind of creepy. So there I am willing myself to be invisible in this alien, porn-like environment, when I felt a bump at my back and I hear a man mutter, "Excuse me." I turn and there at eye-level and inches away from this gentleman's startlingly large man parts. He didn't mean anything by it. He was just making his way through a crowded room to the bar.

So that was my first date with Robert.

Later I traveled with him to Mexico where we hung around with the film director Alejandro Jodorowsky during the filming of *The Holy Mountain*. Jodorowsky was a mesmerizing presence, tailor-made for the experimental spirit of an era in which everything – mystical, spiritual, and pharmaceutical – seemed worth exploring. He was as revered an artist as he was controversial. His film *El Topo* was an art house hit but he was also rumored to have raped an actress on the film.

The magazine had paid my way on the trip since Robert told them I was his photographer. Much preferring the role of photographer to hanger-on girlfriend – though I knew next to nothing about photography – I borrowed a professional-grade camera from an artist friend, Tony Hudson (whose cute little boy Slash would grow up to be a member of the band Guns-N-Roses). On the plane I read the camera's owner's manual as well as the instructions that came on the boxes of Kodak film.

Once in Mexico Robert and I spent a lot of time on the set and in the house where Jodorowsky was living at the time. I occupied myself chiefly by fiddling with Tony's camera to see if I could coax a few good images out of it.

For some reason Jodorowsky ended up taking a liking to me and invited me to sit next to him taking my pictures while he was shooting his movie. And once we got back to L.A., after all the high jinx of stumbling through Photography 101 on the fly, Robert and his editors liked my photos, some of which ended up running with the *Rolling Stone* feature.

A month or two later Robert and I flew north to San Francisco. He was now working on a book about the Rolling Stones, his second, which would be called *Stones Touring Party: Journey Through America with the "Rolling Stones."*

Just after we arrived I got a call from my sister, Barbara Jean. She said mom had done something strange – had driven herself nearly three hours from Yuba City to San Francisco General Hospital.

"What's wrong?" I asked.

Barbara Jean said she wasn't sure. Mom had always been very tight-lipped about any difficulties she might be having. Talking about her health was part of a long list of things she didn't discuss.

It was a few hours before the Rolling Stones concert. I'd been excited about seeing the group for weeks but now all that anticipation was replaced with dread, sensing that something much bigger than Mick Jagger might be coming at me.

After taxiing to the hospital I met my brother and sister where we had a chance to confer with a doctor involved with mom's case. He didn't soft-petal it; she had pancreatic cancer and had six months to live. If that.

It was like a hammer blow to the chest. The bigness of it made thinking in a straight line nearly impossible. It took a while to really grasp what we'd just heard. I remembered how Tim had gone through a mental and physical collapse at the end of our relationship and I hoped desperately not to replicate that right now in front of my family. I wanted to keep myself together but wasn't sure how.

When we went into her room, Mom was Mom. Her skin and eyes were yellow from jaundice and yet her attitude was like nothing special was going on. She refused to speak about the diagnosis and had no time for our tears. Nothing was going to change as far as she was concerned.

Barbara Jean turned to me and said, "You should go to that concert."

I shook my head. How could I?

"There's nothing for you to do here," she whispered. "If we just sit around staring at her, it's just going to make her mad."

It went against every impulse – after Honey had died alone following the same kind of assurances, the last thing I wanted to do was leave her side.

But I knew the situations weren't the same. The cancer wasn't going to end her life in the next few hours. Barbara Jean was right; we'd just piss her off by hanging around. I gave my dear mom a kiss.

As I was leaving she called after me, asking if I'd do her a favor and buy her a nightgown.

"Nothing in yellow," she added, offering the only hint that she was aware that she was presently the color of margarine.

Robert and I had incredible seats of course for the concert, in a box to the left overlooking the stage. There was the most famous band in the world just feet away and yet I was detached. Mick Jagger and Keith Richards put on a hell of a show and they were at their pinnacle in the early 1970s. But in that moment the music and the noise of the audience were not much more than white noise.

After the concert Robert grabbed my hand and led me backstage, where he consulted with one of the band's managers about getting together for dinner. That led to elaborate instructions that I didn't pay attention to. Robert however led me through a maze of backstage hallways and out of the theater where a mob of fans and paparazzi were waiting. There followed a bewildering James Bond-like swapping of taxis and subterfuge to outwit photographers and Rolling Stones devotees to get to a super-secret, super-stoned-out dinner at a restaurant with the band and select groupies.

None of it mattered.

My mom was dying. And I needed to get her a nightgown.

A couple of days later Mom drove herself home and ignored the fact that she was dying, running at her usual pace of life: gardening, keeping the house clean, getting together with her friends for their weekly Bridge games.

At the time I was at a loss to understand this kind of reaction to learning you only have a short time to live, thinking that if it were me, I'd mark lots of things off my bucket list like seeing the sunset on Fiji, taking the Queen Mary to England, or seeing friends I hadn't connected with since childhood. But what I've realized is that the modest rhythms and routines of life are what made my mom happy and so she was spending her final days doing the things she loved. I'd like to think that she lived her bucket list every day, though I suspect that's oversimplifying who she was and underestimating her dreams. Since my dad's death she had in fact done some traveling including the trip of a lifetime to Africa.

Later I would learn that Mom had finally gone to an attorney and worked through a list of important things related to the house, finances, her will, and so on.

I had little idea what was really happening until I got a call from her doctor in Yuba City who said, "Your mom has no idea that she has two weeks to live." Well, she did. She just wasn't going to waste her breath about it with him.

This was my cue. Whether she was going to like it or not, I flew to Sacramento and got a ride to Yuba City. Mom had grown small and frail and I could see the end was not far off. She asked me to tell her friends what was happening to her. I borrowed her car and ran this sad and distressing errand, knocking on doors and delivering the news. One of her friends had already guessed the truth, another took it okay, and a third really fell to pieces.

On one of her last nights at home, Mom and I relaxed and watched TV. As it happened I was on two shows on CBS that night – *Medical Center* at 9 pm and *Cannon* at 10 pm. Back then, if you were in a guest role the wardrobe department would often ask you to bring an assortment of your own clothes to wear. In one show I was a prisoner on a bus and in the other I was a blind heiress. I had filmed the shows a few months apart and without realizing it, I ended up wearing the same green houndstooth jacket. Mom thought that was hysterically funny and we had a great laugh.

She was proud of what I'd become professionally – her little girl who'd displayed so few natural abilities had done all right, which is what I believe I heard in her laugher that night.

A day or so later, I finally cajoled her into calling my brother and sister – she hadn't wanted to bother them. But Mom was ready to go to the hospital. They both came right away and the next day my brother, Lewis, carried her tiny frame to the car and he and Barbara Jean took her. I had decided, with a touch of drama, that I didn't want to go and then after they'd disappeared down the road I was so overwhelmed and disconsolate I thought, "Why am I being so stupid? Of course I want to go."

I hopped in Mom's car and lit a joint to try to keep myself together.

On the way I started thinking of my best memories of Mom ... like riding in the front seat of our car on our way to somewhere falling asleep up against her. Soft and warm...so comfortable and safe. For a small woman she had large breasts. Not sexy, just a mom.

She always wore a housedress with stockings rolled at the knee with a quarter, to get the measurement just right. The only time she wore trousers was when she and Honey traveled in their camper. She had a permanently freckled right arm from hanging it out the passenger window.

She had the same hairdresser for years named Bunny and a perm every two months. She didn't really like the style but didn't want to hurt Bunny's feelings. I had cried when she cut off her long red hair. She wore it braided over the top of her head.

Through the tears in my eyes now, I saw police lights flashing in my rearview mirror. Crap. I rolled down the windows to get the marijuana smell out and flicked the roach into the floorboard.

In true small-town fashion the officer who stopped me was Ron Cardiselli, a guy I'd gone to high school with. I apologized for breaking the speed limit and told Ron about the situation with my mom. If he smelled the weed, he didn't say anything. I still got the ticket.

At the hospital, Mom had already received a large dose of morphine and was drifting away. I sat on her bed and said to Barbara Jean. "God. I just got stopped by Ron Cardiselli. I threw my joint on the floor and if he noticed I was going to say it was Mom's."

From somewhere in her haze Mom gave a burst of laughter.

I turned to her and said, "I'll see you later Mom."

"No you won't," she said, pragmatic to the end.

Chapter 7

Henry and Mary X, Part 1

MY ROOMMATE, DOREEN SMALL, wanted to learn the film business and so became a volunteer at the American Film Institute's film school, the AFI Conservatory. AFI was funded by the National Endowment for the Arts and other big-name contributors, established in 1967 to become the premier institute for the study of American film and to house a graduate-level film school. An institute with a mission this grand was appropriately housed at the very stately Doheny Mansion in Beverly Hills, a huge Tudor-style estate built by an oil baron in the 1920s. Like the Pasadena Playhouse, its alumni list is long and distinguished. Some of the first graduates were Terrence Malick, Paul Schrader, and Caleb Daschenel.

I knew Doreen was enjoying her work at AFI assisting some hotshot young filmmakers and gradually I became aware that there was one student project in particular that she'd become attached to. In fact one weekend she went up to Neil Young's ranch in Woodside south of San Francisco to pitch him on helping to fund this AFI student project. Neil had a lot of interest in film. At the time I believe he was in the middle of editing *Journey Through the Past*, a documentary he directed about a tour with Crosby, Stills, Nash and Young and within a few years would launch his own feature film project, which would be called *Human Highway*. For whatever reason Neil didn't end up writing any checks to help the project Doreen was promoting.

Not long after that she came home to Topanga Canyon and told me that there was a possible role in this film for me if I was interested. I'd worked in a couple of student films through the years; they were always shot quickly, on a microscopic budget and were shown once or twice and then disappeared without a trace. Often the films themselves weren't stellar but the work was almost always fun, letting me stretch my actors wings a bit. I said I'd be happy to meet the director.

Doreen arranged for her student auteur to come over for dinner and we'd chat about the project, see the script, talk about schedule, and all that.

He arrived the evening of February 17, 1972 on my doorstep tall and lanky wearing a Panama hat with a hole in the brim and not one but two neckties – his signature look I would learn. This guy with a wry, loopy grin then, inexplicably, handed me a sack of wheat as a gift. Hmmmm. This was my introduction to the young David Lynch.

David had grown up all over the place in lots of outdoorsy settings – Montana, Idaho, North Carolina, and so on. As a boy he went on to become an Eagle Scout and developed a lifelong interest in forests, wood, and woodworking – all of which the world would see in its fullest bloom in the 1990s in *Twin Peaks* with its eerie owl and spirit-filled forests, drama around the wood mill, Special Agent Dale Cooper's obsession with tree species, and of course the Log Lady.

In the mid-1960s David had gone to Pennsylvania School of Fine Arts in Philadelphia, focusing on painting. He tells the story that one day he was working on a painting that was all blacks and dark greens and as he was looking at it he talks about hearing wind and seeing the painting move a little. And he realized through this kind of hallucinatory epiphany that what he wanted was to create a painting that moved and had sound. With this in mind he produced an animated one-minute film called *Six Men Getting Sick*.

In 1968 he shot a second short film, about four minutes long, called *The Alphabet*, which, like his first film, combined elements of animation and of live action, very much having the feel of a painting come to life.

From there film rather than painting seemed the way forward. While still in Philadelphia David applied for a grant to AFI, showing them his two short films and a script for a new one. He was awarded the grant and with the money shot *The Grandmother*, a 30-minute film in 1970.

That evening in Topanga he gave me the beginning of his graduate level project at AFI, a 23-page script (most full-length scripts are 90 to 130 pages) for a film titled *Eraserhead*.

What I realized later is that David was auditioning me – as much as he auditions anyone. He never does the traditional thing of asking an actor to read lines or do a scene. He just talks to you informally and gets a feel for who you are as a person. Whatever his process is, I apparently passed the audition as the role was mine if I wanted it.

A few days later I read the script – more of an outline than a screenplay really. Then I read it again. Which didn't help because I couldn't begin to understand it.

It seemed to be set in a grim industrial landscape where it was always night. The main character, Henry Spencer, an odd, passive, young man with a pocket protector full of pens had fallen in with a weird and dreary young woman named Mary X (my character). Together they became parents to a hideous thing – a baby? – okay, a baby-like thing, that takes over their lives with its insistent, bleating cries.

I don't have that original script so I can't go back and re-read how the film was originally resolved, which kind of doesn't matter because it evolved so much over time. For example, I do not remember the "woman in the radiator" in the original draft, a character that dominates the final third of the film. I think at some point in shooting David became enamored with the radiator on the set, the light shining from within, the hisses and noises he was creating for it, the possibility of Henry dreaming of a miniature world within.

From this initial read though, I was able to get a sense for my character, which ultimately mattered more to me than whether or not I understood the movie as a whole.

Mary X was an overly-protected, awkward girl. I saw her as someone who made her own clothes but had no sense of style, someone who slouched as though she was missing some bones, looked uncomfortable all the time, and always had a bra strap hanging down. She was easily walked over and put-upon. She seemed to either be ill or imagined being ill in very real terms. She reeked of desperation.

When I discussed this with David he was very enthusiastic about my take on the character and later during filming, before the camera would roll, he would play on the idea of hypochondria by what he called "giving me an ear infection," putting a dollop of glue in my right ear. This acted as a physical reminder that Mary always had a dull, weird ache in her head. It was brilliant. In some of the shots when Henry and Mary are in bed together you can actually see that glue blob in my ear.

Because David only had a small AFI grant to work with, there were a lot of do-it-yourself projects both prior to and during filming.

One of the props we needed was a photo of Mary. At one point in the film Henry pulls two sheets of paper out of a dresser drawer and we see that it's a picture of Mary that has been torn in half. To make the picture I sewed a dress – I made all my *Eraserhead* costumes – which didn't look right. So I made a second one that was less attractive. Bingo. I loaded on make-up for washed-out look and penciled my eyebrows in so that they almost met. Then Doreen, Mary X, and I went to a drugstore that shot passport photos.

Fearing I may have overdone it, I showed David the outfit and the photo and he gave it his total approval with one of his favorite responses: "Neat!" He is one of the most cheerful people I've ever known.

The first time you see Henry approach the house where Mary X lives with her parents and grandmother, you'll notice large dead sunflowers adorning the unattractive front yard. Doreen and I had seen those dried, awful looking sunflowers in someone's yard in Topanga while we were heading to AFI so we stopped and pulled up a bunch by the roots and stuck them in the back of my car. David loved them.

A more memorable prop was required for a moment in the original script when Henry and Mary are in bed. She's asleep and he reaches over, pulls down the bedcover, pushes a hand through her abdomen and pulls out fistful after fistful of umbilical cords. To make this work, David needed a cast of my torso.

Doreen and I went over to his house where he'd set up a bed on a screened-in porch. I stripped down to nothing, laid on the bed, and David and Doreen went to town slathering me from neck to nethers in latex and then waited for it to set up. Once it was dry – with the consistency of one of those rubbery Halloween masks – they peeled it off, which took some doing in my various cracks and crevices. Both of them at one point were digging around between my legs to get it all tugged out. (Hey everybody – welcome to my privates!) Using the latex mold, David poured a plaster cast of my torso, which looked really cool.

Unfortunately, after all that, when we filmed the scene it just didn't work; it looked too much like Henry was punching through a plaster cast. In the end, David filmed it such that Henry reaches down under the bedcovers and pulls out umbilical cords (which were real!), which he flings against the wall each with a wet splat that still gives me the creeps. I still have the plaster cast of my torso – later painting it gold; it sits on my dresser to this day.

By the time of my first scenes in about May of 1972 David had already done some filming with Jack Nance, who played Henry. They filmed a good deal of footage of Jack dressed in his plain black suit with high-water pants and white socks tottering almost Chaplin-esque through sooty, oily, muddy, abandoned warehouses and construction sites.

I'm not sure who else David had had in mind for the part of Henry, but I do know Jack very nearly didn't get the part. Jack had done a lot of theater first in Dallas, Texas, where he'd grown up, and then later in San Francisco at San Francisco State and at ACT. I believe he'd only been in one or two films up to that point. The way Catherine Coulson told it – she and Jack were married at the time – David had Jack come by his house and had done his usual thing of just chatting about this and that, no real auditioning. I think David would rather get a person who he sees as having the natural capacity for a part in their DNA, rather than having to do too much acting. Coming into filmmaking from painting, he comes at things from an all-consuming visual standpoint rather than from a script standpoint. If I had to guess, I'd say he sees actors the way a painter sees color and texture. He sets you up under the lights, in the environment that he's created – among all the other colors, shapes, and textures – and asks you to go through the movements of the scene. I remember while working on *Twin Peaks* he'd offer direction like "Make it more blue," rather than give specifics on how to move or what kind of emotion to shade your voice with.

Anyway, for whatever reason David just didn't seem to think that he and Jack clicked or that Jack quite embodied the part.

As they were wrapping up and walking outside though Jack noticed the cherry wood rack on David's VW and remarked with real reverence at the beauty of the wood and the workmanship. David had made the rack by hand. For some reason this changed David's mind. He saw the spark of a similar bent – a level of obsession with detail that seemed right. Ultimately they became good friends and collaborators. Jack was in every film David made up to *Lost Highway* in the late 1990s.

Other than the exteriors in which Henry slowly meanders through industrial decay, *Eraserhead* was shot on the old family estate at AFI. David had secured permission to use an abandoned two-story structure that had been servants' quarters and horse stables in which to construct sets, to store equipment, set up some office space, and so forth. All the interiors were fastidiously constructed, painted, and decorated by David, with occasional assistance from with his brother John Lynch, and long-time friend, the film's art director, Jack Fisk, (who would also eventually become David's brother-in-law when David married Jack's sister Mary in 1977).

The reason the hallways and elevator in Henry's building are so narrow is because David had to construct them as shells within the already narrow spaces of the stables. It worked beautifully helping to make Henry's world more cramped and soul sucking.

Besides Doreen, Jeanne Field had also come on board to help out in countless ways. By this time Jeanne had a lot of experience in documentaries, having worked in sound and on the crew in various capacities both on *Woodstock* and then on *Journey Through the Past* with Neil Young and Crosby, Stills and Nash.

The real center of the sisterhood on *Eraserhead* was Catherine Coulson, who the world would eventually know as "The Log Lady" on Twin Peaks. As early as *Eraserhead*, David was already dreaming up a character he wanted Catherine to play called "The Log Girl." By the time *Twin Peaks* came along in the early 1990s Catherine suggested he change the name to Log Lady given her age.

Catherine had grown up in Los Angeles around the entertainment business. Her father had been in radio and television and eventually became head of public relations at Disneyland. Her mom had at one time been on the Vaudeville circuit as a dancer partnered with her sister, Margrit Feeligi, who had later been a costumer and went on to became a very successful swimsuit designer.

Catherine had done camera work, an unusual job for a woman then, and in fact became the first woman to join the camera union. During *Eraserhead*'s various hiatuses she did some terrific work for John Cassavetes, who was for a time artist-in-residence at AFI, doing hand-held work on the films *The Killing of a Chinese Bookie* and *Opening Night*. In her post-*Eraserhead* life she would do a lot more camera work, the most well-known project being

Star Trek II: The Wrath of Khan. She was versatile to say the least. Prior to *Eraserhead* she'd done some acting, which is how she'd been introduced to Jack. They'd met at San Francisco State when he was a guest artist doing a play called *Amerika* that had moved from Dallas. They formed a theater group with David Lindeman, who also ended up at AFI. She says they fell in love doing *The Threepenny Opera* eight days a week together and were married in 1968.

On *Eraserhead* Catherine was the glue that held the operation together. I actually didn't get to know her all that well then because she was so busy on so many fronts – from making hundreds of grilled cheese sandwiches for the cast and crew to lighting to finding the right kind of vanilla pudding for various effects to securing actual human umbilical cords, which on its own was no small task. Somehow – probably because she was just so nice – she managed to talk a local hospital into giving her a seemingly endless supply of umbilical cords. She became such a fixture there; she'd don a pair of blue scrubs and wait outside the delivery room until a nurse would come out with a jar filled with cords in formaldehyde.

Her mom would also drive in from Anaheim to bring baked treats for the crew and her aunt Margrit helped David by letting him film images in her swimsuit factory. Plus she didn't mind that Catherine and Jack rummaged through her 17-room house helping themselves to lots of treasures that were used as props in the film such as the vaporizer that Henry uses to try to nurse the baby back to health.

For David there was no detail too small to obsess over. He did numerous test shots of various shades of white, gray, and black to see how they all showed up on film. When you see Henry getting in and out of bed, David had Catherine first soak the sheets in tea or coffee, to ensure that they were the right shade of white-gray (or gray-ish white) on film. Before shooting started he had us come over to AFI to watch the Billy Wilder film *Sunset Boulevard*, primarily so we could see what he wanted to achieve in black and white.

The story of the film begins with insemination imagery. A long sperm like creature drops into a pool of water inside a planet. Then we see a diseased-looking character called The Man in The Planet, played by Jack Fisk. Only seen in half-light next to broken factory-like windows he sits like a sentinel with railroad-type switching gears in front of him. Then to the sound of industrial grinding, he pulls the gears and seemingly sets something in motion.

After that we see Henry living in a decayed industrial wasteland, where no one ever sees the sun. He visits what from the outside looks like a haunted house. This turns out to be the home of slouchy, hollow-eyed Mary X and her family, where Henry has come for a nightmarishly awkward family dinner during which, at various times, Mary, her mother, father, and even the tiny roast chickens – that evening's entrée – each have seizures of varying kinds.

After dinner Henry is cornered by Mrs. X, who demands to know if Henry is going to marry Mary, revealing that Mary has given birth to a baby – at which point Mary interrupts and tearfully reminds her mother that at the hospital they weren't even sure if the baby was human.

Soon enough we see the newborn, which looks like a fetal lama crossed with a frog covered in a sheen of mucus. (Having said that, David swore Jack and me to secrecy about how the baby was made, a promise I've always kept.)

When it came time to film scenes in which I'm in Henry's dingy apartment trying to feed the baby, David kept it covered. I didn't see it until I had the spoon in my hand and David said "action." When it was uncovered I had the same reaction as every other filmgoer – revulsion. But of course this was my baby so in spite of it fighting to move its mouth away from the spoon, and its spitting, its goat-like bleating, and its gut-twisting appearance, I was supposed to love it.

(Although not named in David's script, Jack and I decided the baby needed a name, so we called it Spike. I'm still not sure if it was a boy or a girl.)

So there's Henry in his weird, ugly, isolating apartment with his weird, desperate wife and his hideous baby. It's dark and rainy outside and industrial clanging noises come from the radiator next to the bed. Is it any wonder than Henry gazes into the light of the radiator and, like a prisoner in solitary confinement, begins to dream up alternate realities – such as a tiny singing, dancing woman in the radiator. Or vaguely erotic dreams of the one other woman in the building.

The other woman is a character identified in the script as the "Beautiful Girl Who Lives Across the Hall" – one of my favorite character names. She was played by the truly beautiful Judith Roberts, whom I knew a bit as she had been married to Parnell Roberts, who played the older brother to Michael Landon's Little Joe on *Bonanza*. After they divorced Judith had moved in with my Pasadena Playhouse buddy Josh Bryant in Studio City. As you can see in the film not only does Judith have sensational bone structure but she had the most beautiful skin. I learned her beauty secret too – every night she coated her face in Vaseline.

Unlike Mary X who is wretched and miserable, the Girl Across the Hall is alluring and mysterious. But of course poor Henry is stuck not only with Mary but with the least loveable mutant baby who ever graced the screen.

Mary at some point can't take life with this horrific baby and tugs her suitcase out from under the bed and leaves in tears and wails. Now Henry is left to care for the baby himself. He tries to feed it, only to watch it sicken before his eyes, developing a skin disease that looks like that of Jack Fisk's Man in the Planet character. He unwraps the swaddling around the thing only to discover that the cloth had been holding together the infant's insides, which now ooze out in a mess of polenta-like goo and organs.

When the infant dies, Henry – as far as I can tell – transcends into the world of the radiator, where the Girl in the Radiator, with a puffy, diseased face and bright, shining eyes performs a weird dancehall song and dance number, stepping on spermlike creatures dropping to the stage floor (more umbilical cords).

The problem with describing the action of *Eraserhead* is that it diminishes the film. *Eraserhead* isn't really about the plot. For me, looking at it now, it's like a series of paintings. Every scene is beautifully and perfectly lit. Each moment is carefully structured and framed. People ask me all the time, "What does it mean?" To me that's like asking what Monet's water lilies mean. It's best to experience it and let it wash over you, resonate within you, take you where it will.

Having said that, I completely understand having a sense of bewilderment when entering into the *Eraserhead* universe. In the early days of shooting, I thought a lot of what was going on around me on that set was utter nonsense, such as when we shot the scene with Jack, Mary, and Mary's family around the dinner table. I was struck by how David would simply leave the camera running until the actors weren't sure what to do and he'd capture moments of such awkwardness. At other times I just got pissed off by how unreasonably slowly and meticulously he worked, laboring over details that, I was sure, would never really show up on the screen. It took weeks to shoot the dinner scene, all of it at night.

Because most of us – including me – had day jobs we would get together in the evening, have a meal together, and David would talk us through what we'd be working on. Typically we'd start shooting around 10 or 11 p.m. and go all night through about 5 a.m. In a six-hour period we would get one shot. Maybe two. This excruciating pace was due to the fact that David was painstaking and he did nearly everything himself such as tinkering with lights, with props, with the positioning of actors, discussing with Jack the smallest movements, say, of a hand or an arm. A scene of Mary X just lying in bed would take two or three days, while David set and re-set lights, repainted the walls, positioned the sheets just so and found the right spot for the camera – always a tough thing because we were filming inside an actual structure rather than, say, a sound stage, where you can simply move a wall if it's in the way. Since the *Eraserhead* set was built inside the servants' quarters/stables if a wall was in the way too bad, David (often with Catherine's assistance) had to get creative moving that large, heavy camera into a position that gave him the best possible framing. He didn't believe in the idea of "don't sweat the small stuff." It was like a film directed by a watchmaker. I once heard David joke later that after two or three years "we finally found our groove."

By the time I was in *Eraserhead* I had been working steadily in television and film since the early 1960s. I'd seen – I thought – every sort of director in a broad ranging variety of projects, comedy, drama, mysteries, etc. But in all that time, I'd never come across anyone like David. In the first two weeks of shooting I thought, "This guy is never going to make it as a director." (So much for my career as a clairvoyant.)

No one would dream of keeping actors hanging around for half the night while you fiddled with, for example, the workings of a tiny mechanical roast chicken (which Jeanne or Catherine would operate from underneath the table).

In the scene in which Mary finally leaves Henry and the baby, Mary is about to walk out the door then realizes she wants to take something with her. There's no indication of what it is. She reaches under the bed and begins to tug at something.

When David walked me through the scene he told me to keep tugging until he indicated (off camera) to pull the thing free.

So there I am kneeling down at the end of the bed, wailing, with my eyes on Henry, who is lying under the bed covers not believing that I'm really leaving. And I tug and tug and tug.

I tug 21 times before David gives me the sign and that's when I pull a suitcase free.

While doing it, it made no sense to me.

Now I see it as a quintessential David Lynch moment. It's both tragic and comic and as the director he steadfastly does not tell the audience how to feel. There are no music cues, there's no dialogue to tip you off, no winking at the camera, none of the irony-alerts of other films. As the viewer you get to experience it in any way you like.

Over time, because of moments like this on film, moments when I as an actor had no clue where he was going, David more than won me over. It taught me that if you're working with a great director, you simply do what they ask you to do and don't expect them to sit down with you in the moment and give you a graduate level TED Talk on what it is they're trying to achieve. So much of what David shot was gut feel – letting an idea germinate in the moment – he'd unlikely be able to elucidate exactly what it is he was going for.

It would have been a waste of time to stop everything and have the "What's my motivation" conversation. He was thinking not in words but in texture, grain, light, shadow, and darkness – mechanical vs. organic, wood and steel, disease and life.

Sometimes as an actor you just have to shut up and do your job.

Another reason I grew to trust him was because he helped form us into such a great, hard-working family. It was all for one and one for all. I agree with Catherine who compared working on *Eraserhead* with going to summer camp. There was a lot of freedom and camaraderie.

Part of that good feeling I suppose was that from the beginning David was very vocal that he wanted us all to get paid fairly and had developed a contract, which set up a regular (SAG minimum) wage. About a year into the project as his funding ran out, he couldn't pay us but Peggy, his wife at the time kept track of our hours. Loyalty is sometimes in short supply in Hollywood and even people with the best of intentions forget or lose track. I have learned that it seems to be incredibly easy not to pay people. Whatever the case would be, I wasn't holding out hope for payment though I appreciated that David's heart seemed to be in the right place.

That alone helped weld us into a close, tight-knit group, though I can't say we necessarily got to know each other much outside of the set. While I worked with Jack Nance during the first two years of filming, playing his wife, I really didn't get to know him personally all that well. I really only knew Henry, the character. The only times I saw Jack were on set and on set Jack was always Henry. When we weren't filming he'd often sit in a chair, hands folded, not needing to speak with anyone, not requiring entertainment of any kind. He was kind of a curmudgeonly guy about 40 years older than his actual biological age. I don't think he ever had much of a social life. He didn't get out often, didn't go to parties. His only friends were a few drinking buddies.

And in fairness, all Jack really saw of me was Mary X. During those long hours in between takes, I just hung around and tried to stay in character, adjusting my make-up, and re-pinning my odd, swirled hair.

What I could not know then was how long I would end up being friends with Jack and how intertwined our lives would be, parting and coming together more than once – for better or for worse, in sickness and in health – in a kind of spiritual marriage over the course of 25 years.

Likewise, none of us in the early 1970s could have known that unlike any other student film *Eraserhead* would take not a few days or a weeks or a month to shoot (as I had originally anticipated), but would turn into a project that stretched over years of filming and about another year in post-production. (In the 2000s David would repeat this feat with the five-year period it apparently took to shoot and cut together *Inland Empire*.)

For Jack the role of Henry meant a kind of dedication rarely seen in the history of cinema. As you probably know, the most iconic image from *Eraserhead* is Jack with that upright tower of hair. He maintained that look, like a male Bride of Frankenstein, for four years, his long-suffering wife Catherine keeping it snipped and clipped like topiary.

Chapter 8

Becoming Miss Beadle

FOR ME, SHOOTING *ERASERHEAD* was never a full time job. It was always a night here, a few nights there, so I was still involved in a lot of other things. While I was Mary X in the wee hours, by day I was appearing in commercials for Kool-Aid, Cheer laundry detergent, Jiff peanut butter, Dial soap, Clairol shampoo, Scope mouthwash, Three Musketeers candy bars, the postal service, Gravy Train dog food, etc., playing exuberant moms, cheerful pet-owners, and grateful deodorant wearers.

Eraserhead also overlapped with filming *The Waltons* pilot episode, which caused some problems. As I said, we filmed *Eraserhead* all night, and I drove to a friend's nearby apartment, slept for an hour, then at 6:30 a.m. I had to be on-set at Paramount for *The Waltons*. By mid-afternoon of the third such day in a row we were filming one of those scenes in which every single person in the cast is crammed into the living room and I was so tired, I was practically cross-eyed. I blew a couple of lines and apologized to everyone. Be assured, no one in either cast or crew had any sympathy for my screw-ups because I'd spent the night slumming on a student film.

How did I manage then to also have a fling with Ralph Waite at the same time, you ask? It's that farm girl work ethic.

In addition I was also still making and selling dresses at The Liquid Butterfly and because that still wasn't enough, I had taken up a new occupation – I was a proud waitress. Jeanne Field had opened a café in Topanga Canyon called Everybody's Mother, which featured large photos of the moms of everyone who worked there. My mom, the late and beloved Alice Stewart, was of course properly recognized and celebrated. Jeanne liked to call Everybody's Mother "food as theater," including the featured role played by Mickey Fox at the front counter. With her Venus of Wilendorf figure and larger than life personality, most patrons assumed Mickey was in fact "Everybody's Mother." During the gas crisis in 1974 people would get up early, line-up their cars at the gas station and walk across the street and have breakfast at the café. It was a Topanga thing.

Actually what I was doing at Everybody's Mother was a swap with Jeanne. She was working at The Liquid Butterfly for nothing and so I was supporting her by serving up piping hot breakfasts for nothing. That's what hippies used to do in the '70s. God, I miss that sometimes – sharing work, sharing homes, sharing weed, sharing boyfriends.

Not everything in my life was groovy though and I would open up to Jeanne and other friends about this. Even though Tim and I had separated in 1969 and our divorce finalized in early 1971, I still felt terrible about what had happened. No matter what else was going on in my life – how fun or adventurous things were – my role in the downfall of that relationship, how I had hurt him, stuck around inside me like a dark cloud.

Then I got a dinner invitation from Tim's brother John – remember John who had been such an angel going with me to Mexico for that horrific abortion? He had a great heart. Anyway, John and his wife, Toby, invited me to their house in Pacific Palisades for dinner and I learned they had invited Tim. Knowing John, this was no accident.

We had a great time. It was fun, relaxing dinner and afterwards John and Toby just sort of disappeared and Tim and I went outside at sunset and took a walk there along the ocean, which was spread out gigantic and gold. I was able to pour out my heart to Tim and tell him that I knew I'd done so much to hurt him and how terribly sorry I was. By now Tim had gotten to a new place in his life. He was happy again and it seemed like he enjoyed being on his own, making new friends, and having fun again. Finally the rift between us closed and that miserable chapter ended. A new one began as friends.

Tim started coming to the Friday night poker games at my house in Topanga Canyon, becoming one of the regulars along with Kit Carson, an actor friend, Peter Butterfield, who lived with me, and others. Tim even spent the night a few times. And now I had an open invitation to the soccer games he organized on Sunday mornings at the UCLA fields with family and friends. No one famous, just people from all parts of his life of every size, age, and sports ability.

I'm so happy that Tim and I have remained good friends ever since. When he married Willie, his wife of many years now, they had a small family wedding followed by a larger reception, to which I was invited.

I've been a guest at their house many, many times and it usually ends up being Willie and me in the kitchen making food or cleaning up while Tim and his "car buddies" are outside checking out engines and kicking each other's tires or whatever the hell car guys do.

***

In November of 1973, I spent four days shooting an episode of *Gunsmoke* called "The Schoolmarm," in which I played the role of Sarah Merkle, a kindly teacher at a one-room schoolhouse in Dodge City in the 1880s. Sarah cleans black boards, she's gentle with students, and she looks mighty fine in a prairie dress. Hmmm. Sound familiar? At the time I didn't think much about the role and in fact when I see the episode today I can't even remember filming it. But looking back I can't help but wonder if that guest role, which aired on February 25, 1974 on CBS, put something out there in the ether, a vibe that resonated a couple of months later.

In early May of that year I got a call from my agent with an audition for a project being created by Michael Landon with Ed Friendly's production company. It was called *Little House on The Prairie* set in the late 1870s in Minnesota.

Having never read the books, I knew little about the character, other than she was a teacher who worked in Walnut Grove's one-room schoolhouse. With so little to go on it can be challenging to breathe life into the dialogue on the page but I'd learned to go with my gut and that it never hurt to display a little audacity, which nearly any character needs in one way or another.

I drove over to Ed Friendly's office at the appointed time and found a waiting room filled with actresses in prairie dresses, bonnets, and other outfits of the period. I'm sure it sounds ridiculous outside of Hollywood but with so much talent to choose from a producer is often less concerned about acting ability – that's taken as a given – but on a person's look, their skin tone, eyes, hair color, facial structure. With so much riding on appearance it can make sense to "dress the part" for an audition to help the sometimes overworked, tired, high, bored or otherwise unfocused producers choose you over someone else.

On this occasion I hadn't bothered to track down the right dress or any of that. I just showed up in one of my usual flowy, flowery, running-around-Santa-Monica outfits. I'd been playing roles on TV and film since the 1960s and had lost interest in the various tricks actors can employ. These guys had seen my work. Part of being a professional, in my opinion, is to let the work speak for itself.

At least that was what I told myself. The real reason I didn't go to great lengths to get the part is that I thought it was just a "movie of the week" and if I didn't get it, no big deal. But as I looked around the waiting area at all the other actresses decked out in period hats and dresses, I did begin to wonder if there was something they knew that I didn't.

When it was my turn, I went into the office, said hi to Ed Friendly, the show's producer, and to some of the assistant producers. But it's a funny thing, with all those other people, my eyes went straight to Mike Landon. His presence owned the room. Some people just have that kind of enigmatic eyeball-drawing magnetism and he had it in a way only a few people do. I met both Tom Cruise and Denzel Washington years later and they had it too. What is that?

When given the chance to do my lines, I first asked Michael and Ed if I might re-arrange things in the room a little bit. Michael grinned and said, "Sure," and wanted to know what I had in mind.

Well, what I had in mind was to be a teacher and take charge of the classroom. I scooted Michael and Ed out from behind the big desk and arranged everyone like they were my pupils. I scolded them for talking and laughing and making noise. I mandated that they all be quiet and mind their manners while I ran my lines. Michael was giggling and I figured if nothing else I'd broken up their afternoon with a little comic relief.

By the time I arrived home an hour later, my agent called and let me know I'd gotten the part – then came the real surprise. This *Little House* gig wasn't so little. What I'd thought was just a quickie "Movie of the Week," was instead slated to be a major television series and they wanted me to sign a four-year contract which guaranteed seven out of 13 episodes per season. I believe my jaw actually, physically dropped.

Four years was forever. It was as long as high school. A presidential term. My marriage to Tim. I was stunned. It was like winning the lottery.

Okay this just got serious, I thought. I'd better learn something about the books.

A couple of days later at a swap meet in Topanga Canyon, I spotted one of the *Little House* books, bought it, sat down, and started reading. In Chapter One everyone has scarlet fever, Mary goes blind, Pa shaves her head, and the dog dies. "What the hell?" I wondered. And I thought *Eraserhead* was dark. Eventually I realized that I'd picked up *By the Shores of Silver Lake*, book 5 in the series, while the TV show was kicking off somewhere in the middle of book 4, *On The Banks of Plum Creek*. Things on the TV series wouldn't begin in quite such bleak territory.

Within a few days NBC messengered over a copy of the first script, I signed that lovely four-year contract, and on May 30, I drove to Paramount for my costume fittings. The costume department is a wonderland – rows upon rows of racks of clothes towering overhead and it just seems to go on for miles. This is where I first laid eyes on a girl named Melissa Gilbert, who would play Laura Ingalls but who was mostly called "Half-Pint," a nickname that had belonged to Laura Ingalls but was so on-the-nose that it now belonged to Melissa both on and off camera.

Half Pint was a buck-toothed, freckled, sparkly-eyed nine-year-old whose mouth was wide open as she stood gazing up in wonder at this towering cathedral of dresses and gowns. She was just adorable. I also met Melissa Sue Anderson, who everyone called Missy (to help clear up the confusion of having two Melissas in the cast) and she was poised and lovely with a bright smile that tended toward a shade or two of shyness. Maybe, I thought, working with these kids wouldn't be too bad.

The wardrobe crew took lots of measurements though I learned I wouldn't exactly be drowning in dresses over the next four years. People who lived on the prairie in those days didn't have a lot of money for life's niceties – like clothes. As such Miss Beadle's wardrobe in that first season would consist of a grand total of two dresses, one red plaid, and the other gray, along with four blouses and four skirts.

In scenes that called for Miss Beadle to wear glasses, I got permission from Mike Landon to wear my own round wire frames, the same glasses I could be seen in when sewing and hanging out at The Liquid Butterfly. I've never heard any complaints that they weren't right for the period. Apparently there was some stylistic crossover between 1870s schoolmarm and 1970s flower child.

Later when shooting started I would realize that Miss Beadle was a fashion plate by Walnut Grove standards. By contrast Karen Grassle, who played Laura and Mary's mother, Caroline Ingalls, always wore the same dress at home unless she went into town where she snazzed things up with a bonnet. Mike Landon wore the same thing show after show – woven britches, a flannel shirt and suspenders. The real fashionista was Alison Arngrim, playing uber-brat Nellie Oleson, who often went about her business in flamboyant, frilly dresses that were totally at odds with the plainness of everyone else's clothes – to her eternal delight.

Next it was time to do something about my hair and I met with Larry Germain, a hairstylist I'd bumped into very briefly years before when I did that episode of *The Virginian*. No one knew more about hair than Larry as he'd been in the business of making wigs, snipping, clipping, dyeing, and keeping secrets since the early 1940s. He'd done it all from *To Kill a Mockingbird* to *The Ghost and Mr. Chicken*.

Larry and the producers of the show had a pretty clear idea of how they wanted Miss Beadle presented and that involved making a partial blonde wig. The tricky thing for Larry was two-fold: I had really straight hair and I had just cut it prior to getting the part. Larry and Mike Landon wanted their teacher to have some curls and whoop-dee-whoops in her hair that were right for the period. But in this case, unlike when I did the Toni Home Permanent ad, they couldn't say "come back in a year." I had to go in front of the cameras in just a few days.

Because the wig would be for the top and back of my head (including a braid), Larry had to incorporate it seamlessly with the rest of my natural hair. To get the color right Larry and another hair stylist, Gladys Witten, took clippings from all over my head, giving them the overall color palate and they created a wig from there.

Once the wig was complete, we had trouble getting it to stay attached because my hair is so pencil straight. I tried curling the front with curling irons but the thing just wouldn't stay. Finally came the orders I had sorely hoped not to hear. I was told I had to get a permanent, which would give me some curl in front and would allow Larry to get the wig to stay attached for a full day of shooting.

Ugh.

A frizzy '70s perm.

A perm I would have to maintain for the next four years.

Suddenly I felt like Jack Nance having to sport that head of crazy hair for all those years of shooting *Eraserhead*.

I wasn't the only one with hair issues. Karen Grassle had short hair too and in the opening credit sequence of the show you can see her and Mike pull up in a wagon while Karen is busy tucking that short hair back inside her bonnet. The Oleson ladies, Katherine MacGregor, as Mrs. Oleson, and Alison Arngrim, as daughter Nellie, were also outfitted with wigs. To get the full story on Nellie's wig – which was practically its own character in the show – you'll have to do yourself a favor and go buy a copy of Alison's brilliant memoir *Confessions of a Prairie Bitch*.

Another part of the preparation was doing make up tests with Allan Schneider, whom everyone called Whitey. This guy was a legend who had been Marilyn Monroe's personal make-up artist, working with her on films including *Gentlemen Prefer Blondes*, *How to Marry a Millionaire*, and *The Seven Year Itch*. It was Whitey who had designed her signature bedroom eyes; it's a very specific swoop of eyeliner that gives that look – what a virtuoso move. Whitey demonstrated it on me once for fun but ultimately you may have noticed that Miss Beadle did not get bedroom eyes on camera.

My first day of shooting at Paramount Studios was on Sound Stage 30, an area of the lot formerly part of Desilu, where I'd filmed *My Three Sons*. If you take the Paramount tour today, there's a sign on the exterior of Sound

Stages 30 and 31, telling visitors that *Little House on The Prairie* was filmed there along with *Top Hat* and *The Gay Divorcee* both starring Fred Astaire and Ginger Rogers (back when the lot belonged RKO), *The Godfather*, and much later *Addams Family Values*, and about a ten thousand films in between. So it had been seasoned with a lot of great film and TV history.

This sound stage, as nearly all I've worked in, was a large eggshell colored industrial building, not terribly interesting from the exterior, designed to block out all light and sound from the outside world.

Sound Stage 30 measures 107 feet wide, 90 feet long and 35 feet high. Back in the 1930s, when it was RKO, the interior walls would have been sound proofed with mattresses behind chicken wire but by the 1970s that had been replaced with a thick material called Instaquilt. There's an odd thick feeling to the air inside because of the complete deadening of sound. It takes a bit of getting used to. In the rigging overhead you'll see dozens if not hundreds of lights of various colors, shapes, and sizes all designed to create a specific mood in whatever interior scene you're shooting – whether it's Fred Astaire and Ginger Rogers on a gorgeous, glittery dance stage or the dim and menacing inside of Don Corleone's office. It can make the world suspended above you, as an actor, look like a thick jungle of black light housings, armatures, and electrical cords.

The huge "elephant door" at the front of the sound stage measured nearly 24 feet in height. Those big, sliding sound stage doors apparently got the name because back in the old days they were big enough to walk an elephant through – if that's what your scene required. Mostly though they're that size so that a crew can build sets and slide them in or out. Once those elephant doors close, the outside world is gone and there is only the world that has been painstakingly built, painted, costumed, and lit.

On that day, Monday, June 24, 1974, it was the interior of the Walnut Grove one-room schoolhouse in the 1870s, which was welcoming two new students to the classroom – Laura and Mary Ingalls.

My call time was 6:15 a.m. and after getting all put together – hair, make-up, costume – I took a look around the sound stage and saw the chairs set up for the various actors. There was one with Michael Landon's name, one for Melissa Gilbert, Karen Grassle, etc. And finally I saw one that one that had the word "Teacher" on it. I made myself comfortable in that chair until an assistant director came by and said in a low voice, "I'm sorry you can't sit there. That's for the teacher."

"Yes, I know," I said. "I'm the teacher."

"No, it's for the real teacher."

Ah.

With so many kids on the series there was in fact a real teacher who was running a real classroom each day on set after the kids had shot their requisite four hours.

I eventually found a chair, though not one with my name emblazoned upon it.

***

> "Nellie Oleson was very pretty. Her yellow hair hung in long curls, with two big blue ribbon bows on top. Her dress was thin white lawn, with little blue flowers scattered over it, and she wore shoes.
>
> "She looked at Laura and she looked at Mary, and she wrinkled up her nose.
>
> "'Hm!' she said. "Country girls!'"
>
> — *On the Banks of Plum Creek*, Laura Ingalls Wilder

My first episode on *Little House on the Prairie* was called "Country Girls," which would first air on September 18, 1974. In this case "country girls," as you can infer from the quote, was an insult hurled sneeringly by, of course, Nellie Oleson at Laura and Mary on their very first day at the schoolhouse in Walnut Grove.

This was Nellie's way of establishing the pecking order, letting the new girls know that she was a sophisticate who not only owned more than one dress but that all her clothes were store-bought and not – gasp – sewn by her mother. (Nellie Oleson was basically Walnut Grove's Kim Kardashian.) It didn't end there. Not only did Nellie have a closet full of fancy, flouncy dresses, she was smart and knew how to read. Laura by contrast could only barely get through a single sentence, a fact that she was at great pains to hide. Oh, and Nellie would be making Mary and Laura's lives hell if they didn't kowtow to her. And so the die is cast between the girls from the first moment.

If a show's success is fueled by its antagonist, *Little House* was off to a good start, I thought.

What's interesting is that this dynamic between Laura and Nellie is there in one of the books – *On the Banks of Plum Creek* – buried on page 148 (in my copy) in a chapter simply titled "School." It's a credit to the genius of Mike Landon to recognize that story element, practically tug it out of the book with tweezers, and make it the engine of a show that lasted nine seasons.

The trio of kids that most people remember is of course that of Melissa Gilbert (Laura), Alison Arngrim (Nellie), and Melissa Sue Anderson (Mary). They had great chemistry on screen, which is all that really matters to fans. Like most children the world over, however, they did not always get along. Missy tended to do her own thing and keep to herself, while Alison and Half-Pint got along pretty famously. They were all terrific at playing their roles, bringing a lot of honesty and emotion to the screen. I doubt any group of kids would ever all get along without a hitch – if the trio of Barbara Jean, Lewis, and Charlotte Stewart back in Yuba City was any sort of guide.

While shooting that first episode, I realized what a find Melissa Gilbert was. She was a great scene partner. There's one moment in particular where it's just Laura and Miss Beadle in the classroom. Laura is reading haltingly out of a book. Miss Beadle is encouraging her, gently trying to build her confidence, while kindly and evenly pushing her to do better. At one point Half Pint stops reading and fixes me with those big, brown, nine-year-old eyes and shy smile and the camera, the lights, and the crew all just vanished. You can feel the adoration pouring out of her. In that moment we weren't at Paramount Studios on Melrose Avenue in Los Angeles. We were a teacher and student in Minnesota in the age of kerosene and wagon wheels. If America loved Miss Beadle, it's because Laura Ingalls loved her first. Even watching those scenes today, I am struck by Melissa's focus and authenticity. How do you do that when you're nine?

Maybe too it has something to do with the fact that Miss Beadle's empathy was real. When filming those scenes I remembered how I had struggled in school back in Yuba City, how I'd felt stupid, felt like I was letting my parents down, and was fighting to hang on to a shred of dignity in the face of schoolwork that had seemed like a breeze for my brother and sister and other kids. I knew Laura's embarrassment, I was rooting for her, and I wanted Miss Beadle to be the teacher I wished I could have had.

"Country Girls" set a pattern for how Mike would construct nearly all of the shows. While Laura and Nellie were having their battle about who would call the shots in the schoolyard, their mothers, Caroline Ingalls and Harriet Oleson, were being snippy and passive-aggressive over their own pecking order. Caroline brings a dozen eggs to sell to Harriet at the mercantile and their bicker over the price is a not-so-thinly veiled power struggle. Later as Caroline fingers a pricey bolt of cloth on display in the store, Harriet says with a domineering smile and triumphant tone that that fabric is surely something the Ingalls family can't afford. They both know it's true but Caroline sets her jaw and buys it.

Time and again you see mirrored storylines in which what's happening with the kids is also happening with the adults, one storyline taking the more emotional and dramatic path, while the mirrored storyline usually serves as the comic relief.

Another good example of this is "Bully Boys," a show in the third season. When a boy and his two much older adult brothers move to Walnut Grove, the youth establishes himself as a bully at school, at one point punching Mary in the face and giving her a black eye. Meanwhile the two brothers are swindling everyone in town and when Pa physically goes after them (for making Ma spill her fresh eggs on the Walnut Grove bridge), they send him off in a wagon badly beaten up too.

In the end the kids in the schoolyard finally have enough of their bullying and gang up and beat the living crap out of him – literally something like a dozen kids press in around in a scrum hitting and kicking him. (Miss Beadle is inside presumably cleaning chalkboards and spritzing herself with lemon verbena somehow not hearing the sounds of violence just outside her window.)

In the adult world, the townspeople finally have a showdown with the two older brothers and march them out of town all singing "Onward Christian Soldiers."

After my first couple of days shooting interiors at Paramount, I had on June 27 my other big "first" with the show and that started at about 5 a.m. Getting up and driving an hour out to Simi Valley to Big Sky Movie Ranch.

The Ranch is huge and hilly, more than 6,000 acres in size, and it looks like you're a thousand miles from any city. By 6 a.m. I parked in a gravel lot with the other actors and crew. A van picked me up and drove me over a hill to a collection of white trailers for costume, hair, and make-up.

There Larry Germain got my hair and wig just so, Whitey Schneider did my make-up, and Richalene Kelsey got me into that day's costume. Once I was all packaged up as Miss Beadle in my wool skirt, petticoats and golden hair, I walked to the top of the next hill where the sky was sprawling and blue, the air was clean, and the only sounds were the crunch of dry grass and dry soil under my lace-up boots. There wasn't a power pole, TV antenna, or a paved road in sight. I crested the hill and there spread below in a pretty little valley was Walnut Grove. My breath caught in my throat. The store, the mill, the church that doubled as the schoolhouse, all painted in early morning sunlight. I still get goose bumps thinking about it. I walked down and crossed the bridge spanning the busy stream and it was as though I'd passed through a magic doorway into another time. It seemed so real.

I struggle to put into words why this had such an effect on me. In the late 1800s my grandmother, Nana, had come to California from Iowa in a covered wagon and I felt a powerful connection to her. The sight of that beautiful little frontier town, me in these 19th century clothes, the connection to my family, to the past, maybe even in some way it called up some of my deepest memories growing up in Yuba City with its farmland and broad valleys dappled with the same grasses and scrubby plants, the same bird sounds and scents of nature. I felt as though I'd been there before.

Over the next four years, every time I would crest the hill and see the town, I would have the sensation that somehow I had been lucky enough to travel back in time to this very ordinary and yet very special place. Even now, some 40 years later, I'm nostalgic about that moment. I loved being out there.

Eventually, of course, the moment would pass and I was indeed at work. There was the big camera on a dolly, reflectors, barrel-shaped HMI lights, make-up people, crewmembers hauling equipment, the usual hustle of a film set.

As I explored the Walnut Grove set that first morning it reminded me of filming *Gunsmoke* or *Bonanza* in that the buildings were more or less false fronts. When you see cast members climbing the stairs into the church (or school), once the doors open there's a dark wall in the center with entrances to the left and right. The positioning of that wall allowed actors in and out of the building but kept the TV audience from seeing that inside the building there was simply a hollow, open space. There were no church pews or chalkboards though there were modern folding tables and chairs set up as this is where the younger members of the cast had their actual on-set school on days we shot at the movie ranch.

When we'd go up the steps into Oleson's Mercantile, you can see a sprinkling of items for sale in the front window but it was a very shallow space inside. Any time you see the inside of the Ingalls's cabin, the store, the school, etc., all those scenes were shot back at Paramount Studios.

One thing I still love about Walnut Grove is the water wheel on the mill. I realize that may sound pretty random but I know that Mike had to fight for it. One of the producers or perhaps the studio had said no to his original request to the mill's waterwheel – not sure who – on the grounds it would be a large, needless expense, saying that you could easily build Walnut Grove without spending god-knows-how-much on such a thing. Instead of giving up, which was not in his nature, Mike cooked up a scheme. Without telling anyone, he used his own money to purchase the mill equipment, created a fake rental company, and rented the water wheel, the mill works, and all things necessary to create the stream that appears to power it (all fake as Simi Valley is bone dry). I believe that by hiding the cost as a rental instead of a purchase, he got it past the bean counters. Once it was part of the series, it was too late to go back. I always admired Mike for fighting – if not outright pranking the studio – for that waterwheel because he was right. It's a detail that helps brings the town to life.

As beautiful as the movie ranch was, there were challenges shooting out there. Depending on the time of year the place is naturally brown and dry so any greenery – such as the grass and plants around the pond or along the streams – had to be brought in. For that matter all the ponds and streams had to be created too.

In the show's opening title sequence when you see little Carrie bobbling down the hillside through the grass and flowers and she takes her famous header, all those flowers are fake and their stems are wires. Apparently as they were filming her running down the hill, Sidney Greenbush's right shoe got caught on one of the wires and perhaps the most famous tumble in TV history was born.

We all learned pretty quickly you had to take some precautions on a shoot day in Simi Valley, where it got very hot. For example, in "Country Girls" you can see that Missy has a sunburn – no, that's not bad '70s TV make-up. In the previous episode she'd be allowed to hang around in the sun too long and she turned lobster red. After that the producers made sure all the actors had plenty of shade in between takes.

Later in the series we shot an episode called "In the Big Inning," and at about midday we were all in baseball stands watching a game. Of course there I was in 100-degree heat in my long skirt, petticoats, and all the other layers. When the director called for a break everyone got up but me. I sat there unmoving. Someone realized I had heatstroke and – being our second summer at the movie ranch – the crew was prepared. They put wet washcloths on the back of my neck, soaked in a blend of water and witch hazel, which brought me back around.

Much has been made of the fact (mostly by Alison) that Mike Landon didn't wear underwear while he worked. Well guess what? Neither did I – at least not in Simi Valley, where temperatures were regularly out of control. Unlike Mike, who wore his woolen pants like a glove, and often left little doubt regarding his gender, my commando status was as discrete as could be. Though once I nearly gave the cast and crew quite a show when my skirt was invaded by a wasp. It happened in front of the schoolhouse while a lot of people were milling around between takes. My first terrified impulse was to throw the skirts up over my head and get the thing out. Fortunately Richalene Kelsay, the wardrobe person, grabbed my arm and dragged me around the back of the church, where we could flush the beast out and I could avoid advertising my wares.

One of my other wardrobe contributions, which you can kind of see in that episode of "Country Girls," among others, is that I wore a bra that I really liked, as it was comfortable and fit well – something that's important for long shooting days. Plus as someone who was a hippie at heart I often went without a bra in my daily life. The downside to this thing of comfort was that the thinness of the material tended to show my nipples. And depending on the blouse I was in, well, there they were. Should that be a big deal? We all have them. It's not like Miss Beadle was some kind of outlier born without all the usual parts.

I figured given the nature of the show Mike or one of the producers would eventually ask me to re-think this choice. But no one said a word, though fairly often, under the right lighting conditions when they were shooting me "from the jugs up," I would see Mike and the cinematographer take turns peering at me through the camera's eyepiece discussing something just above a whisper. The only thing I'd hear is Mike murmuring to the cameraman, "It's fine, let's shoot it."

***

For anyone who was a kid watching *Little House on the Prairie*, it was probably easy to imagine that the lives of the actors who played Mary, Laura, Nellie, or any of the others were really fun and exciting. The truth is it was mixed. I should mention right off that Mike Landon was in many ways a kid at heart and was a great mentor to some of the child actors, being especially close with Melissa Gilbert. He would break the tension of a long day with a joke or a prank and make the kids laugh.

For the most part though life on the *Little House* set was hardly a play land. The show was run as a tight ship in all ways including expectations for the children. They were either shooting scenes, in their on-set school, or on a union mandated break. There was very little goof-around time except scripted moments in front of the camera. It was always fun to see the genuine joy in the eyes of someone like Jonathan Gilbert, Melissa's real-life brother, in his role as Willie Oleson when he got to terrorize the girls at school with a big frog.

I didn't get the idea that any of them were particularly unhappy. They all seemed up for the daily challenge. But I often wondered how they were doing since their lives stood in such contrast to my own childhood back in Yuba City, a time when life was so easy and free.

On top of that I'm not sure that being on the show necessarily translated into any added status in their personal lives. When you live in Hollywood, you're surrounded by lots of people who work in entertainment – your mom and dad, your parents' friends, aunts and uncles – and it takes the shine off. It'd be like growing up in Napa Valley where half the people you know work in the wine industry, in Detroit around automobile manufacturing, or Washington DC in the fishbowl of government. Hollywood is a factory town. And Alison talks about how if anything, beyond the typical trials of teenage life, being on television actually added to the social challenges she dealt with rather than giving her a sparkly carpet ride of coolness. She'd be in school on set for two weeks straight and then back in regular school for a couple of days when not shooting. Or she'd be in real school for three weeks and then back at her *Little House* school for four days. The lack of continuity in either direction played havoc with her friendships and social well-being.

Growing up on the set came with other unusual challenges as well. At one point both Alison and Melissa Gilbert had braces, which of course didn't exist in the 1870s. The make-up people solved that by applying white candle wax to their braces, requiring the poor girls to spend the end of their day getting that gunk out of their teeth in addition to shedding the pounds of pancake make-up we all wore. If you keep an eye out, you can sometimes see the braces. There's a scene in "Bully Boys" in which Melissa Gilbert sits up in bed at night with an idea she wants to tell Mary about. The light hits her teeth just right and you can see the glint of metal.

Even with these and other things to deal with, the young actors all rose to the challenge. They knew their lines and worked hard to respond to a director's instructions; no one messed around. When I was playing Miss Beadle, whether in the classroom or outside while the kids were "playing," I was always the adult, feeling that if I gave into my own impulses to goof around with them, it would ultimately work against the chemistry we had on camera.

I only remember one child actor in my four years on the show, who was cast in a guest role, who showed up not knowing his lines and thinking that this was a place to have some fun. He was replaced after one day.

It's fun today to watch those episodes with scenes in which the townspeople gather in the church and recognize so many faces. Ruthie Foster, who was my stand-in when they would set up lights, is often in one of the pews and was so good on camera that Mike eventually gave her a role as Mrs. Foster, one of the townspeople you might see at the Mercantile buying eggs from Mrs. Oleson. A lot of the kids you see were the children of the crew including those of the directors who would come in to direct an episode or two. Once when directing episodes that aired in December 1975 ("The Voice of Tinker Jones" and "Money Crop"), Leo Penn brought along his oldest son Sean Penn, who has an uncredited role, as one of the kids in the schoolhouse.

It was a real gift to get to work with all of them and I love to see them at the reunions and fan events that we get to do. Alison and I clicked early on. Unlike her character she doesn't have a mean bone in her body but ate up her juicy role as the meanest girl on earth. She could bunch her face up like a fist and scare the bejesus out of all the other kids.

Both Alison and Half-Pint have written books about growing up on *Little House* and about their private experiences growing up in their real-life families. They each lived through heartbreak and terrible challenges. Alison experienced sexual abuse on a level that is hard to imagine – and yet she has emerged with her humanity and chutzpah intact and works as a fighter for causes benefiting children and AIDS-related charities.

One of the funny things I noticed about Alison when we first started is that when we'd do scenes together she would never look at me directly in the eyes. Partway through a scene I'd realize that she was looking at my nose or a little off to one side. She was a funny kid. She could be very outgoing and sort of enter a room with a real sense of tah-dah and yet she also had some shyness to her, something that was held back a bit.

Melissa Sue Anderson, as discussed in both Alison and Melissa's books, was never a girl who seemed to fit in with the rest of the kids, nor particularly seemed to want to. She was always ready to work, nailed her part, and was prepared, so I didn't have any difficulty working with her and in fact I liked her a lot. She seemed like a very normal, healthy, non-Hollywood kid. She wasn't there to hog the spotlight or to razzle-dazzle anyone. Some of this may've been due to her family. Unlike the other kids, many of whom had a paid caretaker with them on the set, Melissa's mom was there almost all the time. She was my favorite of the actor-kids' moms on *Little House* – some of whom were either big, over-the-top personalities or were just basket cases. In fact she and I and Melissa Sue went out to dinner a few times and had nice evenings together.

I wasn't there to become anyone's surrogate mother but I did see Missy's aloofness (or perceived aloofness) between takes and, over time, her isolation from some of the other kids. In many ways she carried herself like a young adult from early on. To this day I have no idea of the causes of any of these dynamics and can only speculate. Melissa Sue Anderson has also written a book about her *Little House* experiences but, like her presence on set, it doesn't allow the reader to look too deeply into her life.

Because most of my scenes were filmed with the children in and around the schoolhouse, it took me some time to get to know the adult members of the cast.

When I started working with Karen Grassle, I felt like a complete bumpkin around her. She had earned not one but two degrees at U.C. Berkeley (my sister Barbara's alma mater) in English and Dramatic Arts – which made my internal inadequacy alarm bells ring. She had also done a broad range of theater from Shakespeare both in the U.S. and in England to a stint on Broadway. The only thing we had in common really was that she'd taken part in the summer program in 1961 at Pasadena Playhouse.

Where my little heart had always been with film and television, Karen was a theater person – so much so that she has talked publicly about the fact that she was almost totally unfamiliar with U.S. television. In early 1974 she'd just come back from doing Shakespeare in England and her agent called, saying that Michael Landon from *Bonanza* was putting together a show based on *Little House on the Prairie* and Karen had to ask who Michael was – being unclear which character he had played on the show.

She took her work seriously, was always prepared, and managed to look lovely and even elegant in the plain palate of costumes and make-up the producers gave her character. You can actually see much of her personality on screen as there wasn't a huge distance between Karen and her character in terms of stamina, smarts, and focus. In other ways she's very different – more outspoken, a better advocate for herself, and more adventuresome.

She was terrific as Caroline Ingalls and she and Michael always had excellent chemistry on screen. Unfortunately in real life, Karen and Mike didn't always get along. He would tease her without mercy for being serious-minded and I think she got tired of not only his joking around but of the easy-breezy approach he took to acting in general. Mike was an actor who did not seem to sweat at all in terms of his craft. Time and time again I saw him joshing and joking around with the crew, drinking vodka out of a coffee mug in the middle of the morning, and moments later he'd be in front of the camera as Pa with tears streaming down his cheeks in a scene about a dying colt or some disappointment suffered at Christmastime.

I had heard that when Mike and the producers were casting key roles for the show, the role of Caroline Ingalls very nearly went to Hersha Parady, who would have made the part her own, perhaps a bit earthier, finding little comedic touches, a bit like Mike really. Hersha landed a part later in the show's run as Alice Garvey, married to Merlin Olsen's character, Jonathan Garvey.

I have to say that one of the things that worked well with Mike and Karen were in fact their differences. There's nothing more boring than watching two characters who are too much alike. Sparks often happen in that space between two actors where there's friction.

One of the other differences between the two was that Karen – and she's talked about this publicly as well – thought the show was a bit too lightweight in its exploration of themes such as family, marriage relationships, the harshness of prairie life, and so on. She wanted the show to be grittier, as she said once in an interview, adding that at one point she felt like the show was "Let's Pretend on the Prairie." She says she's come to see it differently with time but it's a legitimate point and gets to a tension that exists any time you produce a show intended for a very broad audience.

"Country Girls" is a good example. On one hand it took a look at what it's like to be illiterate with Laura's embarrassment about her inability to read. It also revolves around issues of social class, a theme the show would return to again and again both dramatically and with a sense of humor thanks to Nellie and Harriet Oleson lording their supposed aristocracy over the Ingalls family and other townspeople.

At the same time a fairly rich vein of fantasy runs through the episode with its portrait of idealized family life. Laura is shown as adoring Miss Beadle and of course her mom. At one point she's at the dinner table and she says to Pa, "Miss Beadle is the most beautiful woman in the world."

Then Mike shoots his eyes in the direction of Karen and Half Pint takes the hint and adds, "Next to Ma, of course."

In the meantime Caroline Ingalls is looking over that costly length of blue fabric she purchased at the mercantile to make herself a nice dress – and let's be honest, doesn't Ma deserve to have at least one nice thing? Ultimately though, in a generous change-of-heart – because she's the perfect parent – she uses the fabric to make dresses for her two girls instead.

The real fantasy bit though comes later in the episode when Laura enters an essay writing contest at the school to prove she's up to the task of reading and writing. In a big moment in front of the whole town Laura reads her essay in which she lavishes rich praise on her mother for her self-sacrifice, hard work, constant attention, and loving kindness.

It is a moment that brings tears to the eyes of Ma and Pa Ingalls. And no doubt to many parents watching because who wouldn't – at least secretly – love to have that moment when your child entirely on their own, unforced, and un-coached steps forward to declare in amazing and eloquent detail how fantastic you are in front of everyone you know.

In the real world, it's pretty unlikely that a nine-year-old would take that kind of notice of what mom or dad does for them, much less trumpet for all the world to hear, unless heavily prompted. And probably bribed with cookies and chocolate milk. Not because they're bad kids but because in reality children take their parents for granted because they're mom and dad – and they just naturally do mom and dad things. Just like the sun rises and grass grows and water is wet.

So there's the show – reality and fantasy spun together in a way that millions of people have found very appealing.

Ultimately Karen – and everyone else – knew that it was Mike's show and he would produce it the way he wanted to. I think everyone in the cast agrees today that he worked some magic in terms of touching a lot of hearts. Something we did not always see at the time and really wouldn't know until years, and in some cases, decades later.

When you're in the middle of a show like that – which is happening within the swirl of your actual life – you don't always think about the larger life of the show. What it's saying. How it's affecting others. You're doing your job, playing your part, trying to sit in the right chair, get into the moment while hundreds of lights are dangling over your head and the all-seeing eye of the camera is staring you down.

While I initially found Karen intimidating, she turned out to be wonderful to work with and always ready with an act of generosity. Because of her starring role on the show, NBC sent a car to her house to pick her up in the morning on days when we were shooting in Simi Valley. Since she was the only one in the vehicle, she was kind enough to offer me an open invitation to jump in alongside her. I'd get to her house at 5 a.m., and we'd ride out to the set together. It was a great way to arrive at work much more relaxed and ready to go. The only issue was then the night before I could tell myself that since I didn't have to drive to the movie ranch I could have four or five extra drinks. Those morning drives were often accompanied by a brutal hangover.

Karen was one of the few cast members from *Little House* that I hung out with outside of work, having dinner occasionally with her and her boyfriend at the time, who I knew as Tuie, but discovered later went by William Kinsolving on the covers of his novels.

Another one of my favorite people on the *Little House* set, and one I also spent some memorable time with, was Katherine MacGregor, who was brilliant at playing the preening, self-centered, peacock Harriet Oleson, the proprietress of the Walnut Grove dry goods store.

Katherine's background, like Karen's, was largely in theater and she brought an almost academic seriousness to her work. She'd gotten her start in New York as a dance instructor in the 1940s and went on to work steadily in regional theater and on Broadway. By the start of *Little House* her film and television resume included a small, uncredited role in the Elia Kazan film *On the Waterfront*, and then a smattering of guest roles on TV shows including *Mannix*, *All in the Family*, and *Ironside*.

At some point in the series I was having a respiratory problem and decided to do what you did in the '70s, which was to go to a health farm; Katherine and I thought it'd be fun to go together. She was a great aficionado of health spas with a special preference for The Golden Door in Escondido. The place we went on this trip was down near San Diego called Hidden Valley Health Spa (or something like that). We drove down and spent five days at this place sharing a room, which is when I discovered Katherine was a devout Hindu. She didn't make a big deal about it but it was an important part of her life. In our shared room she set up a little shrine with a candle where she'd meditate each day.

Meditation was also part of our daily regime at the health farm as was eating almost entirely tasteless vegetarian food. After a day or two we got such a strong craving for flavor she and I hiked up to a garlic farm that we found nearby and did a little surreptitious harvesting. We took back these huge garlic bulbs that had a delicious, delicate flavor and soon everyone at our table was clamoring for a slice or two.

Every day the health farm staff had us walk barefoot through green grass, then through a trough of cold water, then a trough of sand, and finally back across on the grass. All of this was to stimulate our feet.

So Katherine and I got our feet stimulated, foraged for garlic, and laughed a lot on that trip. The whole thing was so ridiculous, but because I was with her it was a hoot.

You really couldn't find someone more different than the character she played. I found her to be such a serene soul, very warm, funny, and unpretentious.

I learned too that she was also so kind to her fans. Even though she was in one of the top shows on television, there she was listed in the Hollywood phone book. Fans would call her up at home and she'd chat with them for hours.

She loved playing Mrs. Oleson and threw everything she had at the part, physically and emotionally. Once the show was over she says she just felt wrung out. She didn't do any more television or film, instead she got involved with a children's theater company in Hollywood and moved into a little apartment on Vine St. across from her beloved Vedanta Society, a Hindu temple and worship center.

I have a feeling that Mike secured so many of his actors from the theater world – Karen, Katherine, and Richard Bull, who played Mr. Oleson – because they were so solid and so right-on-the-money. At the same time a television audience wouldn't associate them with any other previous TV roles or shows.

Even those of us with long backgrounds in TV and film were not, in the minds of a general audience, associated with any other characters or shows. Although someone like Dabbs Greer, who played the Reverend, and whose TV and film credits went back to the late 1940s, or Kevin Hagen, playing Doc Baker, who'd gotten his start in the 1950s, were at most only vaguely familiar faces.

Ultimately this approach to casting accomplished a few things. First, Mike got us pretty inexpensively by Hollywood standards. (Mind you, these were the biggest and most consistent paychecks of my career.) But even Kevin Hagen said publicly once that they "got us cheap." The second thing is that since none of us brought any identification with other shows or films, it was easy for the audience to see us more purely as characters in the world of Walnut Grove. For example, you didn't look at Mr. Oleson and say to yourself, "He's good here but he was great in *My Favorite Martian*" or anything like that. Finally, and I'm not trying to be snarky by saying this, it ensured that Mike was the star of the show – though it was a billing he would eventually share, quite comfortably, with Melissa Gilbert.

The show, it should be said, was Mike's from start to finish – every piece of it. On that first day at the costume department, I realized that all the costumes were new, nothing had been borrowed from any previous film or TV production as is a common practice especially with period pieces.

Later I realized that Mike allowed none of the *Little House* costumes to be sold or rented to any other productions. He didn't even want anyone to use the outdoor sets. In the last episode of the show, he actually blew up Walnut Grove. (I've never watched that episode and never will – there's no way I want to see a place that precious to me destroyed.)

The crew was even his, in a sense. They were completely devoted to Mike. Nearly all of them had come with him from *Bonanza* and would eventually follow him to *Highway to Heaven*. They were all Western guys, good with horses, expert builders, comfortable and effective working at a fast pace, and they liked to drink and cuss and play pranks and do, well, guy stuff. I got along really well with them because they reminded me of my dad's drinking buddies, like the man who owned the local chicken hatchery or ran a Yuba City plumbing company.

Mike was very much the leader of this troop of cowboys and most of the time Victor French, who played the mountain man Mr. Edwards and who directed a lot of episodes, was right there in the mix. And yet in the middle of this testosterone funhouse Mike also managed to, in my opinion, create a new kind of masculinity on television.

Charles Ingalls was tough and hard-working, he was quick to defend his family and his town. Remember when he got the crap beaten out of him in "Bully Boys?" He was a fighter who wasn't afraid of taking a hit.

Being a good dad was important to him. He had fun with his kids. He would listen to them and tried to answer their questions. He was patient. He cared about not just their physical well-being but their feelings. He was fair and optimistic.

Pa wasn't a drinker, didn't swear, didn't gamble, didn't even flirt with other women, much less alley-cat around with them. He adored his wife, his kids, his house, land, horses, his town, his profession, going to church, his fiddle, and Christmas.

He didn't hesitate to say, "I love you," or to hug, hold hands, or cry. Lord, Pa cried all the time. And yet Mike had come from the same world I had – raised by those tough-as-nails parents who'd grown up in the Depression and had kicked ass in World War II. Boys didn't cry. Boys didn't hug or express "girly" emotions. That was unmanly and weak.

Mike totally broke that mold.

Mike said you could be loving, funny, sentimental, silly sometimes, emotional – and yes you could cry. And still be a man.

Had television ever seen a guy like this before?

Fred MacMurray on *My Three Sons* and Ward Clever of *Leave It to Beaver* were both cardigan-wearing, pipe-smoking, problem-solvers, who loved their families but were both a bit aloof and untouchable. Andy Taylor on *The Andy Griffith Show* was a good listener, a great dad, and was insightful in the ways of the human heart but even he didn't have the emotional openness and availability of Charles Ingalls. Perhaps closest was my friend Ralph Waite, as John Walton, Sr., on *The Waltons*. Even so, no one came close to the shiny eyes or outright tears down the cheeks of Mike Landon as Pa.

He was like the embodiment of the Robert Frost poem "A Door with No Lock" – there were no barriers between Charles Ingalls and his emotions.

The thing that amazes me is that Mike seemed to know how to maintain a balance between being a bona fide TV hunk and the greatest dad ever. He managed to be sexy and yet an upright citizen. Those tears always seemed earned and were a reflection of the viewer's own emotions.

People ask me all the time, what was it like to work with Michael Landon. The truth is it was a lot of things.

I admired him for so many attributes – his ability to create, shape, and execute a story that millions of people could relate to. His gift for creating moments on screen that – even if they crossed the line into pure fantasy – rang true and made emotional sense.

He was always looking for ideas, always had a legal pad with him jotting down notes. In fact, I gave Michael an idea for an episode in season two based on my godmother, Pauline, who had been the only teacher in the 1930s in Ft. Bragg, California, a lumber town. A lot of the older boys in the area would work part of the year with their fathers in the lumber business and part of the year they would attend school. It was a difficult transition for everyone. These boys, who were used to sawing, hauling, and milling logs, weren't always happy about being made to sit at desks and learn the basics of reading, writing, and arithmetic.

One night some of the older boys decided to have fun terrorizing her by hurling rocks at the door of the schoolhouse while she was inside feeling trapped, unsure what would happen to her if she tried to leave. Life as a pioneer teacher was tough and the everyday challenges weren't always pretty.

I could tell Mike liked the story idea because after I told it to him, I watched him go to work on that yellow legal pad, writing very quickly, outlining the basis for an episode that would be called "Troublemaker."

As a writer Mike always worked at terrific speed. It seemed like the words he wrote in longhand couldn't ever come out of the pen fast enough to keep up with his thoughts. The dialogue he wrote always had great rhythm and music to it and even though we were playing characters from 100 years in the past, the lines always fell so easily out of me. I don't ever remember having a moment thinking, "Wait, this doesn't make sense" or "This doesn't work" or worse, "Miss Beadle would never say this." The dialogue matched the character and the situation. Mike never overplayed the script, never tried to show off as a writer. It was all clear, clean, and direct. And because he was running the show, if dialogue could ever be cut and the scene played better for its emotion without it, that's where he would always go.

The episode Mike created from my godmother's experience remains one of my favorites because we got to see so many sides of Miss Beadle. The way Mike structured the final televised version the townspeople – mainly Mrs. Oleson – decide that Miss Beadle isn't up to the task of managing a classroom with older boys in the backbenches. The trouble that's brewing is that with the end of harvest even more older boys from outlying farms will return to the schoolhouse and God knows what will happen then.

The school board decides that a man would be better suited to handle the classroom management situation and they vote to fire Miss Beadle. As she is not present at the meeting, it's up to Pa to deliver the news.

We see Miss Beadle waiting for the verdict in what appears to be a small, pretty boarding room seated on her fancy brass bed reading a book.

When Pa knocks, she opens the door and there he is, his face filled with regret and she already knows the news. He lets her know that the vote was not unanimous. There are tears gleaming in his eyes.

Victor French, who was not only a tremendous actor but one of my favorite directors on the series, took me aside after a take or two filming this scene and gave me a great note. He said quietly, "Don't let him see you cry." It turned out to be a moving way for the audience to see both Eva Beadle's strength and her vulnerability at the same time.

So the unthinkable happens – Miss Beadle leaves the school, much to Laura's regret, and is replaced by the imposing Hannibal Applewood, played by Richard Basehart, who had such a great, powerful voice and presence. Richard had been in movies going back to the 1940s such as *Voyage to the Bottom of the Sea*, *La Strada*, and *Moby Dick*. He'd even played Hitler. Well, he certainly brought a touch of the Third Reich to Walnut Grove, focusing his sadism and ill-will on Laura Ingalls, punishing her by making her fill the chalk boards with spelling words, slapping her hand with a ruler (twice!), and even expelling her from school – all for crimes she had not committed. Well, you don't treat Half-Pint like a juvenile delinquent and not expect Pa to eventually open a can of whoop-ass. Which he does demonstrating the truth of the words "Beware the anger of a patient man."

Miss Beadle is looking pretty good about now to the townspeople as well as the kids in the school – even the boys in the back who like to cause trouble.

The school board meets again and there is a showdown with Applewood in which he reveals himself, under questioning, to be a complete crackpot. They don't get the chance to fire him because he quits. They bring back Miss Beadle and all is well in Walnut Grove once again.

Beyond his ability to put together the building blocks for a captivating story, something else I admired about Mike is how he valued efficiency. He'd never shoot anything he didn't have to. Most directors will work their way through a scene getting a master shot and then shoot close-ups, a medium shot, a three shot, whatever, so the editors will have lots of footage to work with; it's a kind of safety net should something be missing or if, say, a reaction doesn't work well. Not Mike. He'd shoot a quick establishing shot and then move in for close-ups and other shots as needed. No extra footage, no safety net. He edited in his head all day as he went and I doubt he gave his editors much to do. Not a moment was wasted. He consistently came in under budget and every day – unlike any other show I'd worked on – we wrapped at 6 pm. He valued time with his family and friends – he wanted to have a life. He valued our time as well, which we all adored him for.

Years later I heard a classic Mike Landon story. He was guest starring on a show in the 1990s, I believe it was *Touched by an Angel*. And he grew restless and irritated by how slow the director was working. Without asking anyone's permission, he grabbed some crew and went off and shot a bunch of second-unit material for the show. The director was, apparently, furious but was of course checkmated. NBC appreciated all of Mike's extra, cost-saving work and it all ended up onscreen.

Having said all of these things, Mike was not a saint nor do I think he aspired to sainthood and would, I believe, balk at the level of glow-y virtuousness that is becoming his legend.

He could be a bit vain. The hairdressers were always at their wit's end with what to do with Mike because he dyed his own hair at home – covering up the onset of gray with color out of a box. They hated the result. I suppose, though, if you're Mike while you may be okay weeping in front of the crew you may not be as cool with them seeing you get your hair treated. That's just my guess.

He did wear those wool pants pretty tight and if you'll notice – as Alison pointed out in her book – whenever Pa gets injured, it's never in the shins, it's always his ribs. This necessitates the shirt coming off, bandaging, and sexy winces, while Doc Baker, tells him he'll be fine in a couple of weeks.

I remember at one point maybe in the second or third season, the show was becoming popular in Europe, especially in France and Spain, and Mike was dragging his feet at going over to do publicity. While he was a big star here in the U.S., he wasn't famous over there. Over there he was no more well-known than anyone else in the cast.

Beyond all those very normal traits Mike did, just once, let me know that he was up for a roll in the hay, if I was interested. It was the end of the day and I was gathering myself up to leave the set. I could tell he'd been drinking. And this was a time in his life between marriages so he wasn't breaking any rules; maybe he was just seeing what a quickie here and there would be like. I don't remember the exact words he used but it was specific enough to let me know what he had in mind and yet vague enough to let me wriggle out if I wished. I was shocked – there had been no lead-up, no hint in our past to suggest this was coming, no flirting. And it took what felt like a long time for my mind to process what exactly was happening.

I liked Mike and I know Mike liked me. He always called me "Beadle" on the set, which I enjoyed. But we didn't hang out. We didn't socialize on weekends. Ever. One time in the week before Christmas I happened to run into him in Beverly Hills where we were both doing holiday shopping. It was really fun to see him away from work – it was a totally different feeling from how we interacted on the set. He was very sweet asking what I was buying, whom I was buying it for, and all that. We walked together for a little way and that was that.

To Mike I was a chess piece that he moved around the *Little House* game board. I was an underling. An employee. Sleeping with the boss wasn't my idea of a good time and I've never regretted that choice and I don't believe he held it against me.

I don't mean to be unkind by saying this. I mean to make the point that Mike – like all of us – was human. He worked in an industry in which sleeping around, at least in the '70s, was as remarkable as going out for ice cream. There was plenty of alcohol on the set and lots of guy-talk. The fact that this only happened once is probably more noteworthy than the fact that it happened at all. Context being everything.

Honestly I would think that, rather than being remembered as a saint, Mike would rather be known for his incredible work, his work ethic, his friendships, his jokes, and his devotion to his crew, his friends, and his family rather than being remembered for something false – that he lived some kind of idealized life that came with a halo.

***

In my personal life I was also grateful to Mike for casting me in the show, as it gave me house-buying income. While I'd loved my rented home in Topanga Canyon, the drive was killing me. With my *Little House* paycheck I was able to purchase a home in Beachwood Canyon located just below and to the left of the H in the famous Hollywood sign. It not only gave me homeownership but it positioned me minutes away from Paramount and the other studios.

To get there you had to drive way up the hill past lots of houses stacked practically on top of each other. I had a big backyard with a Jacuzzi and a sauna with a sun deck on top. In fact on the first night that the place was mine, before I'd even moved in, I took my Corgi, Elmer, and a sleeping bag up to the deck over the sauna planning to spend the night up there just soaking it all in – a girl and her dog. Elmer had less dreamy plans as it turns out. In the middle of the night he tore off barking like crazy at something, which set my heart racing. In the darkness I heard snarls, growls, hisses and all kinds of noise and then came the acrid, overwhelming, sickening stink of skunk.

It was something like two in the morning. I didn't have a single towel, blanket, scrub brush or anything in the house. I had to pack Elmer up, take him back to Topanga and give him a bath in tomato juice.

Still. It was pretty cool to finally own a home and I owed it all to Miss Beadle and Mike Landon.

***

Toward the end of my run with *Little House*, Mike came up to me one day with two photographs – headshots of two different male actors. He asked, "Which one would Miss Beadle marry?"

This was in preparation for an episode I still get lots of wonderful fan reaction for called "Here Come the Brides," which aired December 5, 1977. In it Miss Beadle is swept off her feet by a sweet, handsome pig farmer named Adam Simms. At the same time Nellie Oleson, now in her late teens, falls in love with his son Luke, a strapping country boy who goes about in overalls and bare feet. Mrs. Oleson's full powers of outrage and disgust are given full vent (Katherine was never better).

I looked at the two photos of the actors in Mike's hands and saw that one of them was Josh Bryant, my long-time friend from Pasadena Playhouse. Of course I picked him.

After all the years of knowing Josh, it was the first chance we'd had to actually work together.

Josh and I rehearsed our scenes away from the cast and crew and were able to fall into those moments so easily. It was a lot of fun and I think that real friendship shows up on the screen.

As with most episodes the two storylines mirror each other. The relationship between Adam Simms and Eva Beadle (yes, Adam and Eva) is reflected in that growing between Nellie and Luke. Of course Nellie and Luke's was comedic and fraught with peril, thanks to Mrs. Oleson.

Nellie invites Luke to the grand Oleson house for dinner. Thinking that Luke is going to be on their social level, Mrs. Oleson puts on a fancy spread and ensures that the entire family is dressed in their best. When Luke shows up in their doorway with his shaggy hair, overalls, and big, old bare feet – the very archetype of the sort of hayseed she despises – Mrs. Oleson cannot mask her revulsion and alarm.

Nellie – her Nellie – falling for a hick?!?!

The sky is falling.

Meanwhile I got to shoot a fun scene with Josh out at the Simms pig farm. It's one of the few scenes in which I got to pull up in my own little carriage pulled by my beloved Jack – he was my horse for the four years I was on the show. As I tug on the reins, slowing Jack, and pull into the farm, the horse goes out of frame, the carriage halts neatly, and I hop out.

The reason it halts is because Hal Burton, our horse wrangler, is standing off camera catching Jack and holding him in place. It makes me look like an expert.

A quick question though – where does Miss Beadle keep her horse and carriage? At her boarding house? And where is that boarding house exactly? Is it the one over Doc Baker's office? Hmmm. Miss Beadle has secrets.

Adam greets me warmly in his understated way and we chat about Luke and Nellie a bit. Miss Beadle has trouble masking her attraction for this kind, thoughtful farmer. As she's gathering up her skirts to go, Adam presents her with a gift: a smoked ham.

Well, ladies, I ask you – whose heart wouldn't melt?!?

Later the two couples enjoy a picnic together near one of the movie ranch's manmade ponds. Adam and Eva go on a little walk and Adam can't hold back his feelings any longer. In spite of her advanced years (Miss Beadle is in her 30s after all), he asks her to be his wife. For a schoolteacher who was pretty sure the joys of marriage had passed her by, it's a big moment.

Meanwhile Luke has proposed to Nellie but in an uncharacteristic moment of self-doubt, she says she needs to think about it.

She finds Miss Beadle on a swing – God, if this was a musical imagine the big number they'd be belting out just then. She asks the schoolteacher questions about love and comes around to the idea of not being quite the right age. Nellie naturally means being too young but Miss Beadle's mind is on the other end of things – the idea of being too old. With conviction, Miss Beadle tells her that age should play no part in love.

Taking that bit of advice to heart, Nellie and Luke do the unthinkable – they elope.

When Nels and Harriet Oleson realize Nellie has run off with Luke, they grab a shotgun, hop on a horse, and ride like thunder for the Simms pig farm.

As the horse approaches the farm at a gallop you see Katherine slide off, pulling Richard Bull down with her. It's a funny moment on screen however it was unrehearsed, not performed by stunt people, and not in the script. In fact Katherine got hurt pretty badly and they had to run her to a hospital. Richard, thankfully, was fine.

As the scene continues you'll notice that Mr. and Mrs. Oleson approach the front door of the farmhouse filmed from behind. While it is indeed Richard Bull as Mr. Oleson, the woman you think is Mrs. Oleson is actually Ruthie Foster in Katherine's dress and bonnet. The trick works because Katherine later recorded her dialogue and they dubbed it in. Ruthie did a great impression of Harriet Oleson's physical mannerisms and it all works pretty seamlessly.

A few days later, when Katherine was up and around again, they filmed the remainder of her scenes.

I would guess that the physicality of the role, along with injuries like this eventually took their toll, leading her to retire from film and television when *Little House* was over.

While all that's happening we see that Nellie and Luke have awoken a Justice of the Peace in the next town over in the middle of the night to marry them. He does so in his nightcap and then off they go to a hotel room where they awkwardly prepare for bed and presumably a pretty un-steamy night of amore.

Before that can happen though, the Olesons, with Miss Beadle and Adam Simms in tow, have tracked them down. Mrs. Oleson bursts through the door of the hotel room with Nels holding the shotgun.

Mrs. Oleson points at Luke and shrieks, "Nels, make her a widow!"

When Nels characteristically shrinks from her, simpering that he can't shoot Luke, she grabs the gun and blasts a hole in the ceiling. Luke makes an escape in his long underwear.

Everyone ends up back at the Justice of the Peace where Mrs. Oleson demands that man who married the kids unmarry them. Which he does simply by tearing up the marriage certificate.

At this point Adam Simms turns to Eva Beadle and says while they're there at the Justice of the Peace's office, they might as well get hitched.

And they do and Josh and I share a lovely on-screen kiss.

For reasons I can't remember, Bill Claxton, the director, wanted to get one more take of that scene, which is when Josh and I cooked up an idea.

We told the cinematographer that after Bill said 'Cut,' to keep the camera rolling. When he did, Josh and I kept kissing. And kissing and kissing and kissing. Until the whole crew was busting up. Every now and then we'd do stuff like this for "the party reel" – a collection of bloopers and pranks we'd show at a cast party. Usually it was moments when the set would fall over or someone would flub lines.

Josh stayed on for several episodes in Season Four as my husband and, as you know, things move quickly in Walnut Grove. Two months later Miss Simms (as everyone now called Eva Beadle) was pregnant and Caroline Ingalls learned she was pregnant too in the episode "A Most Precious Gift," which first aired on my birthday, February 27, 1978.

There must've been something in the water.

Miss Simms starts to feel her contractions in the schoolhouse and hands over the classroom to Mary (who is old enough now to be acting as an assistant teacher) and promptly and without drama gives birth to a boy – Matthew Adam Simms. Fortunately he was a much healthier child than Spike, the quasi-human baby-creature I had with Jack Nance in *Eraserhead*.

***

After his stretch with *Little House* Josh invited me over for a party at his house, where I met his buddy Richard Dreyfuss. Richard and I had some chemistry and the next day he sent a limo over to pick me up so I could come over and play. What a fun guy to hang out with. Besides the fact that he's devilishly smart, charming, and good-looking, we found we had a lot of mutual interests, such as sex, alcohol, and cocaine. Oh, and backgammon.

We both liked going to a restaurant/bar called Ports, which was located across from Goldwyn Studios, where we'd do cocaine (in the bathroom) and play backgammon all night long. It was a surprisingly popular combination at the time. One night I played backgammon forever with the composer Paul Williams and I cleaned him out – we played for money. When he'd run out of cash he finally gave me a ring off his finger. (A couple of months later his girlfriend called and asked if he could have it back – not sure why Paul didn't make the call himself. Of course I returned it.)

I made a lot of friends at Ports, such as Nicholas Meyers, who wrote *The Seven-Percent Solution* and Coleman Andrews, who would go on to become the editor of *Saveur* magazine. Coleman wrote a great chapter on Ports in his book *My Usual Table: A Life in Restaurants*. In it he recreates the feel of the place in which he says the patrons you'd run into there were people "you'd last seen in Tangier." You would see Francis Ford Coppola at one table, Andrews writes, and Rip Torn, Kinky Friedman or young Oliver Stone at another. If Nickodell, where I'd enjoyed memorable lunches with Bill Frawley, was Old Hollywood, Ports was New.

Richard Dreyfuss, you may recall, was having an amazing career stretch having filmed *Jaws*, *The Goodbye Girl*, and *Close Encounters of the Third Kind* one after the other.

Even while we were partying together, Richard had some interest in getting sober. It's hard to keep all the plates spinning on a successful film career *and* fully dedicate yourself to the twin cause of drugs and alcohol. There simply aren't enough hours in a day. One time he checked himself into a well-known spa that had strict rules about vegetarian diet. He called me because he wanted me to try to sneak him a hamburger. So I bought a burger and drove over to this place; it was in a huge Victorian mansion in Venice Beach. I met him as he was coming down a grand stairway and as we were talking I heard a fruity, imperious voice boom down from the top of the stairway. It was Gloria Swanson, looking very much as she had in *Sunset Boulevard*, enunciating like a vampire, "R-r-r-r-richa-aaaaaard, who have you got there?"

Richard and I eventually drifted out of each other's lives though I did see him once more a few years later when he invited me to an event to hear people talk about getting sober – something that had transformed his life.

At the time, I was happy to go, assuming that Richard simply wanted to spend time with me. My friend Jeanne Field pointed out to me in her blunt fashion, "It wasn't a date, Charlotte, it was an alcohol recovery meeting."

It never occurred to me that he had perhaps invited me along because he thought sobriety was something I could benefit from. I just thought he had a thing for me.

Jeanne was still busy, as always. She'd given up running Everybody's Mothers in Topanga and had moved on to various other projects including a short-lived television show called *TVTV*, a sort of experimental guerilla comedy program that was way ahead of its time, using techniques like fake news and documentary style that would go on to be staples of comedy later on.

She worked with a bunch of great young comedic actors on the show, including a guy named Bill, whom I only vaguely remember from *TVTV*. Unfortunately the show only lasted a short time, less than a full season, and everyone went their separate ways. Bill ended up going back to New York for a part on a TV show that he'd gotten.

A few months later though he was back in town and Jeanne and Bill and I ended up going out for the night – went to Ports and then decided to head to a dance club in Hollywood. When we arrived I let out a groan. It was a really hot club and the line to get in was long. I thought we should go somewhere else – it would take forever to get in. But Bill was feeling confident and took us up to the front of the line where the bouncer recognized him. We got right it. Well, that was pretty cool. I made a mental note to check out the show he was on, as I'd not yet seen it.

The three of us had a great time and at the end of the night Bill decided to go home with me. Rather than Jeanne. I could tell she was annoyed and hurt by this; I didn't think it was a big deal.

I liked Bill. He wasn't conventionally handsome but he was a lot of fun, very smart, and sexy in a way all his own.

The next day was Sunday and I wanted to go to Tim's weekly soccer game. Bill said he'd see me there and took off in his car. I put on my soccer clothes and drove out to the field at UCLA expecting that all the fun of the night before would carry on into this morning. Once I got to the game though, it was like I didn't exist. Bill and Jeanne hung out at the sidelines together and talking and laughing, having a lovely old time. I could tell Jeanne was still mad at me and she wouldn't look in my direction or speak to me. And Bill didn't give me the time of day. It was like he'd never seen me before in his life. I was crushed.

And now I was mad at Jeanne.

For the first time since we'd met – after rooming together on and off in Topanga Canyon, working together at Everybody's Mother and The Liquid Butterfly, after all the men we'd slept with practically at the same time – now this. Now this one guy comes along and suddenly we're not speaking to each other anymore.

The angry silence between us lasted about three weeks. Which was just dumb. Finally I saw Jeanne at a party and thought, "This has to end."

I walked up and gave her a hug.

"I miss you," I said.

She said she missed me too and we both cried a little bit.

"No guy is worth this," I said.

Not even if Bill was a guy the rest of the world knew as Bill Murray from a show I finally got around to watching called *Saturday Night Live*.

***

Back on the *Little House* set, another of my favorite co-stars was Victor French, who played Mr. Edwards. A lot of fans never got to see past the bearded, backcountry, yee-haw charm of the character he played to know what a passionate and fine actor he was.

In 1959 French had worked with Leonard Nimoy, Richard Chamberlain, Vic Morrow, and others to found a nonprofit theater company in L.A. called Company of Angels, which offered Off-Broadway style productions in the intimate setting of a 99-seat theater. (It's still open today and is the oldest repertory theater in Los Angeles.) He was also a private acting teacher with a great reputation. More than anything though, he was a big, sweet, funny, loveable teddy bear of a guy.

Victor was very much inside the Mike Landon and crew frat group, and he wrote and directed quite a number of episodes. The two had a big falling out later in the run of the show when, without Mike's blessing, Victor left to star in his own sitcom called *Carter Country*. You can't blame Victor for taking a shot at some more income and giving his star a bit of a boost.

But Mike was pissed off and felt betrayed and he wrote Mr. Edwards and his family entirely out of the show.

Unfortunately for Victor, *Carter Country* did not do well in the ratings and after two seasons, it was history.

He and Michael patched things up and Mr. Edwards and his family miraculously reappeared in Walnut Grove. Well, all but one – Radames Pera had played Mr. Edwards's adopted son John Sanderson. When Radames heard the news of Victor and the Edwards family coming back to the show he naturally saw it as a return for his character as well. He drove over to Paramount to reestablish contact with the production and as he was walking onto the lot he ran into another actor, who greeted him with the words, "Hey how you doing? We just buried you!"

His character was dead and Radames was collateral damage of the Michael-Victor falling out.

Unfortunately for Victor, it wasn't the only relationship shake-up he would face while shooting *Little House*. At home he was dealing with the end of his marriage with his wife Julie and was absolutely devastated by the divorce.

I knew it was hard on him but I had no idea until out of the blue he called me one night at home. Poor guy, it was clear how torn up he was. I told him to come over to my house in Beachwood Canyon. We sat up for a long time drinking, talking about marriage, divorce, and life. And he ended up spending the night. Which was the start of an occasional thing between us. Usually Victor would call and say he was having dinner with one of the producers, Kent McCray and his wife, and would I like to come along? We'd go out, have a good time and he'd stay over. It was never a romance – I was never after him – I simply adored him. We had a lot of fun together – how could you not with Victor? Sometimes we'd lie in bed and joke about what fans would say if they found out that Miss Beadle was hooking up with Mr. Edwards.

***

Though I never drank during a day of filming, I showed up hung over more than once. I would ask my make-up guy, Whitey, if he could put make-up on my private life too. The drinking ritual I had on *Little House* was as soon as they were finished with me for the day, whether we were in Simi Valley or at Paramount, I would head to the prop truck where the bar was always open. I finished each day with a belt of vodka and would then head home for more.

Alcohol did get me in trouble a few times during this era, though. In mid-1977 I landed a role in a TV movie called *Murder in Peyton Place*, which was shooting during the same week I was scheduled on *Little House*. My part was small in that particular episode – I was only supposed to appear in a Walnut Grove church scene to satisfy my contract – so I asked Mike if I could get out of that week's shoot and he had no problem with it, so off I went.

The night before I was supposed to appear before the *Peyton Place* cameras I was at home drinking rum-and-cokes and snorting cocaine (as one does), when I was overcome with the need to move my television from one side of the room to the other.

This was a big TV set I'd gotten out of the blue the Christmas before. Mike Landon often cooked up a surprise for the cast each year of one kind or another. One year we all got special *Little House on the Prairie* belt buckles, all specially made for us. I wish I knew where mine was today! The following year the show must've been doing well because just as shooting ended on Christmas Eve, a truck pulled up stacked with television sets for adult members of the cast.

Not bothering to take off my high heel wedges, I hefted the bulky thing, which must have weighed somewhere around 50 lbs., and I tottered around the room. A heel went sideways and I fell backward. As the TV came down with me, a corner drove into my forehead just between my eyes. I think I must have passed out for a little bit and when I came to I was drunk and bleeding everywhere and flying high from all the cocaine and knew that somehow I needed to get myself to an emergency room.

I called my financial manager, Syd Crocker, and he and his boyfriend came over and drove me to General Hospital, where I got five black, Frankenstein stitches in the middle of my face.

I dreaded showing up at 6 am the next day for my call time at the studio. As fate would have it, the train tracks in my forehead actually played second banana to a bigger disaster – our director had died at home the night before.

The whole production was put off for a few days in order to find a new director who could pull the project back into shape. This lull in production allowed me to go to a plastic surgeon who took out my original ER stitches – ouch – and do a much more skillful and subtle job of sewing me back together. Nevertheless, I ended up with a Harry Potter-like scar that I carry to this day.

Fortunately the first scene of me on the movie was a long shot and they covered my stitches with flesh-colored tape. Throughout the remainder of the shoot the hairdresser employed strategic use of my blonde bangs to cover the damage.

Murder in Peyton Place aired on October 3, 1977 in the time slot just after *Little House on the Prairie*. Another Charlotte Stewart double-header.

***

My last day shooting *Little House* was August 22, 1977. The final scene was at Paramount on the Oleson's store set for the episode "I'll Be Waving As You Drive Away (Part 2)," which would air on March 13, 1978.

Mike made sure I had a good moment to end on.

Mary Ingalls, who had lost her sight in the first of this two-part episode, has been away at a school for the blind and has come home one more time before leaving Walnut Grove for good to go teach at a new school for vision-impaired children.

Eva and Adam Simms are also leaving Walnut Grove to find their fortunes elsewhere.

Mrs. Simms (the schoolmarm formerly known as Miss Beadle) comes into Oleson's mercantile to say goodbye to Mr. Oleson, Pa, and Mary. She presses a cameo brooch into Mary's hand, saying that it was one that her teacher had given her long ago.

She looks at Mary with tears in her eyes and says simply, "I watched you grow up. And I'm going to miss you."

She turns to Charles Ingalls and Mr. Oleson. "I'm going to miss all of you."

I give Mary a hug and then pull back to look around one last time.

The tears in my eyes were real. Those lines from the script were words from my heart. I had enjoyed being part of this ensemble so much, had treasured my time working at the movie ranch in Simi Valley and on the sound stages at Paramount – had loved the make-believe world of 1870s Walnut Grove.

And I had indeed watched Missy, Half-Pint, and Alison grow up. Their storylines had gone from fights in the schoolyard to first loves and marriage.

And then reality crashed the party.

When I walked out the door of the store the director, Bill Claxton, called, "That's a wrap for Charlotte." And there began the usual flurry through the teardown and set-up for the next scene.

And that was that. Four years with *Little House* had, for me, come to a close. Everything and everyone around me plunged forward at the usual, formidable pace. Costume and make-up people busy doing their thing. The crew hustling. Actors moving off to their trailers or to prep for what came next.

The *Little House* set wasn't a place where there were a lot of parties so I had no expectations of Champagne and confetti. But a hug – a real hug, not a scripted one – would have been very welcome at that moment. Some well-wishes for the future. But I knew I couldn't really expect that either. Everyone had a job to do – there were only so many hours in a day and there were always more script pages to get through and a million details to attend to. Putting together a show of that size and scope requires everyone's complete focus at all times.

And it's the nature of the business. People come and go. And sometimes you're the one who goes.

I had been inside Mike Landon's *Little House* typhoon since 1974 and in an instant I was now on the outside, it seemed.

A feeling of numbness came over me. As I walked toward the prop truck I realized that all the relentless forward movement of filming here would continue without me. A new actress was coming in to play the schoolteacher. The cast would continue to grow and change. I suppose in some way that's hard to explain it was like the death of a dear friend.

I reached the prop truck, had my last vodka, and then left my pretty prairie dress and golden wig behind for a final time.

***

A person has to console themselves after a loss like this and I helped myself through this difficult time by flying to New York a couple of days later where I had a fling with a pilot I knew who flew with the U.S. Air Force Thunderbirds. Like all the other pilots in the squadron he was in amazing shape and all the guys wore beautiful uniforms designed by Yves St. Laurent. Needless to say he was hot and it helped massage my feelings of loss.

New York was a place I liked to escape to although I generally got myself into various kinds of trouble. My friend Erica Spellman was and still is a literary agent there who would drag me around to various parties where, inevitably, I'd drink too much and engage in bad behavior and as a result our friendship, sadly, drifted apart. One party in particular comes to mind because I got the chance to meet writer-director Paul Schrader, an AFI alum, on whom I hoped to make an impression and didn't. In the other room was director Martin Scorsese, who was having an asthma attack and was simply trying to breathe. Poor guy. I'd met Scorsese years prior when he was doing sound with Jeanne and Larry on the *Woodstock* documentary. I don't believe I managed to make an impression on either occasion.

Once a friend had asked me to show the writer Anthony Haden Guest around Los Angeles – he's the brother of Christopher Guest, who's created so many great films such as *Waiting for Guffman* and *Best in Show*. Well, Anthony Haden Guest was a bit of a snob as far as I was concerned, although I was probably just intimidated by his writer-cred and his connections with British and American aristocracy and with his literary circles, blah, blah, blah. Anyway, I was in New York once in the late '70s and Anthony had invited me to meet him for dinner. Feeling nervous, I had a drink or three before I went to the address he gave me, a brownstone which I assumed was his house, where I knocked on the front door. I was in for a surprise when it wasn't Anthony who answered the door but his friend, the writer Tom Wolfe, wearing his signature white linen suit.

Tom, his wife, and Anthony Haden Guest and I sat around Wolfe's place making conversation while I drank wine. We went to dinner at Elaine's where I snozzled down a few cocktails and got to that very special place of intoxication that puts one on the dividing line between loss of inhibition and loss of consciousness. I knew that if I tried to excuse myself to the ladies room, I would trip over someone, probably Elaine herself, and make a complete ass of myself. Thus without lead-up or explanation I stood in the middle of dinner, walked out of the restaurant in an alcohol-induced zombie state, hailed a cab, and returned to my hotel. Anthony Haden Guest never called to inquire about my whereabouts or well-being nor did I call to check in with him. That was that.

Except that it wasn't exactly. A few years later I was lying in bed in Los Angeles reading Tom Wolfe's novel *The Bonfire of the Vanities* and came across a scene in a restaurant that was pretty clearly Elaine's (though given another name) in which a priggish writer with three names is at dinner with a friend when the three-named writer's date who is drunk gets up and leaves without explanation. She is described as "a humorless little American dimwit …" and the writer is humiliated in front of his friends.

My contribution to great literature. You're welcome.

***

Remember *Eraserhead?*

Throughout my sojourn in 1870s Walnut Grove, Henry, Mary X, and Spike lived on.

My involvement with the film had ended at some point in the first half 1974 – in fact on a few occasions I would rush over from Paramount to AFI, where I would scrub off my Miss Beadle make-up and get prepped to inhabit the skin of Mary X. In terms of film sets and characters this represented two worlds that were about as far apart as you can get.

When David Lynch had shot everything with me that he needed, shooting and then editing continued on and off through late 1976. I may have my dates a little wrong since I wasn't there but I continued to hear about the progress of the film through Doreen and Jeanne, who were both involved much longer than I.

After about the first year of production, David's AFI grant ran out and he had less and less money to work with. Apparently he got some funds from his Dad and he built sheds around town to make money (Hollywood needs sheds – who knew?). Both he and Jack got a paper route, delivering copies of the *Wall St. Journal* in the small hours of the morning. If David was excruciatingly slow to set up a shot, he apparently exhibited lightning speed when it came to his paper route. It was supposed to take about four hours and he whipped through it in two. Jack only lasted a few weeks as a paperboy.

David secured financial help from actress Sissy Spacek, who was art director Jack Fisk's wife (they had met while working on the Terrence Malick film *Badlands*). Sissy covered the cost of film stock, without which the movie would not exist. Jack Fisk helped pay for things out of his own pocket too.

At one point David moved in with Jack Nance and Catherine Coulson and at another he was actually living on the *Eraserhead* set, making the bed [*that*] the Henry and I shared his own.

Eventually, even though Catherine and Jack divorced, they stayed friends and her relationship with David remained strong.

When funding ran short, Catherine pitched in financially with wages from her waitressing job at a restaurant in Beverly Hills called Barbeque Heaven. She also ~~went around and~~ raised money from friends, family, and even her dentist.

Sometimes David would come to the restaurant where Catherine worked and she ~~says~~ [*said*] he'd do odd jobs, like repair the roof, in exchange for a sandwich and fries.

It was clear, to me and I think to all of us from early on, that not finishing the film was not an option for David. And not simply finishing it but completing it in a way that remained true to his vision. After the AFI money was gone I've heard him say that he actually considered building miniature sets and creating a small Henry figurine and filling in unfilmed portions using stop-motion animation. He'd successfully mixed live action and animation with some of his early experimental films and I could see him making something like this work.

It was a long, challenging haul for David and I have nothing but admiration for that kind of unbreakable will that I believe marks a lot of true artists.

The thing, I think, that has made the film an enduring success is that you can't pin it to any particular era. Given the style of filmmaking it could have been made any time between the 1940s and today. It doesn't look "'70s." Unlike a lot of my friends – the guys from Crosby, Stills and Nash for example – David wasn't a hippie. He wasn't especially political either in life or in his work.

The thing you do see in his films is the return, over and over again, to certain ideas, images, and sounds. The industrial hiss and clang so much in the background of *Eraserhead* is heard in *The Elephant Man*. The chevron carpet that you see in the "red room" in Twin Peaks makes its first appearance in the lobby of Henry's building (albeit in black and white).

A great example that a lot of people don't know about, is the connection I see between David's 30-minute film *The Grandmother* and *Eraserhead*.

David showed me *The Grandmother* before we started filming *Eraserhead* and it's tremendously odd and idiosyncratic but I really liked it. I was already a fan of a lot of the avant garde film coming out of Europe and what I saw in *The Grandmother* helped me see where David might be headed.

What I didn't realize until much later was the amount of connective tissue between the two films. Like *Eraserhead*, *The Grandmother* starts with lots of birth imagery, much of it animated – two adults emerge from the leaf-covered earth and then a boy of about 11, all of whom are pale white with Kabuki style makeup. The parents, if that's who they are, are primitive. They grunt, growl and bark. The mother has seizures. The boy, by contrast, always wears a black suit, white shirt, black bowtie and we see him over and over in isolation in a small, dark bedroom with only a bed with gray-white sheets, a dresser and a few stick-dry plants. Sound familiar? It's like Henry Spencer's boyhood.

In his parents' bedroom the boy finds a bag labeled "Seeds." He finds a large one he likes, piles dirt on his parent's bed, puts the seed in and waters it. Something like a large potato grows and grows until it gives birth – very wetly – to another person, also dressed in black, also with Kabuki makeup – a woman looking to be in her late 60s. At last there's someone in the boy's life like him. She's loving and sweet to him in total contrast to his parents who are like wild dogs.

There are shots in which the grandmother's white face with its bright eyes and large round cheeks I swear she looks like the woman in the radiator without the skin disease.

Perhaps I'm reading too much into this but *The Grandmother* feels a lot like a prequel to *Eraserhead* and anyone who loves David's films should check it out. It's one of the many great extras on the Criterion edition of *Eraserhead* that came out a couple of years ago.

A few months before *Eraserhead* had its premiere in Hollywood in 1977,

David showed a few of us an early cut. At that point the film was still about three hours long. David asked me what I thought and I said, "David, it's like a toothache."

"Swell!" he said, beaming, considering this an immeasurably high compliment.

Even so, he kept refining it and eventually cut quite a bit until the final version was just 89 minutes. Gone was a scene of Catherine Coulson tied to a bed being tortured connected to battery cables. Gone was a scene when Mary X's parents force her to return to Henry and the baby. Also excised were things like Henry stroking a dead cat.

Good riddance. It was all extraneous. The final version holds together like a sonnet.

No one had ever seen anything like *Eraserhead* before; it was a film of enormous intelligence combined with visceral brutality, like an opera glove filled with organ meat.

Like all great art it can be viewed and understood in lots of different ways. It comes as close as I've ever seen to diving down into the dreamy subconscious with a camera and capturing it on film.

While I still can't claim to understand the film, you can see David's take on a lot of themes and influences. At the start when you see the diseased god-like "Man in the Planet" pulling the train-yard switching levers, for me that has the feel of Shakespeare. Like Macbeth, Henry finds himself caught in the machinations of fate – something outside himself, something supernatural, like Macbeth's entire life being spun into a whole different direction by the Weird Sister's prophecy (the word weird in Shakespeare's time meant fate). Henry's passive reaction to everything around him for nearly all of the film feels like Hamlet. And like Hamlet, that apparent inability to do anything turns suddenly into an act of gruesome violence at the very end.

There's also an element of virgin birth. In the first minutes of the film a sperm-like creature (one of Catherine's umbilical cords) seems to emanate from Henry's head and then drops to the planet. Soon afterward it's revealed that Mary X has given birth. When Mary's mother corners Henry and demands to know if he and Mary had sex, both seem very confused by the question and neither of them actually admits to it.

There are elements of Frankenstein. Near the end, with lights blinking on and off and electricity sparking – like a mad scientist's laboratory – Henry examines "the creature," the thing that he created.

Henry finally reaches for a pair of scissors, cuts open the swaddling clothes that bind the baby (another infant Christ visual) and he finds that it has no skin and inside the wrapping is a salad of organs and mush. When he stabs the baby, its death becomes a transformation and seems to return to The Man in the Planet.

These are just a handful of images and ideas that the film brings to my mind but of course the beauty of it is that *Eraserhead* isn't just a collection of literary symbolism and cannot be reduced to any one interpretation. It challenges you with its combination of familiar and alien, it images of disease, isolation, and desire. Yes, it's influenced by Kafka and other writers and artists, but ultimately, *Eraserhead* is its own macabre, horrifying, wonderful thing.

For those who are reading this as fans of *Little House on the Prairie*, I completely understand why *Eraserhead* may not be your idea of a good time. It's disturbing and dark. But I would like to suggest that *Eraserhead* is not just about bleak isolation, an exploration of the subconscious, and gross-out weirdness but in an important way, it's about love.

I think Henry finds something – God knows what – to love in Mary X. In spite of her spasms, her agonizing awkwardness, and emotional brokenness, he wants to be with her. He loves her. And when Mary leaves him and Spike, he gingerly and tenderly tries to care for the baby – the ugliest and least loveable infant in all of movie history. He exhibits love and care for this creature that shows no ability to love in return.

To love the unlovely, to love the thing that cannot return love – in all major religions and philosophies, this is the highest form of love.

To me it's no surprise that while David has long refused to discuss the meaning of the film, he has remained steadfast that this is his most spiritual work.

On release, *Eraserhead* caused a sensation. It got a big reaction at the Los Angeles Film Festival. It was polarizing. And audiences had a gut reaction that was either love or hate.

It joined *Rocky Horror Picture Show* as one of the top grossing midnight movies of that era. It showed every Saturday night for at least four years in L.A., New York, and other cities around the country. People would shout goofy instructions and encouragement to Henry and Mary up on the screen and audience members would dress like us and act out scenes from the movie while it was playing.

As you might expect, though, it was not met with universal praise. *Variety* called it "sickening" and "gory" adding: "*Eraserhead* consists mostly of a man sitting in a room trying to figure out what to do with his horribly mutated child."

The New York Times called *Eraserhead* "… a murkily pretentious shocker" and added, "It runs for two hours but because of its excruciatingly slow pace and the under-lighting of all its scenes, it seems to be twice that long."

Well, harrumph, harrumph.

One of the people who loved the film, however, was Mel Brooks, who was gearing up to produce *The Elephant Man*. Yes, Mel Brooks of *Blazing Saddles* and *Young Frankenstein*. Mel hired David to direct *The Elephant Man*, which like *Eraserhead* was shot in black and white, featured a main character in a kind of terrible isolation, and contained some of David's signature ominous background noises of machines hammering away somewhere two floors below.

My early prediction about his having no future as a director were, I am happy to say, completely off the mark. And you may quote me.

Charlotte's mother, Alice Stewart, in an image from the 1930s

Charlotte's dad, Willis Stewart, as a young man

Charlotte's parents, Alice and Willis Stewart, in the early days of their marriage

Charlotte Stewart shows her readiness for the spotlight, posing on the back of her dad's flatbed truck

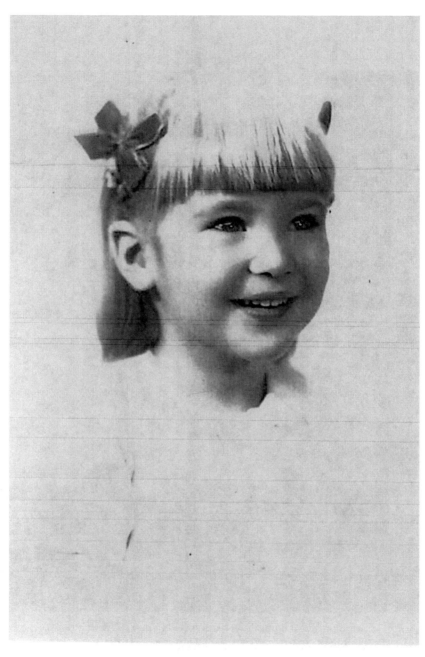

A childhood portrait of Charlotte Stewart

Charlotte with her brother and sister at their home in Yuba City, CA.
Left to Right: -Lewis Stewart, Charlotte Stewart, Barbara Jean Stewart

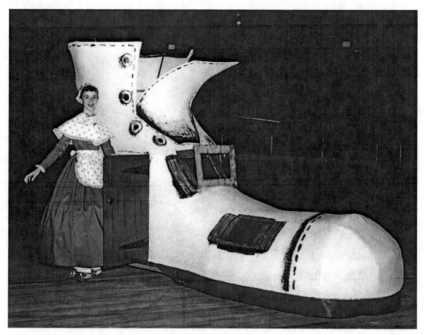

Charlotte Stewart as The Old Woman Who Lived in a Shoe posing by the shoe built by her father, Willis Stewart, for her Yuba City competitive rollerskating team

Left to right: Charlotte Stewart, William Frawley, Willis Stewart, and Alice Stewart
on the set of *My Three Sons*

Charlotte Stewart, Tim Considine and their many attendants at their wedding in Bel Aire in 1964

Charlotte Stewart and Tim Considine at their wedding in Bel Aire in 1964

Charlotte Stewart and Tim Considine as newlyweds out on the town

An image of Jimmy Stewart and Charlotte Stewart in character on the set
of *Cheyenne Social Club*

Joni Mitchell (left) and Charlotte Stewart on the back porch of Charlotte's house in
Topanga Canyon in the early 1970s

Charlotte Stewart (left) and her roommate Doreen Small (right) on the back porch of the house they shared with many other drop-ins in Topanga Canyon.

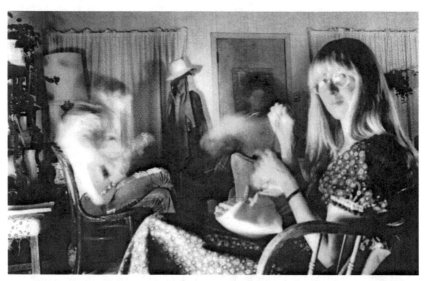

A candid shot of an evening in Topanga Canyon with Charlotte Stewart. Blurred in the background with a guitar is Peter Butterfield.

A photo by Julian Wasser at The Liquid Butterfly. Left to right: Two unidentified people, Dani Senator, Charlotte Stewart, and Jeanne Field

Jim Morrison, lead singer of The Doors, from an image taken from a Super 8 mm film Charlotte shot on a road trip they took together in November 1970

Charlotte Steward as Mary X and Jack Nance as Henry Spencer in an image from the film *Eraserhead (courtesy of David Lynch)*

Charlotte Stewart playing soccer in the weekly game organized by Tim Considine in the 1970s at the UCLA fields

Charlotte Stewart and Tim Considine finding friendship after their divorce

Charlotte Stewart (right) and Patty Elder (left), Charlotte's stunt double
on the set of *Little House on the Prairie*

A candid image of Charlotte Steward shot near the schoolhouse on the set
of *Little House on the Prairie*

Charlotte Stewart as Miss Eva Beadle and her long-time friend Josh Bryant as Adam Simms, the pig farmer Miss Beadle marries on *Little House on the Prairie*

Charlotte Stewart and her second husband, Jordan Hahn, dance at their wedding, held in Kit Carson's and Karen Black's backyard.

Neil Young as Lionel Switch and Charlotte as Charlotte Goodheart in Young's classic *Human Highway*, originally released in 1982
Courtesy of Shakey Pictures

174

Charlotte Stewart and long-time friend Jeanne Field in 1984 soon after Jeanne's divorce and Charlotte's stint in rehab.

An image of Jack Nance after he embraced sobriety and roomed with Charlotte Stewart

Charlotte Stewart and David Lynch on the set of *Twin Peaks* in the early 1990s

The Briggs Family on the set of *Twin Peaks*. Left to Right: Don Davis as Garland Briggs, Charlotte Stewart as Betty Briggs, and Dana Ashbrook as Bobby Briggs

Jack Nance (without pants) and Kelly Van Dyke at Charlotte Stewart's "bad taste"
50th Birthday Party

Charlotte Stewart and Don Davis at Charlotte's 50th "bad taste" birthday party.

Screen and Broadway star Patti LuPone gives Charlotte Stewart a hug
on the set of *Life Goes On* in the mid 1990s

Charlotte Stewart looking pretty pleased to be standing this close to Kevin Bacon on the set of *Tremors* in the 1990s

Charlotte Stewart and her third husband David Banks pose for a shot soon after their marriage in the early 1990s. He is seen here, as he nearly always was, in a straw Panama hat.

Chapter 9

Any Port in a Storm

In September of 1977, I was out with some friends one night at Ports, doing cocaine, drinking, and playing Backgammon, and saw a good-looking guy there performing magic tricks. I watched as he cracked an egg into a glass and made it disappear. And then it reappeared in someone else's glass. Pretty slick.

Jordan Hahn was a professional magician, a good one too, and we started hanging out and having a lot of fun. He was a member of the Academy of Magical Arts, which meant he could take me as his guest to The Magic Castle, a private L.A. club for members of the Academy of Magical Arts.

We had a lot in common. We loved to drink, do cocaine, and hang out at my house and watch *Battlestar Galactica* (which starred Lorne Greene from my old *Bonanza* days).

The first time I'd ever done cocaine was in the early 1970s at Elliot Robert's house. I remember doing a couple of lines and announcing that it didn't affect me in the least – and then I cleaned his entire kitchen.

Mainly, I liked coke because I could afford it and it allowed me to drink more. It was my wingman drug. Eventually, I'd worked out a pretty neat barter system. My dentist had access to pharmaceutical-grade cocaine but he preferred cocaine that was cut. My therapist had cocaine that was cut but preferred pharmaceutical grade. Enter Charlotte, the coke fairy. I was able to help them facilitate a swap on a regular basis and got some coke out of the bargain.

And no, it never occurred to me at the time that having a therapist who relied on me to secure his drug of choice might indicate I was working with the wrong therapist.

Within a few months of first meeting, and having a great time together – there's nothing like doing nothing to bring a couple together – Jordan and I took a trip to Mexico where we did more nothing together and had a good time and got engaged.

In retrospect it happened pretty fast and without a lot of thought, but at the time it seemed like the most perfectly natural thing to do. We should not have gotten married; we should have just thrown a party.

I was, though, thinking clearly enough to realize that we needed a place to get married that would be easy and fun – neither of us wanted a church nor did we want a place that would be too expensive. We needed to save our money for more important things like drugs and alcohol. We had priorities.

I put a lot of thought into trying to figure out where to have the ceremony until I had a flashbulb moment. My mind went back to the poker nights at my house in Topanga and to my buddy Kit Carson, who was both an actor and was turning out to be a very gifted writer. At the time he was working on a screenplay that eventually became the 1982 film *Paris, Texas* among other things. Kit was married to the actress Karen Black and I knew they had a beautiful backyard. Karen, you may remember, had appeared in a string of great films including *Easy Rider*, *Five Easy Pieces*, *Nashville* and *The Great Gatsby*.

I called up Kit and told him what I was calling about and he said, "Well, ask Karen." So he put Karen on the phone and she was just fine with it.

This phone call must have triggered something in Karen's mind because she called me back a few days later.

Here was her question: "Kit was telling me about these little houses he used to eat at your place. I was wondering if you could tell me how to make them?"

Um. Houses? That you eat?

Back in the Topanga Canyon days Kit had spent the night any number of times and my mind went back to what I may've cooked up for breakfast. Drawing a blank.

"Houses?" I asked.

"Yeah, you know. He said you made these houses. With cheese. I think he called them houses."

"Do you mean quesadillas?" I asked, taking a wild stab in the dark.

"Yeah, maybe that was it."

And so I explained the approximately three steps it takes to make a quesadilla.

I liked her a lot but sometimes she was a bit on Planet Karen if you know what I mean.

Our wedding in their backyard was on a perfect, warm, sunny L.A. day. There were lots of guests, many of whom I barely knew or not at all. Including Harrison Ford although for the life of me I cannot think why. He must have gotten dragged along as someone's date.

In front of all these people we promised to be true to each other for the rest of our lives.

It was a terrible idea.

***

I don't know what it is with me getting involved in film projects that take years to complete. Right around this time I was cast in one of my favorite films, which almost no one has ever seen, called *Human Highway*. This time instead of David Lynch throwing five years of his life at a movie, it was Neil Young.

Neil loves movies and had already shot a couple: *Journey Through the Past* and *Rust Never Sleeps*. This time he really wanted to make something creative, anarchic, something he was excited about, and that had some meaning.

He'd come up with an idea in rough form and had gotten together with actor friends Dean Stockwell, Russ Tamblyn, and Dennis Hopper. From the start Neil knew he didn't want anything scripted. He wanted to catch moments as they unfolded naturally in front of the camera. In the late 1970s they'd spent a few months in and around San Francisco and Taos, New Mexico, shooting scenes for a kind of road movie, which Neil eventually hated and finally walked away from.

There are two ways of looking at this first attempt at shooting the film. The first is this – these guys had all lived next to each other in Topanga Canyon and that first on-and-off film shoot was just a typical Topanga thing – a bunch of hippies getting stoned and grabbing a camera, going out on the road and seeing what happened.

The other way of looking at it is that these guys really knew the movie business. Remember that Russ Tamblyn had been acting in film since the late 1940s, as an eighth grader, and had later been a song and dance guy in musicals such as *Seven Brides for Seven Brothers* and then in *West Side Story* (with my old friend Richard Beymer) as well as in straight dramas such as *Peyton Place* and *How the West was Won*. Likewise Dean Stockwell got his start as a little kid in the mid-1940s shooting the big-budget musical *Anchors Aweigh* with Frank Sinatra and Gene Kelly. At age 12 he'd starred in *The Boy with Green Hair* and appeared in one of the *Thin Man* movies with William Powell and Myrna Loy – he'd grown up in the Golden Age of Hollywood – and had gone on to build a huge resume in TV and film.

Dennis Hopper had gotten his start rather famously in the 1955 blockbuster *Rebel Without a Cause* and had gone on to roles in a string of now-classics such as *Gunfight at the OK Corral, Cool Hand Luke,* and *True Grit.*

These guys were hardly naïve flower children when it came to the film industry. What they saw I'm guessing, with the success of Dennis's film *Easy Rider,* was that something was "blowing in the wind." There was an audience hungry for movies with a completely different feel – something grittier, less perfect, and more like their real lives.

The remnants of that first attempt at *Human Highway* appear in a 20-minute dream sequence in the middle of the final film and, in my opinion, it's great stuff. Weird but great. There's a whole extended performance of "Hey, Hey, My, My (Into the Black)" with Neil and the band Devo, which is trippy and pretty cool.

I was only involved a little bit in that first round of filmmaking. It was a scene shot somewhere near Neil's ranch in Woodside in which Neil and I are apparently married and live in this odd little white clapboard house. He's leaving in the morning and something like a dozen of our kids are streaming out past me as I stand in the doorway waving goodbye.

As Neil is taking off, the actor David Blue shows up dressed to the hilt as a milkman in a snappy white suit. Once Neil and the kids are gone, the milkman and I dash inside and shut the door. (Wink.)

It was fun but I had no idea what it was about and as I would later learn, neither did anyone else.

In spite of something like $1-million down the drain, Neil decided to start over but he didn't quite know what to do. He bemoaned the fact that in the first version of the film he'd made the mistake of casting himself as a musician and he just didn't think anyone would find that very interesting.

Jeanne Field meanwhile, who never seems short on ideas, had a concept that she thought might work and wrote a treatment for a new version of *Human Highway* that she described as a rock-n-roll Wizard of Oz.

Neil liked this new direction a lot and used it as a loose – very loose –

roadmap for what became the final film, a dark, spoofy, cartoony anti-nuclear-power film.

We shot the new version at Raleigh Studios, which sits across the street on Melrose from Paramount. The good-looking studio manager from Raleigh named Kevin kept an eye on our production, rented Neil lights and equipment, kept things cleaned up, and would sometimes hang around to watch us work. At some point we all eventually learned Kevin's last name, which was Costner.

Every morning we'd show up to the sound stage and Neil would outline what the upcoming scene was about, what he was looking for in terms of what would happen, how it would advance the story, and then we'd wing it. Once we'd filmed the scene in a way that worked, someone would write down the dialogue so that the screenplay was actually written after we shot it.

Neil played two characters in the new version, a grease monkey mechanic named Lionel Switch, a completely clueless dork, and Frankie Fontaine, a rock star, who is too cool to even emerge from his limousine. He saw the idea of playing Lionel, something totally the opposite of his onstage persona, as being a much more interesting proposition for an audience. For those of us who know Neil, playing a nerd wasn't a huge stretch. If anything, it was simply revealing a side of himself that audiences hadn't seen. This is a guy, remember, who when he got money did what? Built a barn and filled it with model trains. He loves them so much he bought an interest in the Lionel train company. And note the name of the character – Lionel Switch.

I loved how Russ Tamblyn put it once in an interview saying that in *Human Highway* Neil got to play two characters, "Himself and himself."

Besides starring and producing the film, Neil directed along with Dean Stockwell, who played Otto Quartz, the new owner of the Rail Café in Linear Valley who appeared to be up to no good. Dennis Hopper remained in the cast, along with Russ Tamblyn, who, since he was the resident song and dance guy, was now tasked with choreographing a big dance number that takes place just before the world blows up.

Elliot Roberts, who makes an appearance in the film as the manager of Neil's superstar rocker character, produced along with Jeanne.

Elliot and Neil hired Sally Kirkland, Geraldine Barone, and me to round out the cast, as waitresses in the Rail Café and my friend Mickey Fox as one of the café's more memorable customers.

One of the producers very nicely asked if I wanted my new husband Jordan to work on the film and I said absolutely not. Which I realized later was not a good sign.

I played Charlotte Goodheart, a waitress in the greasy spoon café, who dreams of becoming a chanteuse and is the object of Lionel's goggle-eyed, slack-jawed desire. I wore heart earrings, a heart necklace, and a heart apron. I was blonde and breathy and had a ball.

Early in the film Lionel Switch drops by the café to see Charlotte and for a full minute of screen time (time it if you don't believe me) we are treated to the sight of his eyes bugging, his face twitching, his mouth open and moving, trying to form words at the sight of his heavenly Charlotte.

Well, what actress doesn't want a bit of that?

Human Highway was the first and only time I got to sing on film. Before shooting the scene where I sing "Moonglow" to Neil as Lionel (he joins in whistling) I sang that song everywhere I went – in the car, cleaning my house, walking down the street. When we finally filmed the scene everyone was stunned that I could actually carry a tune. Nailed it on the first take.

The film also includes a subplot with guys from the New Wave band Devo as jump-suit wearing workers from the local nuclear power plant – the one that's about to blow. They glow red as they move red glowing barrels of nuclear waste in a truck that also glows red, all the while performing their version of the Kingston Trio hit "A Worried Man."

Devo were big at the time, thanks to popularity of "Whip It." Elliot had been Neil's manager for a long time and now also managed Devo, so he was bringing a lot of his clients together on this. Plus, Neil really like the Devo guys and loved performing with them. *liked*

Dennis Hopper, who played Cracker, the twitchy, talkative short order cook, was always high, drunk or both during filming and was usually a pain in the ass. This was, I believe, the last movie he did before going into drug and alcohol recovery. On set he was not that different from his character in *Apocalypse Now*, always in his little kitchen banging stuff, pots, pans and implements and always jabbering away maniacally and nonsensically and driving us all crazy.

One day Sally Kirkland had had it with him. Dennis was banging the metal counter in his kitchen with a large knife. She grabbed it by the blade, thinking perhaps that it was a dull prop, but no, it was good and sharp and it sliced right through her, severing a tendon in her right index finger. It was pretty bloody and awful.

They got her off to the hospital and bandaged up. A day later several of us from the film went to see her in a play and there she was on-stage with a cast on her hand and arm, gamely ensuring that the show would go on, seeming to do pretty well.

Something like five years later, in December 1985, she filed a $2-million lawsuit in Los Angeles Superior Court against Dennis claiming that he'd intentionally knifed her. She also named Neil and Elliot in the suit, claiming they had been negligent in not keeping Dennis under control. My friend Mickey Fox, who played Mrs. Robinson in the film, and I had to go testify.

In court Dennis's lawyer didn't dispute that the knife incident had happened or that his client had been high at the time but maintained that it had been an accident.

In February 1986, Superior Court by Judge Stanley Malone found Dennis not at fault along with Neil and Elliot and the whole thing was dropped.

The final film, meanwhile, was released in September 1982, shown first at the Mill Valley Film Festival and later in Los Angeles. The reviews weren't great and it wasn't embraced by the film industry at all.

The tone, the look, the feel of it, the politics, it just wasn't cool in the way things were supposed to be cool at that moment. Perhaps if it had been released 10 years earlier or 10 years later it would've received a different reception. In 1982 Ronald Reagan was president. Margaret Thatcher was the prime minister in the UK. Punk music was on the rise. The world had shifted since *Human Highway* had first started filming back in 1978. The average moviegoer was seeing *E. T.*, *Poltergeist*, *Blade Runner* and *Porky's*. Film connoisseurs were seeing *Diner*, *Gandhi*, and *Sophie's Choice*. No one that year was in the mood to see a group of Topanga friends sing and dance their way through a comedic, experimental, anti-nuclear-power film.*

*I am thrilled that as I'm sending this book off to the publisher, I've just learned from Elliot that Human Highway *is slated to show in 400 theaters in March, 2016 – finally getting the spotlight it deserves.*

Chapter 10
Henry and Mary X, Part 2

BY THE TIME I'D STARTED *HUMAN HIGHWAY*, my life had taken on a new reality. For the first time since the late 1950s my indomitable work ethic was faltering. My appointment books from this era offer a glimpse of this. A normal year for me was, say, 1975, in which in addition to filming *Little House*, I also managed to appear in more than 20 television commercials, including Bounty, Shake-N-Bake, Mr. Clean, Cool Whip, Pillsbury, Morning Star Farms, Mountain Bell Telephone and more. In 1978, page after page is empty, with only a notation here and there for a dinner party or a visit to my therapist.

In September of 1978, I was hospitalized as I'd done so much cocaine I ended up with vaginal bleeding that wouldn't stop, and had to get a D and C.

About the worst thing you can give a person with addiction issues is lots of money and free time. Idle hands, as my mother would say, are the devil's workshop.

When I had lived in Topanga the hour-long, winding trek between my house and just about every studio in town mandated, though reluctantly, a level of sobriety. Even when I moved to Beachwood Canyon, though the commute was dramatically cut, the work on *Little House* demanded specific periods of sobriety. Sometimes for two or three weeks at a time I had to be to work at 6:00 a.m. either at Simi Valley or at Paramount and know my lines and perform at a high level. I felt responsible to the cast and crew to show up ready to go, even if I was hung over.

For four years the show gave structure to my life and put money in my bank account. With the end of the *Little House* and with nothing like it in sight, it was now up to me to get out there and hunt down more work.

Unfortunately it seemed that four years on a hit show had done little to give me a career boost. *Little House* was not widely watched in the entertainment industry. It wasn't a show that other producers or executives were watching. It didn't get reviewed and it didn't win Emmys or any other notice at the awards shows.

Alison Arngrim likes to joke we were "the ugly stepchild of the entertainment industry" and to find actual viewers you had to leave Los Angeles County – once you crossed the county line there they were.

A few years after my stint on the show had ended, I went to a bar on Melrose where I often ended up around lunchtime. The bartender and I had become good friends. One day a young, LA, hipster couple were at the bar next to me and the bartender, by way of introducing me to them said, "Do you know who this is?"

They said no.

She said, "This is Charlotte Stewart, she played Miss Beadle on *Little House on the Prairie*."

And they burst out laughing. Snotty, derisive, "How stupid is that?" laughter.

Which put the whole thing in perfect context.

What I'd done for those four seasons on the show counted for nothing. My work on *Human Highway* went unseen and wouldn't see the light of day again until the mid-1980s when it got a limited video release.

If I wanted a job, I'd have to get out there like the thousands upon thousands of other working actors in Hollywood and beat down doors, show up to auditions, and all the other legwork that goes into finding a job.

You know what's a lot more fun than spending the day sitting in producers' outer offices chasing parts you're not going to get? Staying home and drinking and doing cocaine and watching TV.

Especially when you're married to someone who wants to do exactly the same. It's a bonding thing.

At least for a while. And then something clicked and I started to get mad *angry* and disgusted and bored with him.

While the truth is that neither of us were working or looking for work, in my mind Jordan was more negligent than I in this regard. His not-working meant that he was living more and more off my income, which was the accumulation of decades of hard work.

I decided to go on a trip to Mexico with my niece and I told him that I'd come back when he'd found a job. About a week later over the phone he told me that he'd landed a part-time gig at the Magic Castle so I moved back in.

By the time I'd finished *Human Highway* though, I wanted to get away permanently. I wanted to end my second marriage and I decided the best thing to do was to leave town. Employing a kind of magical thinking, I labeled all my issues "L.A. Problems" reasoning that all I really needed to do was to get out of town.

I met with my financial manager and long-time friend, Syd Crocker, whom I'd worked (and partied) with since about 1973 when he'd moved to Los Angeles from the Carolinas and was in the first flush of discovering that he could live openly there as a gay man. The freedom and joy he felt were infectious – I adored Syd. He'd done a great job of managing my monetary affairs all the way through *Little House*. Over the years Syd had helped invest my money so that I owned a house, I owned an apartment building, and had other holdings to secure my long-term future. I liked him so much I talked him up to friends and as a result quite a few made him their financial manager too – friends such as Josh Bryant, Stuart Margolin, Tim Considine, and several others.

Syd was a ball of energy, he was a lot of fun, and he took some pride I think in the idea that he wasn't a stodgy, boring accountant. Financially he'd make moves that were probably more creative than most, like I remember him doing things like moving a few thousand from my account to Josh's account to cover a temporary shortfall and then moving it back. But he always checked with me when making a move like this, so I didn't mind.

When I told Syd I was going to move to San Francisco, he set up a system in which he would take care of all the monthly payments in L.A. for things like the mortgage on my Beachwood Canyon house and the building I owned, plus various forms of upkeep etc., and at the same time he would take care of paying my rent for my San Francisco apartment, the utilities, and so on.

I packed up my yellow Pacer (complete with 8-track player) and drove to San Francisco, found an apartment just off Haight Ashbury, where I would live for more than a year – an era which comes back to me now in not much more than a blur, which is why the details in this portion of the story become a bit thin.

One night I remember drinking so much at a restaurant that a waiter had to walk me home. Once I got there I couldn't get my key into the lock and I stood there stabbing at it unsuccessfully and he kindly and patiently took the key, unlocked the door and helped me inside.

On another occasion I had been out drinking and woke up in the morning with a horrific hang over. Once I stumbled out of bed, the sunlight pounding my eyes, I discovered that my front door was standing open – anyone off the sidewalk could have come in. My car was parked at a sideways angle to the curb, the driver's side door was standing open and my purse with all of its contents lay on the sidewalk as I had apparently left it the night before.

I had moved to San Francisco to escape L.A. and to be closer to my family but at the same time I was drinking myself into a kind of blindness. My family was very worried about me. I knew somewhere in my haze that I wanted to quit. Or at least slow down.

I went to a health spa in the South Bay to try to pull things together. The place offered transformation through meditation and a vegetarian diet – and of course drugs and alcohol were not on the menu. As part of the in-take, I was asked to fill out a personality profile. The next day the director asked me into his office to discuss the results. The answers, he said, indicated that I was suicidal. Which I thought was crazy. How could that be? Something was laughably wrong with their test.

Later I went to another health spa, this one down south outside of San Diego. The staff asked us all to do a skit on Saturday so I asked Dolly Parton, the country singer, who was also staying there at the time, if I could borrow her wig. She was more than happy to offer one up – a large blonde thing – and I did a skit in which I played Holly Spartan.

But health spas weren't solving my problems.

Jordan and I divorced when I was living in San Francisco and I managed to do a miniscule amount of work. I had a small part in the Billy Wilder film *Buddy, Buddy* with Jack Lemon and Walter Matthau. I also managed to pull myself together enough to play roles in a couple of episodes of *Eight is Enough*. But if you look up my career on IMDB.com, you'll see work was scant.

I cannot blame this on Hollywood. I can't fault the industry for having a built-in disinterest in actresses over the age of 35. This was good old-fashioned substance abuse doing its career magic.

And then things got worse. The owner of the apartment where I lived in San Francisco contacted me looking for a rent payment. Huh? Syd was taking care of that. I called his office to see had happened but I couldn't get him on the phone. This game went on for a few days.

What

Then I came back to Los Angeles to find something totally frightening. Without my knowledge, my Beachwood Canyon house had gone into foreclosure. It now belonged to the bank, not to me.

I was panicking and got a call from a friend, Liz Barron, who'd known Syd nearly as long as I had. Syd had encouraged the former model and single mom to go to law school, which launched a law career that lead to a position as a state judge. She adored Syd as much as I did.

"You've got to get away from Syd," Liz said. "The statements you're getting aren't real."

She meant the monthly statements of income and payments, which he'd prepped and sent to me for years.

The question then was – what happened to all the money? Where had it gone? He was still somewhere in town but I couldn't track him down.

Soon I discovered that Syd's cocaine habit had spun wildly out of control and that to fund his addiction he'd been moving funds around from one client's bank account to another – as he had in the past from time to time but now he didn't pay it back. It had all gone up his nose. He had been desperately trying to hide it all in a kind of shell game in which the statements were falsified and the numbers were cooked.

He'd ruined me financially but worse, he'd ruined all my friends – people who were only with Syd because I was with him. And I'd been too drunk and too high in San Francisco to maintain a solid hold on the situation.

I felt sick and scared for myself and I felt heartbroken and utterly responsible for what my friends were now dealing with.

Syd wasn't a bad guy. He was a good guy with a bad addiction. Everyone was doing cocaine – everyone. But unlike most people he'd become completely dependent on it. And like so many addicts – like me – he'd chosen drugs over friendships, drugs over career, drugs over doing what was right.

A spiral had started. My house was gone, the building I had owned was gone, and my investments were gone. Everything I had worked for and earned since the early 1960s had vanished. I had gone from a beloved role in one of the biggest TV series in history to a homeless alcoholic.

Not sure where to go or what to do, I talked everything over with Jeanne. Her new husband Stephen Peck (Gregory Peck's son) had an idea and introduced me to French director Jean-Pierre Dutilleux, who said I could have a room in his large house on Mulholland Drive in exchange for maid duties such as mopping, picking up his clutter, and scrubbing his toilets. That only lasted until a friend of mine and I threw a small party when Jean-Pierre was away for the weekend. That got me thrown out.

I reached out to my old Pasadena Playhouse teacher, Kenneth Rose and his wife Helen. They had a one-room apartment unit on their property in the Hollywood Hills, which they said I could rent. With what money? I didn't get that far.

So my dog Fudge and I moved into that little apartment. But soon after Ken made a comment like, "Are you sure you should be drinking so much?"

And that was it.

Anyone who pointed out the fact that I drank too much was cut right out of my life. I found out years later that Jeanne and Mickey Fox would often say to each other, "What are we going to do about Charlotte?" They knew I needed help, needed an intervention but were afraid to do it because they knew what would happen – they'd never see me again.

I left Fudge at Ken and Helen's apartment assuming they'd take care of him and I tracked down someone I knew I could drink with and wouldn't have a stick up his ass about it – and that was Jack Nance. He still lived in the apartment house I had once owned on Pico near the 405, where I'd set him up as the building manager, a job he was uniquely suited not to do. He had developed an elaborate capacity to hide when tenants needed him.

The success of *Eraserhead* as a midnight movie classic hadn't worked in Jack's favor. He'd only managed to land a couple of small film parts, one in a Chuck Norris movie called *Breaker, Breaker*. The truth is he was far more interested in drinking than working, which made him precisely the sort of person I wanted to hang out with.

I told Jack I really needed a place to stay and he was as agreeable as a curmudgeon can be. His apartment looked like the site of a bombing –

piles of magazines, weird knick-knacks, old books, garbage and overflowing ashtrays.

Jack and I didn't do much. Mostly stayed in the apartment with the drapes shut and stayed drunk and watched TV. Other than the calories from alcohol, our food supply came from shared hotdogs at the Wienerschnitzel a couple of blocks away.

At one point Jack decided he wanted to go fishing in Mexico so we packed his car with booze and took a road trip. There for a few days in Ensenada he fished and I soaked up the sun.

Once we got back to L.A. we did manage to roust ourselves out of the apartment for the running of the Olympic torch through Los Angeles. In a highly intoxicated state we dashed out in front of the torch runner, dancing and skipping and strewing handfuls of rose petals in his path.

In a way it was as though Henry and Mary X had reunited only this time our hideous baby was alcoholism.

I had cut off contact with my family, with nearly everyone I knew. They would all try to make me feel guilty for drinking. They'd remind me of the world outside of the boozy sinkhole I was in. Who needed that pressure? My agent didn't know where I was, so of course I wasn't getting any calls about work. Somewhere inside I knew that things weren't going well. Everything I'd worked for was slipping away. Everything I had once loved was a memory.

I was getting thinner, weaker, and sicker. But I was doing exactly what I wanted. No one was telling me when to get up, to learn lines, to put on a happy face, or that I was drinking too much. I had graduated now to smoking crack – the form of cocaine that you smoke instead of snort. Crack was cheaper and wildly successful at helping to keep the hatch open for even more vodka.

Who knows how long this would have lasted, one dim, blurred day giving way to another.

The morning of August 16, 1984, though, something snapped. Jack woke up at 7 a.m. with wild hair and a dangerous, crazy look in his eyes and he growled at me, "You better leave, Charlotte, or we're going to go out into the desert and kill each other."

In a strange way I knew what he meant. He wasn't a violent person but Jack did own a gun and something in his voice said that the game had changed.

I was scared and felt sick. I didn't say anything. I just nodded that I understood and I walked out of the apartment with the sense that everything was collapsing in around me.

I had no money.

No place to live.

I was ill.

I was hung over.

I had run out of people.

I returned to the apartment at Ken Rose's house and just stared at the walls for a while. Numb. Then without really thinking or making a conscious decision, I reached for the phone and called my doctor. Dr. Paul Cohart had been my GP since the days I was married to Tim and I don't think he'd ever realized the level of my drinking. If anything even close had ever come up in that regard, I had lied to him. In fact, I realized now, I'd been lying to my doctor for 20 years.

I had been lying to myself for even longer.

I was a highly advanced liar.

While I waited for my doctor to pick up the line, things around me didn't quite seem real. I felt detached from myself and dazed. I'd gone past some point, some point that had always been in the distance, some emotional, spiritual, or moral point that did not have a name. But passing it meant that something was about to change.

Something was on the verge of happening.

Dr. Cohart picked up and words fell out of me. Words that hundreds of times had nibbled at the edges of my mind and that I had always fought away. Words that I had always hated and feared.

Yet now even as they tumbled out they were oddly comforting, though finally saying them out loud was like uttering the first syllables of a foreign language.

I said simply into the phone, "I think I have a problem with alcohol."

Chapter 11

New Beginnings

Dr. Cohart gave me the number of "New Beginnings" at Century City Hospital, a six-week live-in drug and alcohol recovery program. I made the call and they said they'd send a cab right over but I had four things to take care of first.

1. I wasn't sure if I still had insurance through the Screen Actors Guild. I had been doing very little work and was well behind on dues. Miraculously, after a phone call I learned that my insurance was still good.

2. I needed $200 for the deductible and I was flat broke. I drove over to Mickey Fox's apartment and told her what I was doing and that I needed money. Mickey was elated for me and even though she was living on social security and barely had two dimes to scrape together at that moment, she and two of her friends were able to pool their cash and loan me the money.

3. I went back to my apartment at Ken Rose's house and apologized for not arranging for my dog Fudge's care while I was off with Jack and asked Ken and Helen if they could continue to care for him over the next six weeks. They were more than willing.

4. I went back to my little apartment and drank a half-pint of vodka – a wimpy amount for a true alcoholic but I didn't have the money for any size larger.

The next morning, August 17, 1984, Ken drove me to Century City Hospital and I checked myself into the program.

First things first. At New Beginnings they gave me a full medical checkup, something I hadn't had in a long time. They found I was suffering from anemia, malnutrition, and the first stages of liver disease.

After that, they went through my suitcase and all my belongings to ensure I hadn't tried to sneak in any drugs or alcohol and then they took everything away, except for the clothes I'd wear and a few other essentials. My private room was essentially a hospital room – no swanky health spa setting here. The bed was a standard issue hospital bed and the room had a lot of the functional trappings of a typical medical facility.

They kept me on a mild sedative and in isolation for the first two days so the medical staff could keep me under observation and see how I managed the physical and emotional effects of alcohol withdrawal.

While I felt weak, I hardly felt terrible. The idea of life without alcohol was not a daunting prospect, nor was it sad, disappointing or awful. It was something else altogether.

It was as though for years I'd been wearing a suit made of bowling balls and when I entered New Beginnings, they had all fallen off and gone crashing away. It was the biggest relief you can possibly imagine. It was like getting out of jail. Like escaping from kidnappers. I felt totally liberated. There was no more hiding. No more lies. No more pretending I didn't have a problem.

The idea that I could be in control of my life – instead of the thing inside of me that craved alcohol – was freeing and transformative. For the first time in a long, long time, I was happy.

More than happy, I was euphoric.

I called my brother and sister and other family members and the response from all of them was relief too. They said things like "Thank God we have you back." Alcohol had put barriers between us. Now I had returned to their lives and they were welcomed joyfully and tearfully back into mine.

I called Jeanne and other friends and told them things like, "The food here is so good!" Looking back I realize it was pretty standard, ho-hum hospital food like turkey and mashed potatoes with gravy. But after such long neglect, living on a diet of vodka and hotdogs, this food was rich, solid, nourishing, and dazzling. I'd forgotten what it felt like to actually feel good.

After my brief isolation I was judged ready to mix with the others in the program, to attend the meetings held throughout the day, have meals in the common area, and take part in the other events.

One of the things my counselors stressed was the idea of learning how to tell the truth. Anyone with an addiction like this becomes a world-class, overachieving, Triple-A-rated liar. And the worst lies are the ones you tell yourself.

I have to say, it's pretty hard learning how to be truthful.

One of our exercises was to write our feelings every day. And I had to learn to write the real things I felt – not to write things other people wanted to hear, not to gain something, not for the effect it might have, not for the image I hoped to create for myself.

This is hard for anyone though I have a tendency to believe – perhaps in a self-centered way – that it may be harder for actors. We want to be liked. We spend our careers obsessing over winning people over whether it's an audience watching us on the big screen or a casting director's 19-year-old intern who's operating the video camera during an audition in a nondescript office.

A lot of the people in the recovery program were younger than I was and were coming off of profound addictions to drugs such as amphetamines, barbiturates, and heroin, drugs I'd never taken and had no connection to.

We all told our stories in the group meetings – or pieces of our stories or versions of our stories. We were all taking those first steps into the strange unknown – telling the unprettified truth about ourselves, which is scary and awkward. In one meeting I stood up when it was my turn and related how after I'd come back to Los Angeles and was bouncing from place to place after I lost my home and was housesitting for a friend. I'd run out of unemployment money, there weren't any residual checks coming in, I was just eking by, and how my dog Fudge and I were living on packages of hotdogs. I realized while relating this that I was hearing someone crying. I looked around the group and saw girl in her 20s who'd burst out in tears as I was talking about my dog and me living on nothing and I remember looking at her in confusion, unsure why this would make anyone cry. I'd just been talking about how I'd made it through a rough spot; it hadn't occurred to me that that level of poverty would move someone so much. But we were all raw and new and our emotions were wobbly and wonky. I know mine were.

An important step, they told us, was to admit that you were an alcoholic. Yep. I was. No problem with that. Another was to admit my helplessness in the face of alcohol, to understand that I would never stop wanting it, there would be no finish line to cross and that for the rest of my life I would require support – the support of others in recovery, of friends and family, and of a "higher power." I did indeed find such powerful support in the program and made many new friendships.

My relationship with myself changed. We are the stories we tell ourselves about ourselves. And I began to see that the story I'd always told myself about myself – my internal autobiography – was completely different than I'd ever imagined.

The new and truthful central story of my life was this: when I was born there was a tiny seed implanted in my brain, something I'd inherited from my dad, that sweet, kind, quiet man who started his day with bourbon and kept cases of Jim Beam in the barn and my mom, who had cocktail hour all too often. Hell, it came from their parents too. I remember my grandmother on my mother's side always had a little brown bottle with her, which she called her heart medicine. I hadn't realized what it was until one day she went to the pharmacy in Yuba City to get a refill and was complaining about the price. The pharmacist, who apparently had no use for euphemism, said pretty loudly, "Well, ma'am, the price of brandy has gone up."

When I was a child and I hung out on the fringes of those weekend cocktail parties that make up my first memories, and I would take sips of those drinks, the seed stirred. Later in high school when I drank beer with my friends, the seed cracked open and something peeked out, liking what I was doing. In college, at the Pasadena Playhouse, I started to drink in earnest. The umbilical-cord-like worm that came out of that seed grew, stretching itself out lazily across the top of my brain. Over time it continued to grow, nourished and strengthened by the alcohol I kept feeding it. And eventually it had a voice and it was my voice and it had thoughts and desires and they were now my thoughts and desires. It was telling me what to drink and when to drink. It told me that Tim Considine was totally off base, controlling, and no fun at all when he said we should stop drinking. It told me that he was the wrong guy for me and that better things were to be had outside our relationship. It said drinking was more important than Tim, more important than my marriage. Later, as I entered my thirties, it became clear that I couldn't keep drinking and ever have children. I had seen Barbara Jean caring for her seven beautiful kids and I knew somewhere inside that I could barely take care of my dog. And so I got my tubes tied because the worm mandated that drinking was more important than children. But we both came to an agreement, the worm and I, that my career was still important. We struck that bargain. And while shooting *Little House* we stuck to that deal. I would say, "Okay I have to work now but as soon as I'm finished filming, then we can drink again." But after *Little House* was over, the worm had no more patience and it told me I didn't need to go to auditions or show up to meetings with my agent. In fact I didn't need to work anymore. I needed to devote myself fully to the worm and I needed to start the day drinking and I needed to take cocaine in order to increase my capacity to drink and to feed the worm. Then it told me I needed to marry Jordan. The worm liked Jordan because we both liked to stay at home and drink and do cocaine and drink more. Somewhere in the haze though, I wanted to quit all this, something didn't feel right, and I moved to San Francisco and I tried to stop and I went to that spa but the worm said, "You can't quit, you need me. You have to drink. Who will you be without drinking? What will you do? Drinking is your life."

Back in Los Angeles, after I'd lost everything, the worm told me it was no problem if I didn't have money – vodka was cheap and smoking crack was cheaper than cocaine and just as good. If anyone, such as Ken Rose, questioned my drinking, the worm took great offense and told me to cut those people out of my life. It told me to move in with Jack. I didn't need to go out of the apartment. I didn't need my family. I didn't need to work. I didn't need to eat. I just needed to keep drinking. I had to. Nothing else mattered.

Going into alcohol recovery with its ongoing group meetings, mentoring, and community of support meant that I, Charlotte, the true Charlotte, had reasserted herself and that I stopped feeding the worm. But I couldn't kill it. It was always there. And it would always remain there. Sometimes sleeping but sometimes still whispering, "Go buy a bottle. No one will know. You can hide it. You don't have to tell anyone. It'll be fine. You can handle it. You deserve it."

It was a strange time. The freedom, the new sense of lightness, and the clarity were amazing. But learning to live without alcohol, without the worm, meant nothing short of starting life over. Finding my boundaries, my voice, my likes and dislikes, finding my identity. Even simple things like how did I pass the time? How did I reward myself? How did I prop myself up on hard days? My relationship to the world, to my innermost self, and even to my own body felt tentative, new, vulnerable, and not always clear.

It was like a divorce, a cure, a release from prison, a death, a transformation, and a rebirth all wrapped in one.

At New Beginnings the staff told me that once my six-week stay was over, I needed to change everything in my life. Even down to rearranging the furniture in my apartment. Anything in my surroundings that could remind me of old ideas, old patterns, old ways of thought had to change.

I realized pretty quickly that it was going to be hard to significantly reinvent the look of my one-room apartment. So I was grateful when Jeanne called, to her everlasting credit, and invited me to move in with her.

Jeanne was starting over too. After dating for several years, and just 11 months of marriage, Stephen had broken the news that he wanted a divorce; he'd already, unbeknownst to her, set himself up in an apartment and had another relationship well underway. Nothing had prepared her for this and it smashed through her like a freight train.

So we were both beaten up, both bruised, and starting over. I moved into the house that she and Stephen had shared in Sherman Oaks, which was situated up on a hill, offered a lot of privacy up off the street and was surrounded by trees and greenery. It was an ideal place to begin again.

I knew one of the most important things I could do was to ensure that I didn't have hours and hours of time with nothing to do – as I had done following my stint on *Little House*.

My first job was to go to meetings. I threw myself into recovery, committing to – and succeeding in – going to 90 group meetings in my first 90 days out of the live-in program. I was gung-ho. I went to a group meeting on Radford Street in Studio City and on Thursdays and Saturdays I drove my yellow Pacer over to New Beginnings and took some women who were in the program to the group meeting as well.

Beyond that I needed to fill the hours of my day. The old schedule of working a day or two here and there with lots of days in between to fill – and falling back into old habits – wasn't going to work any longer. Which is why I count myself extremely fortunate to have connected with a great TV and film industry company called Lantana in Santa Monica. Lantana was created by producers Alex Winitsky and Arlene Sellers. They'd produced a strong line-up of films since the mid-1970s such as *The Seven-Percent Solution*, *Swing Shift*, and *Stanley & Iris*. During that time they'd both gotten sick of driving from their home in Beverly Hills up the 405 to their production offices in the San Fernando Valley. The traffic was usually terrible and a ridiculous waste of time so they got the ingenious idea of starting Lantana in Santa Monica which would offer office space, including pre- and post-production space to film companies.

When you're a producer and you've put together your total package – you've got a script, a director, and a couple of main actors – and you get the green light from a studio, what you need to do overnight is create a company that will make the film. You have to get the gears of your project moving right away. It's called a green light because it means go. Now.

You need an office for yourself and other producers, for your writers, you need a casting office and more. At Lantana we were able to offer connected office space in Santa Monica (not up the river of bumper-to-bumper traffic in the San Fernando Valley) and when you came to us and said, "We'd like to rent this block of six offices," the next morning you could move in. You'd have furniture, desks, phones, a computer network, Internet service – everything.

At Lantana I performed a lot of different jobs – as did the entire staff of six people – under the excellent management of Maggi Kelly, who'd been Robert Altman's assistant and had gone on to run his Lion's Gate Films before this. I would show prospective clients the offices, talk them through the set-up we could offer and I could write-up leases. The idea of production offices in Santa Monica was a big hit and a lot of industry people came through to check out our set-up. Tom Cruise came by once while director Cameron Crowe had offices there. Someone had seen Tom walk up the hallway into the bathroom and Maggi let me know she was going to park her bulldog Gladys in the hall, to see if Tom would stop to pet her on his way back out. And it worked. He took one look at Gladys, couldn't resist her charms, and we got to meet Tom. Denzel Washington was another guy all the ladies in the office wanted to meet. When they heard that I was touring Denzel there was more excitement than if the Pope was visiting. I made sure we had to drop by the office to review lease agreements.

Of course not everyone can be a lovely person. We rented space to Shirley MacLaine who didn't seem to like anything about the place and not just predictable things such as carpet color or the style of furniture but, among other things, made it clear that she hated having a window in her second-floor office. What she had in mind was to take out the glass completely and simply have a rectangular hole in her wall open to the noise of traffic, wind, rain, and the elements. Okay. Our crew promptly and efficiently responded to this peculiar demand and removed the windowpane. For our efforts there was no hint of appreciation. There were never any of the little touches of humanity that we gave and got with other people in the building. Even so, when she complained of suffering from some kind of allergy issue I went down to the nearest Rite-Aid and bought three or four different over-the-counter allergy medications, thinking one of them might help. When I offered them to her she practically threw them back at me. "I wouldn't take any of that crap," she said.

She never had a nice thing to say. None of us ever heard a "please" or a "thank you" or anything other than demands. Fortunately the majority of our clients were exactly the opposite.

We were a great crew at Lantana and we've all stayed in touch. Maggi remains one of my dearest friends. Arlene Sellers and I had an odd relationship though. Every Friday at closing time for years she'd swing through the main office and wish everyone a happy weekend and then she'd walk past my desk and say over her shoulder on the way out the door. "Charlotte, we won't be needing you next week."

The first dozen or so times this happened I looked over to Maggi with a sinking heart and Maggi would silently shake her head as if to say "Don't pay any attention to that."

I would show up again on Monday and everything was fine.

Even so, for reasons I still don't understand, Arlene fired me every Friday for a long, long time.

In terms of my acting career, just like everything else it felt like starting over. Could I still act? Could I handle an audition, the pressures of shooting, or decompressing at home alone without alcohol?

Any career capital I'd built since the early 1960s was gone. It didn't matter that I'd been on *Bonanza* or had acted with Jimmy Stewart in *Cheyenne Social Club* or that I'd been in *Eraserhead* one of the most successful midnight movies ever or even that I'd been part of the blockbuster that *Little House on the Prairie* had eventually become. Professionally speaking, I was no one. I wasn't the freckled blonde of the 1960s or the straight haired, sexually charged flower child of the '70s. This was the '80s, the Reagan-era and I was 43. Single. Had barely a penny to my name. I was starting again. At the bottom.

Well, a girl's gotta work. Through a friend I became acquainted with Sally Sussman, who was the head writer for the daytime soap *The Young and The Restless*. Out of nothing more than sheer kindness, she decided to write a role for me on the show. I would play Tamara Logan, a psychic who was the only person who had any information about the kidnapping of one of the show's leading ladies.

That first morning of shooting I was driving down the 405 to CBS and dying inside, totally filled with anxiety.

I'd learned a lot in my recovery group sessions about strategies for handling negative emotions so I started a conversation with myself. I knew my lines, knew where I was going, had my wardrobe with me, knew I'd be on time for make-up. And I decided that this emotional energy wasn't anxiety, it was anticipation.

It felt exactly the same inside of me but calling it anticipation began to make me feel a bit better.

When I was actually in make-up, I realized I still hadn't really transformed this anxiety into something more productive. That's when I noticed a young actor sitting in the chair next to me, who seemed more nervous than I was. I don't remember his name but it was his first gig and he was bubbling over with apprehension, reminding me of Beau Bridges the first time I shot *My Three Sons*. He was playing a waiter and he only had a couple of lines like, "What will you be having tonight?" and "For the lady?" So I told myself that I was going to take all my bundled up nervous energy and I was going to steer it toward helping this young guy.

"Do you want run your lines with me?" I asked him.

"Really?"

"Sure. It's no problem. We can go over to the set," I said, meaning the set for the restaurant.

"It's okay if we do that?"

"Sure, it's just sitting there. We won't bother a soul."

We went over to the set and he ran his lines and burned through some of his worry and by focusing on someone else, I was able to let go of mine.

I have to be honest, I hated shooting a soap. They didn't do re-takes, they shot each scene using two enormous tape cameras, and the worst part were the cue cards – which drove me crazy. No matter what kind of project it is, I show up knowing my lines and there is nothing more distracting than a guy holding up giant cue cards just to the left or right of the camera.

Because I hated it, I don't think I was very good and in good old soap opera fashion they took care of it by giving me a tragic accident.

Yes, Tamara Logan was hit by a car.

My role now was to lie in convincing semi-consciousness in a hospital bed only able to communicate by blinking my eyes – once for yes, twice for no. President Gerald Ford's son, the actor Steven Ford, was on the show at the time – a very sweet, funny guy – and he gave me the nickname "Blinky."

I spent weeks lying in that hospital bed blinking my heart out as the investigation heated up. The truth is it was the best possible acting job I could have gotten at the time in order to get back in the game. I will always be so grateful to Sally.

I was fortunate that my reentry into acting was so gentle as it prepped me for something more stressful just around the corner.

***

My agent called to tell me that Michael Landon's production company was interested in having me play the role of a nurse at a summer camp in two-part episode of *Highway to Heaven*.

Like on *Little House*, Mike played multiple roles on this show – executive producer, writer, director, and star. The premise was that he was an angel sent from heaven to do good works on earth and that Victor French was his human friend and partner. Nearly all of the crew from *Little House* had moved with Michael to *Highway to Heaven*. Whitey Snider was doing make-up, Kent McCray was a producer, Bill Claxton would direct various episodes, etc., so I knew what I was in for.

I liked Mike a lot but he could, on the right day, be a tough guy to work with. I knew that on *Little House* one of the adult cast members had quit drinking, gone into recovery, and never mentioned it. Ever. The reason being there was quite a bit of drinking on the *Little House* set among Mike and the crew. The culture was one of boyish pranks, put-downs, and smack-talk. If Mike knew this cast member had quit drinking, it would be like a weakness exposed and Mike would likely have unloaded with some teasing and smart-assery. I don't think for a moment that he saw it as hurtful – it was all part of the fun in his mind.

As it turned out, all of my scenes were with Mike, who was also directing, and I was very nervous. He was his usual easy-breezy self and tried to joke and make conversation in between takes and I wasn't any good at banter at that point. I needed to really stay focused on my role and my lines and honestly I was more than a little scared that I was going to blow it. Afraid I might expose some personal, fragile part of myself and have it jovially and amiably dropkicked in front of the crew.

Fortunately we made it through and all was well. I was certainly grateful to Mike for the work. And of course it was a pleasure to see Victor again.

Ultimately filming that episode was a healthy challenge that allowed me to start taking risks and regaining my confidence.

Soon after that I was working more frequently. I had a ball playing a well-meaning but slightly dingy activist on a couple episodes of *Matlock*, playing opposite Andy Griffith, who was a real pro and just as warm and great to work with as you'd expect.

On the personal side, as I continued to venture back into the world; I met a guy at a recovery meeting and we started to spend time together. I of course had no real idea how you navigated these waters as the new me, the truthful me, the sober me.

One night our hanging out led to being in bed together. This may well have been the first time that I'd ever had sex sober. I certainly hadn't been sober on that first historic occasion at the Heartbreak Hotel back in Pasadena. And I can't think of any other sexual experience I'd ever had that didn't go hand-in-hand with feeling that roller coaster of alcohol and/or cocaine in my head.

It didn't feel right. I didn't have the aggression for it that came with being drunk. I wasn't game and ready to go. I felt self-conscious, awkward, and uncomfortable. Completely the opposite of how sex should feel or ever had felt.

I ended the relationship after that. I hadn't found my footing.

The new me wasn't ready.

Chapter 12
Henry and Mary X, Part 3

IN APRIL OF 1986 I got a phone call from Jack Nance's brother saying, "Did you hear about Jack?"

Oh God. My stomach knotted. I'd been expecting this call about Jack Nance for a long time. The next words I knew I would hear was, "He's dead."

"He's in a half-way house in the Valley," he said.

Wait. *What?*

I had never allowed myself to hope I'd hear this kind of news. It would be like wishing a donkey could turn into a duck. Jack was far too stubborn, too grouchy, too in-his-own-world, too entrenched in being Jack to ever submit to a recovery program.

I was almost too shocked to feel happy. I knew what a tricky thing sobriety can be and I couldn't picture how it would look for Jack.

I tracked down the number to this place. It was a respected live-in drug and alcohol recovery center for men.

When my call was answered I asked for Jack Nance. I had to wait a long time before the receiver rattled a bit and heard a dry, gruff, "Hello?"

"Hey Jack," is all I said.

There was a pause and he said, "I knew you'd find me."

He then told me the unlikely story of how he found himself in recovery. David Lynch had cast him in *Blue Velvet*, as one of the psycho-henchmen buddies of Frank Booth, played by Dennis Hopper.

The shoot ran February to April 1986, with the entire production in Wilmington, North Carolina. Throughout filming, Jack was drinking as heavily, if not worse, than ever and was suicidal. He talked about wanting to jump off the roof of the hotel in which the cast was staying. This got Dennis Hopper's attention. Between shooting *Human Highway* and *Blue Velvet*, Dennis had gone into alcohol recovery, which turned his life around. When Dennis believed in something, he didn't keep it to himself, which was fortunate for Jack.

Dennis arranged Jack's flight home so they could sit together. He talked about alcohol recovery, while feeding Jack a lot of drinks on the flight to soften up Jack's resistance. When the plane landed at LAX, Dennis packed Jack into his car and drove him from the airport directly to the live-in recovery program, where he left him to dry out and, hopefully, get sober.

A few days later Jack drove over to Lantana to meet me for lunch. Already he looked so much better than the last time I'd seen him – his eyes were clear and he seemed much more together. He was still in the very early stages of recovery but like so many people, at least for now, the idea of living without alcohol seemed like a relief to him.

I knew that he'd need to change everything in his life once he got out of the rehab program, so I asked him if he wanted to move into my house in Sherman Oaks.

By this time Jeanne had moved out as she'd gotten together with John Binder, whom she been friends with since even before the days of hanging out at Elliot Roberts's office across from Electra Records. John was a filmmaker who'd originally been part of that group of East Coast hippies involved with the *Woodstock* documentary. Having seen Jeanne in those dark days after splitting up with Stephen Peck, I was so happy for her.

Jack accepted the offer, appreciative in his non-demonstrative way. Once he was out of the program he moved his stuff to the Sherman Oaks house and set himself up in the extra bedroom. He liked established patterns in his day and he found them pretty quickly. Every night he liked to sit and watch *Wheel of Fortune*. Mostly what he enjoyed was guessing the puzzles before the contestants and then heaping them with contempt, calling them idiots, morons, dumb-asses and goddamn fools. But nothing gave him more joy than when a contestant lost. He would howl with laughter.

He filled some of his time planting and then tending a garden in the back of the house – carrots and corn and a few other things. Two or three months later he and I were sitting in the backyard in lawn chairs admiring his creation and imagining how nice it would be when we could start harvesting some of what he'd planted.

As we were gazing at the garden though, we noticed one of the corn stalks wiggle. Then wiggle again. Then really thrash about and then – plunk – drop four or five inches in height.

"What the hell?" Jack murmured.

Then the stalk next to it did the same thing.

His garden had been invaded by gophers, which were feasting on the young roots of his vegetables. Jack immediately went to war on the gophers – in full Caddy Shack mode – and that occupied a lot of his time.

Inviting Jack to live with me in Sherman Oaks seemed like the right thing to do on a lot of levels. He was a friend trying to create a new life for himself and I wanted to support that in any way I could. Also, it was paying a debt I felt I owed to karma. Jack and I had seen each other at our worst, our darkest, our most addicted. In this odd circular subplot of my life with Mary

X and Henry, we were together again and this time it was about friendship, helping each other, and discovering the joy on the other side of the darkness that was sobriety, enjoying the support and love we both found in the network of others in recovery.

Jack and I never had a romantic or sexual thing. I liked him, admired his work, and was part of a small circle of people who enjoyed the curmudgeon he was.

He was a guy ruled both by chaos and inflexible routines. His room was a fright fest. Clothes, books, magazines, you name it, strewn and unkempt. Just a disaster. Meanwhile, he liked things to stay the same. Change made him upset and uncomfortable.

One day when he was away, I decided to help him out by cleaning his room. It took a few hours but by the time I was finished, all the garbage was gone, all the books and magazines straightened, the bed was made. It looked great.

A few hours had passed when I heard Jack stump into the house and head for his room. A moment later I heard a cry of distress. He came charging out, shouting, "Call the police! We've been robbed!" Somehow his idea of a home invasion robbery included maid service.

He did make an effort at developing good roommate skills. When I was away once on a film project, Jack said he'd mow our nice big lawn. When I came back however, the grass was at least two feet tall and we were the shabbiest looking place on the block. Jack was apologetic, saying that he'd noticed the lawn needed attention so had purchased an electric lawn mower. But then he said, "I lost the power cord in the grass."

While he was piecing things back together in his life, he picked up a couple of small but good roles in films such as *Barfly* with Mickey Rourke and Faye Dunaway (ironic as it was the first film he made sober) and *Colors* with Robert Duvall and Sean Penn.

David Lynch called him up to appear in a short film he was shooting up north of Los Angeles in the Lancaster area. The French Film Society had asked a number of directors, including David, to each shoot three-minute films, which I think would be shown on television in France – I'm not actually sure. Jack and I drove up together. I wasn't in it but thought it'd be fun to hang out and watch. Surrounded by flat fields stretching off into infinity, David shot a bunch of actors, including Jack, sitting on a fence pulling things out of backpacks like croissants, berets, little Eiffel Towers. Then he shot Michael Horse (who later played Deputy Hawk on *Twin Peaks*) striding through one of the fields with beads on his beautiful bare chest. What any of this was about I have no clue. None. I remember meeting Isabella Rossellini, whom David had started dating, and who was as flawless and beautiful as she is in those Lancome ads that she did. She was sweet, normal, and kind of an Earth Mother, as she often comes across. She'd shot *Blue Velvet* earlier that year, had heard about Jack's rehab and was very happy for him.

I heard later that rather than give the French Film Society the three-minute film they asked for, David gave them one that was 20-minutes long and they refused to show it.

***

On March 9, 1988, David Lynch came over to the Sherman Oaks house for dinner with Jack and me. It was great to see him away from a film set, to just relax, and have a nice evening together. David talked about some recent trips he'd taken to Washington State up near the Canadian border and how awe-inspiring the forests were up there, how moved he was by the landscape. He'd spent a lot of time as a boy in rural, woodsy places and, as I mentioned earlier, had even been an Eagle Scout. Thickly wooded mountains, remote lakes, quiet forest paths were, I think, very spiritual places for him. The stories of his recent travel turned into telling us about a new TV project he was putting together with a producing partner, Mark Frost. It would be called *Northwest Passage*, as it was set in a town in rural Washington State, similar in a lot of ways to the setting for *Blue Velvet*. It sounded like he had a pretty big ensemble cast in mind though clearly one of the stars would be Isabella Rossellini, who would play Josie, the owner of a large sawmill operation, which I could easily picture. Isabella was able to play a balance of toughness and vulnerability, which had been at the core of *Blue Velvet's* success. Then because it was a David Lynch production he described some other aspects of the show that didn't make any sense to me but by now David has outlined plenty of ideas that had sounded perfectly hare-brained that had worked out beautifully.

He capped things off by offering Jack and me parts in the show, which of course we were thrilled to hear. David said they'd film the pilot first and if that did well, ABC would pick it up for a season.

At some point in the evening – and it's why I remember the date so clearly – I got a phone call from someone I was close to, who told me that my dear, beautiful friend Mickey Fox had been found dead in her apartment.

It just crushed me. I knew Mickey hadn't been well and was having some kind of health issue she didn't want to talk about. I'd gone to her apartment the day before, where I found her in bed and she was kind of rambling, her words and thoughts not quite connecting. She'd wet herself in bed and I got her up and with the help of another friend got her and her bed all cleaned up.

I loved Mickey so much. She'd been big all her life and it was as though only a body that size would be large enough to hold that heart and that sense of life and adventure. In her youth she'd been a bar girl in Havana, Cuba. Later she'd lived in Rome and if you were an actor visiting Rome – usually to do voice-over work – you knew Mickey. All the American actors would eventually find their way to her house for fun, companionship, a taste of food from home and of course she had the best weed in town.

Later when she and "the Rome crowd," as Jeanne called them, all lived together in a commune in Topanga, Mickey had worked at Everybody's Mother, where she made everyone feel welcomed.

I'd tried to talk Mickey into seeing a doctor but she'd refused both on the grounds that she didn't have any money and she simply didn't want to.

Now she was gone.

So often Life had served up good and bad at the same time. The same night I found out I'd be working with David again, I learned of Mickey's passing. The Rolling Stones concert with Robert Greenfield on the day of my mother's cancer diagnosis. My split from Tim and experiencing my first taste of confidence as an actor. I remember once reading that when Andy Warhol mixed paints to get the colors he was looking for, he always blended in some black – even if he wanted a neon pink or a green apple. It's never all one color, one flavor, one texture. No matter how good someone's life looks from the outside, there's always darkness blended in with the light and light swirled around in with the dark.

You've seen lots of pictures of actors, models, directors, or producers posing in designer clothes at movie premiers. Flashbulbs going off. Paparazzi shouting their names. It's easy to think those people live a dream life. A perfect existence where everything is easy. I assure you that behind those confident smiles and poses are often people who feel vulnerable, stupid, inadequate, unsure, angry, depressed, broken, lonely, overwhelmed, and trapped.

I remember putting down the phone after getting the news about Mickey and just spending a few minutes remembering her, feeling the raw empty place inside of me that her death had created. Then I cleaned up my face and went back to the table and shared the news with David and Jack.

***

Putting a show together for a major network takes a long time and things can evolve in surprising ways. In this case, the name changed from *Northwest Passage* to *Twin Peaks* and David and Isabella broke up and her part went to Joan Chen.

I learned later that during its development, the show caused something of a war within ABC with executives on both coasts fighting for or against it. Everything was a battle – the plot, the tone, even the casting. David wanted to hire actors from soap operas and old movies, people with fairly obscure careers – no big stars. He never auditions, as I've said, never asks a person to read script pages. Often he doesn't really even talk about the project. He talks to people for a while, gets a sense of who they are and casts them if he thinks they've got what it takes to inhabit the part. One day David caught a taxi in L.A. and struck up a conversation with the driver, a guy named Harry Goaz. David liked him so much he cast him in *Twin Peaks* as Deputy Andy Brennan (the officer who cries at crime scenes).

At one point all the main actors had to go to ABC headquarters to be interviewed by top network brass. I didn't have to go, thank goodness, but Jack did and he was nervous. He put on a suit and muttered to me as he left the house, "I don't think I'm going to pass."

But he did, they all did, though the network tried to get David to change his casting to fit more traditional lines with names that were more marketable. But he and Mark Frost were firm. In the end David got the go-ahead to shoot the pilot his way.

We shot most of the two-hour pilot in and around the town of Snoqualmie, Washington in early 1989. My first scenes as Betty Briggs were shot on my birthday, Monday, February 27. After I'd wrapped that evening Jack took me for a celebratory dinner to the Salish Lodge, which was the exterior of The Great Northern Hotel in the *Twin Peaks* world. The schedule had been set up so that I had scenes on Monday and then more on the following Friday and in the middle I'd get to hang out and have some fun. Except that I got a horrible bout of the flu. There's nothing worse than being ill in a hotel room – you just want to be home being miserable in your own bed. At one point I was watching *The Legend of the Lone Ranger* on TV and Michael Horse was playing Tonto – Michael Horse whom I'd just seen a couple of days before on the *Twin Peaks* set. I thought I was hallucinating.

Other than being sick, shooting the pilot was like a great vacation, being around old friends like Richard Beymer, whom I'd known since the day I met him at the commissary at Samuel Goldwyn while shooting *The Loretta Young Show*, my former Topanga neighbor Russ Tamblyn, who had been so much fun to work with on *Human Highway*, Jack of course, and Michael Ontkean, who was playing Sheriff Harry S. Truman. I'd first met Michael in the early 1970s when we'd both hang out with Sam and Annie Melville. I'd befriended Sam when he played a villain on *Gunsmoke* (the episode called "Lyle's Kid").

Michael knew Sam because they were both on the TV series *The Rookies*, which ran from 1972 to 1974. Sam and Annie had the kind of laid-back place in Hollywood where friends would just come over, smoke a little dope, and hang out all day. It was a great place for me to get my head together after my split with Tim.

And in yet another of those who-knows-who oddities in the Hollywood bubble, Michael's manager in the early 1970s was Thor Arngrim, father of Alison, whom I would later work with on *Little House* and decades later would inspire me to write this book.

I loved the humor and humanity Michael brought to his role. He and Kyle MacLachlan (playing Special Agent Dale Cooper) were both great at that – incredibly good-looking guys who didn't play their parts for sex appeal and sizzle though they certainly could have.

I remember once I'd finished up a scene and was walking through the various sets on my way out and came across Kyle standing by himself, wearing a tuxedo, reading a script. The light was hitting him just right and – I know Kyle, he's a really nice, normal guy – but there he was with that coal black hair and that porcelain skin and that jaw from a 1930s Hollywood musical – it just took my breath away.

But as I said instead of playing their parts as TV hunks, he and Michael both looked for the inherent comedic possibilities, often self-deprecating, that worked so brilliantly.

One of the best things about shooting *Twin Peaks* is that it's when I finally came to know Catherine Coulson as a friend, which probably sounds weird because we'd shared such tight quarters while shooting *Eraserhead* in the early 1970s. But she'd been so busy we hardly got a chance to become acquainted.

On *Twin Peaks*, in which she became famous as The Log Lady, we had lots of time during filming to hang out and have fun. Even though she and Jack had divorced in the 1970s, she still cared about how he was doing and was so happy that he was sober – his alcoholism was the primary thing that had driven them apart. She expressed a lot of gratitude for the role I'd played in getting him a place to live in a setting where alcohol recovery was a way of life.

By the way, Catherine and I were convinced that David Lynch had given Jack's *Twin Peaks* wife, Piper Laurie, the name Catherine because on the *Eraserhead* set we'd all heard him say her name in his elongated, nasal drawl that bordered on a bleat, managing to break it into several extra syllables as "Caa-aa-ther-ine ..."

The other thing I loved about shooting the show is that it brought two new men into my life and family – Don Davis and Dana Ashbrook.

Don was a total surprise to me. When I read the script and learned that my character Betty Briggs would be married to a military man named Major Garland Briggs, I think I imagined someone tall, dark, and handsome and when Don walked into the room, well, Don was compact, roundish,and ginger. It was a change of gears in my brain – but once again David Lynch had given me an unexpected gift. Don was a kind, smart, sweet guy to know and play scenes with – a true artist, who produced sculpture and poetry. He wore his military uniform beautifully and created an authentic character that you knew right away, who would evolve in some pretty unexpected ways.

And Dana Ashbrook, who played Betty and Garland's son Bobby Briggs, I just loved from moment one. Those big gorgeous eyes and eyelashes and all that rowdy hair; he's like chocolate chip cookie dough ice cream for the eyes. As an actor he was up for anything – boundless and fearless. You can see that on full display at Laura Palmer's funeral when he cuts loose with a Wolfman howl. It's so much fun to play scenes with him.

While I was thrilled to be part of *Twin Peaks*, I was a little nervous going into it. I knew that for David there was a lot riding on getting this thing right. I wanted to support him, wanted to support the cast and crew. Both Don and Dana were right there for me from the start. Within the large solar system of the cast we were like our own little three-planet orbit supporting, protecting and encouraging each other. The Briggs family might have been wildly screwed up on screen but off we were the best there could be.

Like any production this size, *Twin Peaks* came with lots of trucks, lights, cables, jibs, and tracks, trailers for make-up and wardrobe and all the stuff that makes it feel like the circus has come to town. Even so, shooting the pilot also felt like a lark. We were basically left alone as we were out in the boondocks filming this thing that was, yes, headed for a shot at mainstream television, but it had the surreal nature of David Lynch written all over it. The cast would hang out together and watch filming. We were in and out of each other's trailers. It was that *Eraserhead* feeling of summer camp only more so.

By now David was a name. He'd been nominated for Academy Awards for Best Director for *The Elephant Man* as well as for *Blue Velvet*. He was a familiar figure in *People*, *Newsweek*, and *The New York Times*.

In terms of sheer production size, *Twin Peaks* was *Eraserhead* multiplied by a magnitude of about 100,000. David had all the funding he needed (at least by comparison) and had scads of great assistants, staff, writers, producers, and collaborators to help him power through filming. Where on *Eraserhead* he'd been a one-man band, on *Twin Peaks* he was the conductor of an orchestra. Even so, he was very much the artistic soul I'd worked with in the early1970s. He could be both very specific – asking me to turn my head or my hand, say, in distinct ways. And at the same time, he could be very vague, talking in pictures, if you will, to set the tone of a scene.

What I was reminded of working with him again is that as an actor, I didn't need to understand why he was asking me to move or talk or exhibit stillness. I just needed to do it. I continued to see the influence of his painting background, that for him the actors were part of the lines, shading, color or texture he had in mind. Often in work such as *Eraserhead*, David has talked about feeling the film rather than thinking it. And when you're going for a feel, you may not be able to explain that to an actor. Nor should you have to. It's a waste of time.

On *Twin Peaks*, just as in *Eraserhead*, he was always open to new ideas – eager for them. There was no point in this huge production that I got the idea that the script was "locked." A young actress from Seattle, Sheryl Lee, had been hired simply to play the corpse of Laura Palmer. But as filming progressed David saw something in her – as they shot footage that was meant to show her and her friends hanging out prior to her murder – and the next thing you knew he'd written a part for her as Laura's lookalike cousin. She was a bright talent and brought a great touch to the show.

In another case, a member of the crew, Frank Silva, was doing some set decoration in the set for Laura Palmer's living room and David caught Frank's reflection in a mirror during filming. David found it so startling that he cast Frank as the disturbing, malevolent character of Bob.

Any actor could come to him with ideas that, as long as they felt right, were incorporated into your scene or your character. With David's approval Russ Tamblyn cooked up a lot of the razzle-dazzle of his character, Dr. Lawrence Jacoby – the red and blue-lens glasses, the Hawaiian shirts, the bowties. None of that had been in the script.

Early on while discussing with David the underlying reasons why Bobby Briggs, my son on the show, was so messed up, I laid out his main issues, "Garland is military and I'm super Catholic. He's fucked." David brought that into his interpretation and as a way of delving into that took my suggestion to start a scene in the first season in which Bobby and his dad, Major Briggs, have an important moment together. But the scene starts with Bobby gazing up at a huge crucifix on the wall that's enshrined with fern fronds and candles. At first you think Bobby's in a church but the camera pulls back and you realize he's at home. Yikes.

My time in Washington State flew by and before I knew it I was back on a plane headed home. Looking out the window I saw those endless forests, rivers, and lakes far below and hoped that some of the magic in those trees and wild places would rub off on *Twin Peaks*. It seemed like it had some great potential but nobody would know if it would soar or sink for another year, when the pilot would eventually air in the spring of 1990. In the meantime, we'd all have to wait and see.

Chapter 13

Alone But Not Alone

NOT LONG AFTER DAVID HAD ASKED ME to shoot the pilot of *Twin Peaks*, my agent had called with an opportunity for a role in a movie called *Tremors*. When I read the script it reminded me, in a way, of *Human Highway*, as it was comedic, full of odd-ball characters out in the middle of nowhere under a big, bizarre threat.

Shooting the film meant spending three weeks in Lone Pine, California, which is located up between the Sierras and Death Valley, about 160 miles northeast of Bakersfield. It defines the boonies. All of which you can see in the film.

The town you see in the film was fake – all sets for the film. The actual town of Lone Pine, located nearby, is basically one street with a couple of stores, a café, a hotel, and a few other businesses on both sides. There's a smattering of houses spreading out from the town center.

One of the challenges of working in a place so remote is that I still very much wanted – needed might be the better word – to go to alcohol recovery meetings. By now, about five years into sobriety, I was no longer attending meetings every day, but I still found strength and support in three meetings a week.

I hated the thought of going for such a long stretch of time without my safety net. The desire for alcohol does not go away. Ever. It's always there in some form – sometimes in a whisper, sometimes in an insistent shout – in my head. Spending that many weeks away from "my people" made me feel vulnerable.

At the little hotel where the cast was staying, I noticed a car parked out front that had a bumper sticker with a symbol on it that is identified with alcohol recovery. Based on the age and model of the car it could simply be an artifact from several owners-ago or … and I hardly let myself hope for this … somewhere out here in the middle of nowhere was someone like me. It sent me into Agatha Christie mode. Inside the hotel I asked the person at the desk if they knew whose car that was. After a bit more sleuthing around, I was eventually able to track it to the maid who cleaned my room. The next morning I hung around as long as I could and when she came in to tidy up, I asked her about her bumper sticker. This led to a funny back-and-forth with the little Spanish I knew and the little English that she knew. Finally she pulled another maid into the room, who was able to translate. Both of them, it turns out, were in a local alcohol recovery group and warmly and happily welcomed me to join. I was so relieved and delighted I hugged them both.

The group met in a local church several times a week, their sessions held in English and Spanish; it was a joy to be so far from home and yet even there to find members of my far-flung alcohol recovery family. It set the stage for me to truly enjoy the *Tremors* shoot, which was just as much fun as you might suspect.

The story of *Tremors* is of a small, dusty, high desert town that is terrorized by giant, slug-like, human-eating creatures called Graboids that travel underground at high speed – making the earth shake wildly just before they burst to the surface and devour the next townsperson. In the wrong hands this premise could have played out pretty poorly but the director, Ron Underwood, took this story and really spun out of it a fun, high-speed, and surprisingly human adventure.

The cast was such a great group. Well, mostly.

It was a total joy to work with then 10-year-old Ariana Richards, which was a good thing as I spent most of the movie clutching her, trying to keep her from being gulped by Graboids. (Thanks to *Little House*, I'd long ago abandon my fear of working with kids.) A couple of years later I was very happy for her as she was cast as one of the kids in the Steven Spielberg blockbuster *Jurassic Park*. She and I worked together again in *Tremors 3*, when she was 21, which was pretty cool.

I knew Fred Ward a bit from a movie that Jeanne had produced and John Binder had directed a few years prior called *UFOoria*, which starred Fred and Cindy Williams (who had been Shirley of *Lavern and Shirley*). They shot it primarily up in the Lancaster area and I'd just driven up to hang out with Jeanne and John for a few days.

The first night, I went with Jeanne to see the dailies – the footage that had been shot that day. The screening room was pretty basic, just a screen and six or eight chairs in a couple of rows. Up on the screen we're watching this scene and that scene. Then I see footage of this totally hot guy walk into a room, rugged and fit, and I blurted, "Whoa – who is that?"

From behind me in the darkness I heard a slow chuckle. When I turned around, there sat Fred. The guy I'd just seen on the screen. So, that was our introduction.

As in *Tremors*, Fred is cast in a lot of good old boy or rough-and-tough roles because of his looks but in fact the guy is an intellectual – we're talking

Ph.D. smart. There's often such a funny disconnect between the actor and the part and Fred is a prime example.

I also enjoyed working with Kevin Bacon, who is talented, has a strong work ethic, and gets the job done – a real pro. His wife, Kyra Sedgwick, who I found down-to-earth and engaging, was only on set a few times as she was pretty far along in her pregnancy. When we'd wrapped filming, we had a party and she was out on the dance floor nine months pregnant putting on some pretty flashy moves. After their baby was born, when I got home I sent a gift and a note of congratulations. About a week later the phone rang and the caller said, "Hi, it's Kevin."

I said, "Who?"

"Kevin."

"Kevin who?"

"Kevin Bacon."

It never occurred to me that he'd call, which I thought was awfully nice given everything else he had going on. But like anyone with good social skills he had picked up the phone to say thank you for the gift. He and Kyra are into each other and into their family, both have had long careers in film and television and yet you never see then popping up on the cover of a supermarket tabloid looking trashed or sick and bloated or sneaking out on each other. I have a lot of admiration for actors like that whose careers and reputations are based on their work rather than going for the easy, trashy, look-at-me, sex-tape kind of PR options that are out there.

Michael Gross, who'd made a name for himself as Michael J. Fox's television father on the show *Family Ties*, by contrast, was such a pain on that shoot. In *Tremors*, he played the gun-nut survivalist, married to country singer Reba McEntire, in her first film role. Michael was an actor who questions everything, everything, everything, wanting to shoot and re-shoot again and again. I saw Reba after a day of filming the scene in which the Graboids bust into her and Michael's basement weapons lair. She was exhausted after spending the day with Michael and his fussiness.

But here's the problem with being irked at Michael – he was great in the film. When I saw the final version I just groaned inwardly because he'd been right. He'd added subtle touches, found moments, and pushed the script in ways that make his character and those scenes absolutely shine.

The lesson here is that there are times that being a pain is what it takes. It's not the way I work. Give me my lines, I'll do that character. Done.

But there are times, such as this movie, when his way gets superb results.

He was the same way when I worked with him again on *Tremors 3*. This was a movie that we all knew was going straight to video and yet the Michael Gross work standard remained ridiculously high.

A couple of years ago I saw him at a *Tremors* reunion in L.A. and he was such a sweetheart. He was so fun, so genuine, and so happy to see me and the rest of the cast. I realized I'd never gotten to know him away from the set and had really missed out. I was glad to see him after all these years and hope to see him again one of these days.

Shooting in Lone Pine gave me a chance to decompress. It was remote and so quiet. At night – unlike in Los Angeles – you could see stars thick and full in the sky. They looked like heaps of white Christmas lights against the vast blackness of the universe. I'd brought with me the audio version of Stephen Hawking's *A Brief History of Time* and I would lie outside looking up, listening to one of the greatest minds of our time talk about its mysteries.

It's funny, I was very much by myself but I wasn't lonely or unhappy. For so many years I'd either been married, living with a guy, or sleeping with someone I found momentarily interesting – the shiny new penny. Here I was, in my late 40s, sober, without anyone in my life. And yet I'd lie out there in the desert and I did not feel alone. Instead I had the real sense that something or someone bigger than me was out there and had my best interest at heart.

I would need to hold on to those feelings in order to get me through the challenges ahead that would shake me to my core.

***

When I came home from Lone Pine, I went through the stack of mail awaiting and to my surprise found a card from Victor French. I'd stayed in touch with Victor after *Little House*, mostly through his girlfriend, who was my manicurist. She had two girls and the four of them made a great little family.

On the cover of the card was a photo of Victor with a lampshade on his head. I snorted. Typical Victor.

Once I opened it up, I had to read the card two or three times before I was able to process what I was reading.

It was an invitation to his funeral.

No one had known Victor had been dying of lung cancer. But in wild, loving Victor fashion he'd used his final days to plan out his farewell down to the last moment – food, band, guest list, and a surprise or two along the way.

The funeral was held in the open-air courtyard at the Gene Autry Museum in Griffith Park in Los Angeles and after a few people had spoken, Victor's attorney got up and said, per Victor's wishes, anyone who cried would be thrown out.

Mike Landon, who was a very emotional guy and had been Victor's dear friend, was standing next to me and grabbed my hand at this and hung on for dear life. I've never seen a man fight tears so hard in my life.

"Now," said the attorney, "There's one final message from Victor for you all." And he pointed skyward. We looked up and there above us a small plane pulled a banner that read, "Eat Shit, Love Victor."

Mike held on tight and I squeezed right back, caught between laugher and a flood of tears that wanted to boil over.

It was the last time I'd ever see Mike. And I'm so grateful that if I had to say good-bye to him, had to have a final moment, that that was it – holding hands, looking up at that message from our friend, dear Victor, in the sky.

***

The two-hour *Twin Peaks* pilot aired on April 8, 1990, and I was always so thrilled that the whole odyssey starts with Jack as the mild, hen-pecked Pete Martell, a totally normal middle age guy, who just loves fishing, finding Laura Palmer's body wrapped in plastic on the shores of the lake.

The pilot drew a massive audience ending up being the most-watched movie on television that year. To the total shock of ABC executives, it turned out there was a big young audience that didn't want the same old, same old. They wanted something new and *Twin Peaks* gave it to them.

The overwhelming success of the pilot gave David a lot of money, confidence and free-reign (at last) from the network heads, who couldn't begin to grasp what he was doing.

David had directed the pilot and first episode and then parceled out writing and directing duties to people he knew and trusted. This allowed him to divide his time with *Twin Peaks* and prepping and then shooting his next film *Wild at Heart*, which starred Nicholas Cage and Laura Dern.

David cast a few people from *Twin Peaks* in the film in small parts. I remember Sheryl Lee (who plays the dual role of Laura Palmer and her cousin Maddy Ferguson) was so excited to play a Glinda-the-Good-Witch type role while Sherilyn Fenn (Audry Horne) was cast in a haunting part as a traumatized accident victim.

For about five minutes David considered casting me in the role of Laura Dern's *Wild at Heart* mother. I was at a dinner with David, Laura Dern, Kyle MacLachlan, and Jack when at some point I realized they were all looking at me. I glanced back a little weirded-out, until I realized they that were talking about casting for the part of the mom. Apparently my name was in the hat and they were picturing me in the part. It would've been a great character to play since she was completely bonkers. But David went with Laura's real life mother, Diane Ladd, who was flat-out terrific, and I think it was fun for audiences to see interaction of an actual mother and daughter on screen.

David cast Jack in a small but very memorable part, which I watched him film. The scene was shot outside a rundown hotel in the San Fernando Valley. An intense, surreal moment, straight out of the subconscious.

Jack got right up in Nick Cage's face and with squinty, twitchy intensity ad-libbed the line: "Mentally you picture my dog, but I have not told you the type dog which I have. Perhaps you might even picture Toto from *The Wizard of Oz*. But I can tell you, my dog is always with me."

He was perfectly sober. David loved it of course and it's one of the more memorable moments in a very classic Lynch film.

Jack was in a good place at that point in his life. Besides the work he was getting with David and the new life he'd been given through sobriety, he'd met someone he was crazy about, a woman who was also in alcohol recovery named Kelly Van Dyke, the daughter of comedian and actor Jerry Van Dyke who in turn was Dick Van Dyke's brother. Personally, I wasn't crazy about Kelly but Jack was, so I tried to be happy for him. She was all over Jack all the time, clingy and girly, coy, posing and giggly. Like Betty Boop. She seemed to have an insatiable need for attention, always very exposed and cleavage-y and done up in a lot of crazy jewelry. I remember once she showed up with Jack at a *Twin Peaks* screening in a fully see-through hey-everybody-here-are-my-tits top. It was a bit hard to take at times.

For Jack this was all new – a sexy woman, 15 years younger than him, who just couldn't seem to get enough of him.

Not my cup of tea, but I wished them well.

Back on *Twin Peaks* I was in familiar territory. In part because, obviously, I'd worked with David on *Eraserhead*, but also in a sense from appearing in nighttime soap opera-style dramas such as *Murder in Peyton Place*. *Twin Peaks* was a marriage of both, or, perhaps more accurately it used the framework, character types, and conventions of traditional TV drama as a Trojan Horse that later opened up and Lynch-world invaded your television.

I think what people remember of the show now were the later and more surreal story elements – the Red Room, the Owls, and so forth. The pilot episode by comparison was pretty tame and doesn't venture all that far from the conventions of TV drama of the 1970s and '80s.

The brilliance of the first season is how it takes a measured pace into the surreal. Where in *Eraserhead* David had submersed the viewer in a starkly strange place from the first frames, here he took his time. By the fourth episode you have Special Agent Dale Cooper describing a dream to Sherriff Harry S. Truman that he is convinced is the key to solving Laura Palmer's murder and Leland Palmer dancing by himself at the lodge and screaming, "Someone dance with me!" Now we were in Lynchland.

I loved playing Betty Briggs, the determined optimist, whether she's picking a cigarette out of a piece of meatloaf during a contentious dinner at home to wearing a happy face button to Laura Palmer's funeral.

After the pilot, which was nearly all shot in Washington State, we began to shoot most of the show in Los Angeles. The interiors that had been shot around Snoqualmie were perfectly recreated on sound stages located not far from the Van Nuys airport. So many of the exterior shots took place at night that it was easy work to make L.A. locations work as stand-ins.

Much like my role on *Little House*, my part as Betty Briggs was not a full-time job. I'd be called in to shoot a scene or two once a week or so. My daily life was still working at Lantana, which gave me the chance to see and experience the build of its insane popularity.

Twin Peaks was the "water cooler show" of the season. And I worked in a place where people did literally stand around the water cooler the next day and talk about the previous night's episode – debating who Bob really was, the meaning of the Red Room, whether the One-Armed Man was the murderer, the meaning of the owls and doing impressions of Catherine as The Log Lady or the dance of The Man from Another Place.

The nation fell into the grip of "Who Killed Laura Palmer?" fever just as much as it had been driven crazy by the mystery of "Who Shot JR?" on *Dallas* 10 years earlier.

As the scrutiny of fans and media focused in on the show and specifically the details of the murder, things began to change on set. Now instead of getting full copies of the script for an episode you were in, you would only get the pages for the scenes in which your character appeared. This made it trickier, as an actor, to gauge your performance so that it fit with the overall story. But of course you make it work. The other change was that now we were only allowed on the set when you were filming a scene you were in. This meant the end of the summer camp. The fun of just hanging out with crew and fellow cast members was over and actors like myself were only privy to the same kinds of rumors that everyone else was hearing.

As problems go, this was a good problem to have. It was all about the show's runaway success. The theories of who killed Laura Palmer – what were real leads, what were red herrings – could go on and on. Friends would ask me and I could honestly answer that I didn't know. And secretly I wondered if David knew.

Each week a bunch of us from the show – Dana, Kimmy Roberts, Sheryl Lee, Sherilyn Fenn, Jack and others – would take over a bar and watch that night's episode, often just as shocked as any viewing audience at home. For the season finale we got together at Dana's house and when Agent Dale Cooper is shot we all gasped – stunned – and wondered if we had all just lost our jobs.

Not only did we *not* see this coming but David had filmed the scene three different times with different actors so no one knew the ending until it aired.

When the 1990 Emmy nominations were announced, everyone in the cast and crew were over the moon. *Twin Peaks* had been nominated in 13 categories and in the category for Outstanding Writing, has been nominated twice.

Kyle was nominated for Lead Actor in a Drama Series, Piper Laurie for Lead Actress in a Drama Series, David was nominated for Outstanding Direction, he and Mark Frost were nominated for Outstanding Writing, and Angelo Badalamenti was nominated for Music Composition and for Main Title Theme. The list went on and on including editing, costuming and more. Wow.

To me it felt like the start of a revolution on network television. David's vision of storytelling, his characters, the worlds only he could create, which had begun in obscurity as an art student in Philadelphia in the late 1960s, looked poised to re-write the playbook for American TV.

The Emmy awards that year were held on September 16 at the Pasadena Civic Auditorium, a place I knew well as it is located about four or five blocks from the Pasadena Playhouse. With so many nominations, the contingent from *Twin Peaks* was pretty large. I wasn't among them – I was watching it at home – but it was great fun to see David, Dana, and everyone looking so elegant and snazzy in tuxes and evening gowns. I even got to see Michael Landon, looking very dashing, among the attendees as a movie he'd directed was up for an award.

The Emmys, unfortunately, turned into a big bust. In category after category, the nominations were read and the Emmys went to shows such as *LA Law, China Beach, Star Trek: The Next Generation*, and *Thirtysomething* – all great – but very much "the usual suspects" in terms of award-winning network fare. The one light moment came when the camera focused on Catherine Coulson in character as The Log Lady and she did a short scripted bit in which it sounded like her log needed to use the restroom.

Well. That's show business. The industry giveth and the industry taketh away.

The revolution, as they used to say, would not be televised.

While filming the second season I got to work with a lot of different directors, including one of my favorites, Caleb Deschanel, father of Zooey Deschanel, and a friend of David's from AFI. They were graduates, along with Terrence Malik, of AFI's first class.

As much as I liked a lot of the people brought in to propel the show forward, I missed having David at the conductor's podium. I knew he had a lot of TV and film projects he wanted to tackle but in that second season I began to feel his absence.

About halfway through that season, something happened on set that had never taken place in anything I'd ever done with David: I had to stop the filming and call something into question (uh-oh, I was becoming Michael Gross!). But without David right there, I didn't feel things were on the same sure footing.

Episode eleven opens with Special Agent Dale Cooper and Sheriff Harry S. Truman questioning Betty Briggs about the disappearance of Major Briggs. The way the script was originally written, it indicated that Betty didn't know where her husband had gone and so couldn't give them any information.

This wasn't in keeping at all with the relationship between Betty and her husband, so I asked to speak with the writer.

I had the sense that the second season of the show there were a lot of story elements hurtling off in a lot of different directions – I just wanted to be sure this subplot with the Major was being carefully crafted. When I spoke to the writer, I argued that I thought Betty did know when Major Briggs had gone, where he was, and that she could not possibly share that information with the FBI or local law enforcement. When the writer and director agreed with me, that's how we shot the scene.

Chapter 14

Two Surgeries and One Kiss

A FEW DAYS BEFORE CHRISTMAS, 1990, two months before my 50th birthday, I took my nurse practitioner's advice and got a mammogram. Not fun getting your girls squished but there it is. It's got to be done. After that I flew up to spend the holiday with my sister Barbara Jean and her kids in Marin County.

When I arrived back home to Sherman Oaks the red light on my answering machine was blinking and when I hit play I heard the voice of my nurse practitioner say, "Hi Charlotte, listen, something's come up on your mammogram, I've sent it in for review …"

The feelings that electrified through me are hard to describe but anxiety and nervousness just about cover it. She instructed me to drive to an oncologist's office nearby where I was simply handed a sealed envelope to take back to my nurse practitioner. Back in my car the first thing I did was open up the envelope. I wanted to know what was going on. Now. Inside nested among the medical-ese was news that made my stomach fill with acid – the physician who reviewed the mammogram had written that I appeared to have a malignancy in my right breast.

"I have cancer," I thought. "I. Have. Cancer."

Cancer was a thing other people had.

My mother had cancer. Victor French had cancer. I'd had a cousin who had breast cancer. Cancer of varying types, yes, but still cancer.

And they had all died.

I started my car and commanded myself to drive like a sane, non-trembling person, and dutifully took the envelope to my nurse practitioner. Once she read through the analysis she set me up for surgery, a lumpectomy, for the next day.

She was both appropriately encouraging and at the same time struck a tone of "we'll hope for the best."

I went back to my house and the thought rolled around and around in my head like a marble in a spray paint can, "I have cancer."

I was living alone in the Sherman Oaks house these days as Jack had moved in with Kelly Van Dyke so I had no one to talk to.

Even if I'd had a roommate this had all happened so fast, I don't know what I would've said. I'd gone from nearly 50 years of not having cancer to having cancer in one day.

Over a span of that kind of time you get used to not having cancer. Not having cancer is your normal. You wake up without cancer, you brush your teeth without cancer, you eat, drive, hang out with friends, do your laundry, run a brush through your hair, pick out a new pair of sunglasses, fall in love, fall out of love, do your taxes – all while not having cancer.

You're the sort of person who doesn't have cancer.

In the space of 24 hours that had changed. I was now the sort of person who had cancer. And tomorrow I was going to be the sort of person who has cancer surgery.

And what then?

Would I be fine? Would I lose a breast? Would my hair fall out? Would I die?

Would I have to wear one of those crappy little gowns with my rear end hanging out the back?

Would I be cold?

Would it hurt?

My mind couldn't crunch through it all.

I just wanted it to go away.

Crisis takes us to our earliest influences. And this was no exception. When things get tough, I often channel my mother's stoicism. You remember Alice Stewart, the force of nature, who'd had six months to live and refused to acknowledge it and went about her daily life as though nothing had changed? I simply decided that I was going to be fine. And with that I went to bed.

Here's the thing about deciding that you're going to live. You're only wrong once. So, really, statistics were on my side.

The following morning I got a ride from a friend to Cedars-Sinai Medical Center, where I checked myself in, filled out all the forms, changed into the ridiculous little gown they give you and was wheeled into x-ray. Here they had to pinpoint the location of the tumor, which involved a procedure that, if it weren't for pain meds, would sound like something they did to people in medieval dungeons. They stuck a needle into the front of my breast and stuck another one through the side in order to help the x-ray – which apparently isn't good at picking out soft tissue like this – identify the location of the malignancy. Then the tech left the needles in me and trotted off for what seemed like hours. While away he ran the x-rays by an oncologist who confirmed the location.

Finally the needles came out and I was wheeled into a waiting area that was like an assembly line. There were women in four or five beds ahead of me waiting for similar procedures. When it was my turn I was given a shot of something to knock me out and not long afterward I was again wide awake, hearing that everything had gone well.

The only thing I had to show for all of this was a Band-Aid over a small incision. It was quick, I felt perfectly fine and later that same day I was at home as though nothing happened.

There was some discomfort but I had my hair, all my parts, and I wasn't dying. My hope was that they'd gotten everything.

A few days later I received a call from the oncologist and this time the news was a bit more unsettling. They needed to go back in and "take out the margins," in other words there was still a possibility that there was cancer tissue present. This time besides taking out more breast tissue, they would also need to take out the lymph nodes under my arms and I was being recommended for radiation.

Again, I hitched a ride to Cedars-Sinai, again checked myself in, and all the rest. However this was no Band-Aid surgery. When I awoke my body was well aware that it had been cut up. This time I opened my eyes in the recovery room feeling sick, woozy and disconnected from reality, attached to an IV and monitors. I was all bandaged up and even with all the pain medication was in a fair amount of discomfort.

For reasons I couldn't quite put together, my hairdresser was looming over me. Had I missed an appointment?

That didn't make sense.

I guess I'd told him about the surgery? I couldn't remember.

I recuperated at Cedars-Sinai for the next three days and because I hadn't told anyone – other than my hairdresser – about the surgery, I didn't have a single visitor. Well, that was on me, wasn't it?

Once I was home though I started telling people about my cancer and the surgeries. Dana Ashbrook brought me flowers, what a sweetheart, the best TV son a TV mother could ask for. So many people wanted to bring me food, I created a system that I thought would be fun. You know how you have lots of people from lots of different parts of your life and many of them never meet each other? Well, I thought this might be a way to fix that. I created a schedule and invited two women over each night, who didn't know each other. The result was a series of evenings most of which were a lot of fun, some were quiet, and some were frankly a little awkward but totally worth it.

It was awfully generous of all those friends to bring food and company to the house. The truth is having chunks and bits of you surgically removed does a number on you. I had to do exercises in the shower to be able to lift my arm again. Having those lymph nodes out was no picnic. I was still in a lot of pain and was nervous about going out and about; getting bumped or jostled was a nightmare.

Meanwhile, as someone in alcohol recovery, I was being cautious about taking pain medication. There are plenty of stories of people such as myself who've discovered a new life away from alcohol only to find themselves hurled back into a dark, addicted place with pain medication following surgery or an accident.

I didn't want to be in pain but even more than that, I didn't ever want to be in the grips of addiction.

With all of this going on, I did return to work at Lantana – very gingerly – and at the same time started a six-week course of radiation. This meant going in five mornings a week, which I scheduled at 8 a.m., since my day at Lantana started at 9:30 am.

The first thing they do in prepping you for radiation therapy is to tattoo a blue dot on the spot where they want to aim the rays. I still have my blue dot; I had no idea at the time that it was permanent.

Each morning started in the waiting area with the same group of people. We'd all scheduled our radiation at the same time and were all doing it over the course of six weeks or more. Over that time you get very friendly, all being in the same boat, and I found radiation to be surprisingly social.

Once in the treatment room I'd lie on a table and they'd lower this long, cone-like object over me, pointing at the blue dot. And then without my feeling anything, they'd blast the tumor area with radiation.

Overall it was piece of cake, I told my nurse practitioner, when she checked in on me. She let me know that, yes, there's nothing to it until about the fifth week, when people tend to start feeling tired. And as always she was right. At about week five, right on schedule, I remember being at work one afternoon and just having to lay my head on my desk. It was as though in a single moment someone had tugged all the stuffing out of me.

With cancer eating at my thoughts, the ongoing pain of the incisions, and being in and out of medical offices, I wanted to fight the bleak urge to feel sorry for myself. I didn't want to just wait around for another phone call from an oncologist, or for the results of another text. I wanted to have some fun. So I began to draw up plans for my 50th birthday party.

I let everyone know that it would be a "bad taste" party and for the invitation I used copies of the ad I'd modeled for back in the late 1950s for a product called "Wate-On," a magic pill that would give skinny girls curves.

The bad taste of my friends and family was on full display on March 1 (a few days after my actual birthday) at the Sons of Norway Lodge in North Hollywood. It was a sea of tackiness and tastelessness. I'd dressed for the occasion in an old blue sequined dress with a purple condom tucked into my bra strap. Jack Nance came with Kelley and he wore a jacket and tie but no pants. Jeanne picked her nose throughout the evening and dropped F-bombs. Russ Tamblyn was one of several winners of the bad taste contest – dressing only a bit more outré than his *Twin Peaks* character. A lot of the cast from *Twin Peaks* was there, including Don Davis, along with friends from throughout my life stretching back to the good old Pasadena Playhouse days.

Among the guests was David Banks, whom I'd known since those Pasadena days. David came with his ex-wife Lydia, who'd been my roommate at the Playhouse. Though divorced, David and Lydia remained friends and had been great parents to their son Jason, who also came to the party. David, who was six foot, three inches of Southern gentleman, is someone I'd seen many times over the years since the Playhouse days – at his wedding with Lydia, at various birthday parties, and even at Jason's birth (I was honored to be his godmother). But David had been out of town a lot over the years. At the Playhouse, while he had studied acting, he'd realized that his take-charge nature was much more suited to managing the chaos backstage.

He'd taken both *Rocky Horror Picture Show* and *Jesus Christ Superstar* from initial runs in Los Angeles to Broadway, a massive undertaking as a stage manager. Later he was road manager for a string of great talents including Bette Midler, the legendary Josephine Baker, and the group Manhattan Transfer.

I'd been surprised to run into him about a month or so prior to my birthday party at an alcohol recovery meeting. I'd not realized that had been something he'd needed nor that sobriety was a step he'd taken. This guy was full of surprises.

At the party David and I danced together – a bit delicate given the pain I was still in. But even so I was surprised at how dancing with him felt. He was a friend – a good friend, an old friend. But something about being this close to him felt warmer than that, more intimate. Which was obviously silly though I couldn't attribute such feelings to alcohol, as all I was drinking that night was bubbly water.

What if I liked David Banks as more than a friend? Okay, stop. Just stop, I thought. I needed to blame these thoughts on something, so I chalked it up to cancer. And the lingering effects of pain medication and radiation. Oh, and menopause. You can blame a lot of things on menopause.

A few minutes later another guy cut in and my dance with David was done. So – that had been weird and I tried to shake it off. But then I looked across the dance floor and there was Jeanne and John Binder. They'd been good friends for years, each having marriages and relationships, their own romantic and sexual ups and downs. And now look at them. Married. And happy.

Okay. So sometimes things happen between friends. Fine. It wasn't going to happen to me. I had other things to focus on.

My contract with the Lodge stipulated that we had to be out by midnight so toward the end a lot of people pitched in to clean up and one of the most fun evenings of my life came to a close.

I got home to Sherman Oaks and at about 1 a.m. my phone rang. It was David Lynch. He was at the Sons of Norway Lodge and the lights were off, the parking lot was empty, the doors were locked, and he was wondering where everyone was. Ha.

A few days the other David called – David Banks – and said he'd been thinking about me (or at least my situation) and asked if there was anything he could do, anything I needed. As a matter of fact there was. The following week there was going to be a conference in the San Fernando Valley for those in alcohol recovery and featured some speakers who had been 50 years sober, an achievement I greatly admired. I really wanted to go but the thing stopping me was that I was still afraid of getting bumped into at such a large conference. It had happened a couple of times now and the pain was pretty bad.

David said he'd be happy to drive me to the conference; he'd wanted to go as well and we both made a joke about it being a date.

The morning of the event he showed up at my door dressed handsomely wearing a straw Panama hat, the second David in my life to have a predilection for such hats. If you'll recall, a Panama hat with a broken brim is what David Lynch wore when he first came to my house in Topanga Canyon. I would learn that this David rarely went anywhere without his.

As we drove to the conference, I had to admit to myself that there was something new between us. What exactly? There was the old comfort of a friendship that goes back for decades, the people such as Stuart Margolin whom we'd both known, the ability at this age to compare aches and pains me with my cancer surgery, him with his back surgeries (he'd had five of them). But that thing that was shimmering invisibly in the air between us didn't really come together for me until we got to the conference and found our seats. When we sat down David simply put his arm around me.

That one gesture was everything.

A wave of relief and comfort passed through me. I had gone through rehab by myself. I'd gone through cancer by myself. I'd faced down all the thoughts of age and mortality that come with a 50th birthday.

And now someone had put an arm around me. Protecting me. Caring for me. Caring about me. It was like I'd been walking around this whole time

carrying a Buick on my back and hadn't even know it. And now I felt it slip
away.

For my entire life, I had splashed into my relationships through the
doorway of sex and alcohol and now, for the first time, I found myself entering
through friendship. And it felt … scary.

That night David drove me home and walked me to the front steps of my
house and I kept telling myself that he was simply being nice, simply being
that Southern gentleman that he was down to his bones. (He'd been born
in Pine Bluff, Arkansas, but claimed New Orleans, where he'd also lived, as
his spiritual home.) On the porch seconds before it happened, I knew it was
going to happen and my heart nearly broke my ribs. And then it did happen.
I kissed him. Really kissed him. With the blood pounding in my neck so hard,
I thought my neighbors would hear it. It was one of those kisses that comes
along maybe once – a kiss that puts everything on the line. A kiss that terrifies
you because it matters.

Something in David's face changed. It couldn't read it but it may have
been shock … or fear or dislike or … well, I didn't know. He left quickly and
I went inside and locked the door and felt like crying. Which was ridiculous,
right? It was only a moment. We'd had our clothes on.

After all the sex I'd had with all the men in all the ways possible, how was
it possible for a kiss to feel like a moon launch?

But I knew why. I knew exactly why.

Most of that sex had meant very little.

I'd crossed a line tonight. In the time that David and I had been friends
people had been born, grown up, and had kids of their own. Real friends are
much harder to come by than friends-with-benefits. And now I'd blown it.
I'd spoiled it. In a moment of weakness and vulnerability and stupid, stupid,
stupid emotion, I'd wrecked a friendship.

It was a long night.

The next day David drove over. He came to make sure everything was
okay between us. He'd rushed off last night feeling like he destroyed a
friendship that was precious to him. His night had been identical to mine

– berating himself, sure that a curtain had come down between us, sure that he'd screwed up.

Well, that sounded familiar.

What a relief. That kiss had not been the end of something; it had been the start. We both now realized that we were ready, both wanted something more than friendship. I asked him if he wanted to stay the night. He did and he never really left. Not long after that we let our family and friends know that we'd moved in together. As I told Jeanne, "If a guy waits to fall for you after rehab, breast cancer, and menopause, he's the one."

***

My final day of radiation was scheduled on April 1. I was wheeled in to have the invisible ray blasted into me and the tech looked at a clipboard and announced that things had changed and that I'd need to come in for another three weeks.

What?

Then he smiled. April Fools. It was indeed my last day and after a series of mammograms over the following months, I was declared cancer free. It was news I was thrilled to share with David.

While my personal life was becoming full of joy and love, friends of mine were going through tough times.

My *Little House* family took a hard blow on May 9, 1991, when Michael Landon went on *The Tonight Show* and talked with Johnny Carson about his diagnosis of pancreatic cancer. What a shock to see him looking so good and apparently feeling fine while the clock on his life was ticking. It took me right back to my mother, who had the same diagnosis in 1972. She had felt well enough to drive herself to the hospital from Yuba City to San Francisco and back. On July 1 Mike died. It was hard to absorb the news that he was gone. Someone like Mike seems so alive that the idea of him being gone doesn't make sense. It's like the idea that the sun isn't going to come up tomorrow. Added to that was the speed at which the cancer took him. It gave you very little time to process it. I was glad to hear that Melissa Gilbert had been able to see him before he passed. They'd had a long and important relationship. I was simply left with a feeling of gratitude – so grateful for everything Mike *had* done for me, for the entire cast and crew and really for a whole generation of kids who grew up watching the kind, loving, strong version of fatherhood he modeled through Charles Ingalls.

Also in May 1991, Jack Nance and Kelly Van Dyke were married. To say it was a tumultuous relationship would be putting it mildly. Jack would eventually learn that while he was away on film locations, she was shooting porn films under the name Nancee Kelly. One of them, which must have come as a cruel slap to her father, was called *The Coach's Daughter*. Remember that her dad, Jerry Van Dyke, was a lead on the TV sitcom *Coach*, a role that earned him four Emmy nominations. Beyond that Kelly hired herself out to perform live stripping and sex acts at stag parties.

None of us knew the extent of what Kelly was up to, but you did get the sense that something wasn't right.

On Monday, November 17, six months after their wedding, I'd just arrived at work at Lantana when I got a phone call from Jack. I knew immediately that something was wrong. He sounded destroyed.

"I need you to come over to the apartment with me," he said.

His apartment? I thought Jack was away somewhere filming a movie.

"What's happened?" I asked, not sure I wanted to know.

Jack had indeed been on a very remote film set shooting the comedy *Meatballs 4*. They were at Bass Lake in the Sierras, which is located just a few miles from the southern entrance of Yosemite National Park. That Sunday night, using the one phone that was available at the camp where they were shooting, Jack had called Kelly and she was a mess, hysterical, talking nonsense, angry, sad, and confused. She kept saying that if he hung up, she'd kill herself.

Outside in the darkness, a storm was whipping up and as Jack tried to talk to Kelly over the growing noise of the wind and the trees, tried to calm her down, there was a crack of lightning – in an instant the power went out and the phone line went dead. Remember, this was before cell phones were common, certainly before texting, social media, or any of the many ways you might get in touch with someone in an emergency. Jack panicked, realizing that from her end it would've sounded like he had hung up.

He grabbed the director, Bob Logan, who raced Jack through the storm in his car on treacherous back roads until they found a pay phone where they got in touch with Madera County Sheriff's Department, who in turn contacted police in Los Angeles.

The local police acted quickly and got to Jack and Kelly's North Hollywood apartment as soon as they could. By the time they arrived, however, she'd already hung herself in a closet.

Jack got the news from the local Sheriff. Someone from the film crew had driven him home to Los Angeles and he'd just gotten into town.

"Will you come to the apartment?" Jack asked. "I don't want to go in by myself."

I couldn't believe what I was hearing. I absolutely ached for him.

I drove out to the apartment and there he was looking like he'd been hit by a semi, the life crushed out of him. I gave him a hug and together we went inside. The police investigation was over; they were gone. The coroner had already taken Kelly's body. The apartment looked as it always had, totally surreal in its ordinariness. Jack just walked around the interior of the place heartbroken and in shock. It seemed unthinkable to him that their furniture, their kitchen things, their lamps, their clothes, their bed – everything was so unchanged when such an act of violence and brutality had erupted within those walls hours before. It was like everything should have exploded. We should be kicking through shambles now instead of this bizarre normality.

Jack found out afterwards a lot of the stuff that she'd been up to without his knowledge and it didn't change much in terms of how he felt about her. He understood addiction too well. Understood how it warps you, changes you, brings out the worst.

Of course one of my big concerns was that this would drive Jack away from sobriety, but he hung in there. Though I have to say it physically aged him; it made him quieter, and he was never quite the same.

Chapter 15

Life Goes On

FINALLY, WE HAVE COME to the happily ever after part. Or at least, that was my frame of mind when on January 19, 1992, I married the tall, handsome, funny, smart, good-hearted David Banks.

We were both pretty short on money just then – as those in the entertainment business tend to be from time to time – so we bootlegged our wedding at an old hotel in Pasadena that had been called the Huntington Hartford Hotel in our student days (known today as The Langham Huntington) and where we'd gone for drinks while at the Playhouse.

Bootlegging worked like this: we invited a group of old Playhouse friends to brunch and had a lovely meal, then stepped outside into the flower garden, had a quick service with my friend Liz Barron, who was now a judge. Then we snapped some pictures – all before we were thrown out/asked to leave.

Actually the staff there was very nice, even after they'd figured out that we'd worked around their wedding party policies and pricing.

David and I enjoyed each other so much – things were easy between us. I think getting married in our 50s meant that we had a lot fewer expectations of each other than we might have had we tried to do this in our twenties. Besides loving spending time together and with friends we each got busy in our own spheres. He had become a partner in a construction firm and I focused on getting work.

Not long after our wedding I landed a recurring role on ABC's groundbreaking series *Life Goes On*. Unfortunately I don't think the show is available on DVD or video on demand now but at the time it was a big deal. Pattie LuPone was the mom of a family in which one of the kids had Down Syndrome. And in that regard it was the first show in which an actor wasn't simply playing a character with Down Syndrome but the actor, Christopher Burke, himself had the condition. John J. O'Connor, television critic of *The New York Times*, termed it "sensitively written, wonderfully cast and beautifully executed . . . . in the admirable family-drama tradition of *The Waltons* and *Family*."

In the string of episodes I appeared in, I played the mother of a daughter with Down Syndrome but where Patti LuPone's character was a patient, supportive mom and a stellar human being, my character was a complete bitch and got into it with Patti. I have to say that I really relished playing a mouthy, unlikeable character for a change. I got a sense of how much fun Alison Arngrim had had playing Nellie Oleson.

Patti was a joy to work with; it's always a pleasure to work with a real pro. She brings firecracker energy and smarts to everything she does. She is probably best known for her performances on Broadway in *Evita*. More recently she was in the news because during a Broadway show she actually took a cell phone away from an audience member. Good for her.

Around this same time I landed a multi-episode gig on the sitcom *Coach* where among other people, I worked with Kelly's dad, Jerry Van Dyke. Of course I didn't mention Jack or Kelly to him, assuming that his daughter's death was still a terrible wound. Somehow though Jerry put two and two together and he asked if he could talk to me. I said of course and we found a quiet corner.

While on camera he often plays a complete dope, Jerry in reality is a sharp guy and in this case was actually pretty intense. He came straight to the point asking what I knew about Kelly and Jack. There was no way I was going to tell him that she'd been doing drugs and had been involved in prostitution and porn films. I just said that Jack loved her very much and was devastated by her death.

Jerry had already made his mind up about the situation and was sure it was all Jack's fault. Poor guy, I could see it from his perspective. What father wouldn't rather pin the blame on someone else? The fact was though that besides her drug addiction, to my mind, it seemed like Kelly had some unresolved mental health issues. On top of that I knew what I knew about Jack and what he'd been through and the kind of person he was.

I did my best to let Jerry know that his daughter, at the very least, had been loved, figuring that that might bring some small measure of comfort.

He appreciated my time but I could see he was furious at Jack and convinced that he'd led Kelly down a path that had ended in suicide. If he truly believed that I could not imagine the kind of anger and sadness he must live with.

Above all though Jerry was a professional. I appeared on *Coach* several times, in a role that I really enjoyed, playing an utter dingbat, and it was the only time that anything about Jack and Kelly came up.

In 1995 at some point, Jack and I got together for lunch. I hadn't seen him much since that day at the apartment. Because we'd stayed in touch by phone I knew he'd suffered a stroke and had spent some time in the hospital. He was out now and seemed to be doing better. He was finding acting jobs now and then but to fill in the income gaps he'd taken a job as a clerk at a motel on Ventura Blvd, which also gave him a place to stay – in one of the motel rooms, which he liked because it was private, small, and contained. It also came with maid service, which he loved – and very much needed. He took the job seriously wearing a suit and tie and he looked very dapper.

As we sat down at the table, he asked if I minded if he ordered a drink and I said that I did mind. Very much. I asked him what was going on.

He sighed and said he'd just woken up one day and just couldn't do it anymore. He walked down to a store and bought a bottle of gin.

I tried to stay in regular touch with Jack after that and I do know that he kept going back to sobriety and would be successful for a few months at a time and then would relapse.

In the summer of 1996 I was contacted about appearing in a short documentary about the filming of *Eraserhead* along with Jack, David Lynch, and Catherine Coulson. We were going to film an interview and some other scenes at AFI, where the stable and old servants' quarters still stood, though largely in ruins now.

Jack asked if I could give him a ride to AFI, which of course I was happy to do. David (my husband in his Panama hat) and I drove to South Pasadena, where he was now living, to pick him up. Jack had moved into an old Mission-style apartment house built, I'm guessing, in the 1920s. It stood on Fair Oaks Avenue across the street from a Winchell's Donuts. It had what novelists might call faded glory. When we walked down the long hallway where he lived, it looked just like something straight out of *Eraserhead* – a long, dark, weirdly narrow hallway with Jack's door being the last one on the left.

Jack met us at the door walking slowly with a cane. Six months prior he'd been in a car accident – he'd been a passenger – and it had messed him up pretty badly. He was also drinking again, heavily I assumed given the bottles here and there about the place, and he looked 20 years older than his actual age.

If you want to see the short documentary, it's included on the recent Criterion re-release of *Eraserhead*. You can see Jack moving with measured, careful steps and speaking slowly, though his dry wit is still intact. In the film you can see us, bathed in sunlight, poking around the stables where we had filmed the cult classic some 25 years earlier. It was great to be reunited with those guys. I think you can tell we're having a good time.

It was the last time I would see Jack. And I suppose if I had to choose a place to spend my last hours with him it would be back there in that special place where we'd first met and had created the characters of Henry and Mary X.

On December 29, 1996, something happened to him, the details of which remain a mystery. All the information I have comes from police reports and a couple he'd befriended in the neighborhood – people who'd stepped in to help Jack take care of himself. They'd do his laundry, give him rides to the store, things like that.

That day they said they saw Jack at lunch and that he had a black eye and wasn't feeling well. The story they said he gave them was that he'd walked over to Winchell's Donuts late the night before and he'd been drinking and he mouthed off to a couple of young Latino guys in the parking lot. One of them, he said, had punched him in the face and had then taken off. The story was that the blow had been especially painful because Jack had been wearing his glasses.

He'd told the couple that he'd be fine, he just needed to nurse his eye.

The next morning they came to check on him and found Jack lying motionless in his Murphy bed. They called the police who pronounced Jack dead and since the coroner listed the cause of death as "subdural hematoma caused by blunt-force trauma," the case was listed as a homicide.

The investigation found that there was no evidence that Jack had gone to Winchell's Donuts that night. None of the employees remembered seeing him there and no one recalled a scuffle or a fight in the parking lot. No one could say they'd seen a couple of Latino guys hanging around outside. There was no evidence that Jack had been wearing his glasses. He rarely wore them anyway and they weren't found at Winchell's nor were they in his home.

The investigation eventually sputtered out. No leads. No suspects. Just a middle-aged guy found with a blood alcohol level of .24 dead in his apartment.

If there is any silver lining to his grim and heartbreaking end, it's that I know how totally delighted Jack would be to know that his death will forever be listed as an unsolved homicide.

Chapter 16
Saving Mr. Banks

WORKING AT LANTANA was in a lot of ways like other office jobs with paperwork to fill out and file, phones to answer, budgets that needed to be stayed within, spreadsheets to analyze and all that. At the same time it was totally unlike the grim, cubicles of slow death I've seen at other businesses. Our office was fun and busy with producers, directors, and actors dropping in almost daily. We devoted a lot of energy to putting on great events for all the companies renting production space. At Thanksgiving we'd set out a big dinner with trimmings galore, at Christmas there was always a big tree and celebration. We also did a lot of fundraising for various causes.

One of my favorite tenants was Larry David, who'd rented a block of six offices as production offices for his show *Curb Your Enthusiasm*. Larry would always complain – with a twinkle in his eye – every time we'd come by the *Curb* offices looking for donations. He'd always spout off with something like "Oh God, if I'd left 20 minutes sooner I could've saved myself twenty bucks!"

One thing you learn about tenants over time are their various quirks and eccentricities, which we always tried to accommodate. In Larry's case, we learned that he hated being in the bathroom with anyone else. For a while if he was in the restroom, which was located down the hall from the *Curb Your Enthusiasm* offices, we'd casually post someone outside the door to keep other people from entering when Larry was in there. Later we solved the issue fully by installing a bathroom in his office.

Knowing of this bathroom phobia came in handy once when I had a chance to audition for a small part on his show as a nurse in a proctologist's office.

Knowing that *Curb* was totally improv – and that the audition would be as well – I prepped by going online and getting the names of as many horrible-sounding medical problems as I could find relating to excrement and the anus.

As I'd expected, for the audition I was simply given the set-up for the scene, which was that Larry had just arrived at the proctologist's office and that he did not want to talk to the nurse about his condition. He would only talk to the doctor. The nurse insists he answer some questions first.

It went something like this:

Nurse: Good morning Mr. David, How are you today?

Larry: I need to talk to the doctor.

Nurse: (pleasantly) Yes, of course…but I need you to answer a few questions first.

Larry: No…

Nurse: Do you notice blood in your stool?

Larry: (aghast) WHAT? No… I –

Nurse: Anything black or mucus-y?

Larry: I want the doctor, please.

Nurse: Hemorrhoids? Anal warts? Pain evacuating your bowels?

Larry: No! Stop! I can't talk to you about this! I want to see –

Nurse: Mr. David! You're behaving childishly.

Larry: Aaagh…please go get –

Nurse: (Leaving) Honestly, what a baby…

I waited outside the door for a minute until the laughter died down and poked my head in the room. Larry was staring at me. The only thing he knew about me was that I worked at Lantana. After a beat he said, "That was good … really good."

I said thank you and went back to the office. Ultimately I didn't get the part but I felt great about my audition. I'd made Larry David laugh.

Around this time I landed a small part in a film called *Slums of Beverly Hills* with Alan Arkin and made a straight-to-video horror film in Romania for Full Moon Entertainment called *Dark Angel: The Ascent*. A little of this and a little of that. But as I headed toward the age of 60 the thing that all women in Hollywood talk about happening very clearly did. The roles became less plentiful.

In 2005 I drove over to Warner Brothers for an audition for the TV show *Cold Case*. And I pulled up to the main gate – I'd been entering through the main gate since the mid-1960s on the crime drama *The F.B.I*. But not anymore. I was directed to a parking lot near a secondary side gate for actors like myself who no longer rated main-gate status. Even with this demotion, I gave it my best and did get the part.

I cannot, however, in all honesty lay the waning of career opportunities at the feet of Hollywood. Just as in the early 1980s, when my drinking got in the way of my pursuit of roles now something else had slowly worked its way into my world which meant spending less and less time on my career.

Something that rehab could not cure. Something I could not control and that would weigh more and more heavily on my heart and ultimately send my life into a crash.

***

After we got married, David and I continued to make our home in Sherman Oaks, otherwise known as the San Fernando Valley. The air there is often unhealthy and David began to notice that on some days he had trouble getting his breath. He'd quit smoking not long after our marriage in early 1992 so he blamed the issue on L.A. smog.

By about 1996 though the problem had grown to the extent that he could no longer fault pollution. Something else was going on. It wasn't asthma and it wasn't an allergy.

David hated going to the doctor so he resisted as long as he could and I didn't pester him about it. I wasn't his mother. He'd go when he was ready. When he finally went they ran him through a battery of tests and the diagnosis that came back wasn't good – emphysema. The doctor suggested that David go on permanent oxygen, meaning he'd have to spend his life with an apparatus that connected his nostrils to an oxygen tank.

David came home and said there was no way in hell he'd ever go on oxygen.

About a year later though, much against his wishes, an oxygen tank showed up at our house. He'd hook himself up when he was at home – but never if we were out, say, shopping or going to dinner with friends.

Within a few years his condition had progressed to the point though that he could no longer maintain his end of the partnership at his construction company. He was in bed more and more of the time. And with the decline in his physical ability, the amount of medications he was prescribed went up and up.

As for income we were doing fine. I'd landed a huge deal with a pharmaceutical company as the face for a two-year campaign for a cancer-related drug called Procrit. At one point I was on a special advertising foldout on the front of *Time* magazine – and on the back cover as well. I was on billboards, on television, all over the place. I heard from friends that they couldn't open a magazine or turn on their TVs without seeing me. The only downside was that my Procrit contract stipulated that during the run of the campaign I couldn't do any other TV or film work. Apparently the drug manufacturer didn't want the face of their ad campaign to run out and land the part of a 60-year-old stripper or brothel madam or something like that.

Career-wise, it was not a good time to be off the market but the income was impossible to turn down. After the Procrit campaign ended, I continued to find parts here and there. I spent a fun and memorable day on *The Office* set. It was pretty simple role. I was a shopper at a Best Buy-type store and I simply had to look over at Rainn Wilson like he was completely bonkers. Not hard to do when he was in character; off camera though he was a sweetie.

David's emphysema steadily worsened to the point that the San Fernando Valley had become unlivable. The air was so frequently polluted that it made the simple act of breathing too difficult to be believed. We both knew it was time to move.

Yes it meant leaving Los Angeles, which had been home for me since the Eisenhower years. But rather than being a difficult decision, as many people have asked, it was in fact immensely simple. We had to find a place that was healthier for David. I couldn't keep going to auditions and chasing parts while watching the guy I loved struggle for his next breath.

I told myself that it didn't mean leaving acting behind. It just meant that I'd find parts as I could. Usually the actual shooting was only a day here and there. I could make it work.

With my family all in Northern California initially I thought we might move to Marin County near my sister Barbara Jean and my brother Lewis, but a friend gave us a tip on a house in Napa. It was a great size, affordable, and was located on a quiet, meandering street called Broadmoor.

I knew the town. Napa had been a favorite wine-country haunt for my parents and in more recent decades for me due to the fact that my niece, Mary, lived there where she was a veterinarian.

To our friends in L.A. the idea that a couple in alcohol recovery would move to wine country was the source of a lot of teasing. Still, the move was exciting. It may be a sign of insanity but I've always loved the challenge of a new start. God knows I'd had enough of them.

We arranged for a moving truck and I spent a month getting all of our stuff organized and packed. Once the truck pulled away from our house in Sherman Oaks, there was no going back. The following day we headed north, David driving one car, me driving the other, each with one of our dogs. That first night we made it as far as Harris Ranch. The next night we were in Napa in the Broadmoor Street house; we inflated an air mattress and slept in the living room. It was like camping and our spirits were high.

At the start there was a flurry of activity and there were times that my life in LA didn't seem so far away. I recruited family and friends in the area to come over for a yard cleanup party and a few days later all my old friends from Lantana happened to be in Napa to celebrate a co-worker's 50th birthday on the Wine Train. It was a real surprise when the chef on the train came out and introduced himself as having been one of the children in Miss Beadle's classroom – as a child he'd been an extra on the show.

It was a novelty too to have family so close, to be able to call Barbara Jean or my brother Lewis and his wife and get together for lunch.

One morning, though, after the hubbub of moving was over, I was staring out through the kitchen window at the trees that overhung a stream just beyond the backyard. David was asleep. He was breathing from his oxygen tank and I'd helped him shovel in the box of pills he had to take each morning, including some pretty serious pain meds. Besides the emphysema, David had crippling back pain. When he'd taken Manhattan Transfer through Europe, he damaged his back multiple times moving heavy equipment from buses to trains to the backs of theaters and so on. He'd had so many surgeries his spine looked like it'd been hacked up by hatchets.

The only sound was the coffee maker sighing and bubbling its way through its morning obligations.

I remember thinking, "What now?"

And not "What am I going to do this morning?" but "What am I going to do with myself here? For the rest of my life?"

What does this life look like?

How would I fill the hours of my day?

Away from auditions and studios. Away from a world I'd lived in for the better part of 50 years.

The answer to that came in large part from David. Being his caregiver was nearly a full time job but that wasn't going to be enough. I looked around my new town for things I could do, ways I could contribute, ways I could meet new faces and make new friends.

I found an alcohol recovery group where I felt comfortable and welcomed. For David, I organized four or five guys to come to our house to host a group meeting. Unfortunately this didn't last as long as I'd hoped as David was gradually losing interest in the world around him as his pain medication was increased.

I became involved in an incredible program for cancer survivors, called Reach for the Stars. It is an annual fashion show that both raises money for The Cancer Wellness Program at the Queen of the Valley Medical Center in Napa and showcases the strength and vitality of those who have been fortunate enough to survive the disease – men, women, and children. Putting on a fashion show can, I suppose, sound like a pretty frivolous thing to do but in this case it's an exercise in confidence-building for cancer survivors. Combating the disease can involve some pretty big changes to your body through surgery, radiation, and chemotherapy. Those who survive often come out on the other side with their self-esteem in tatters, their self-assurance crushed. Learning to walk with poise side by side with fellow survivors down that catwalk and to say to the world (and to yourself) "this is who I am, this is what I've got – hear me roar" is spellbinding and beautiful.

I started to sew again, hitting on the idea of reusing and recycling feedbags as shopping bags. Finding outlets, such as craft fairs, to sell these became a project I enjoyed.

At some point, I took some good advice from a friend who'd been a caregiver, which was that it's important to keep your own inner batteries charged if you're going to be any good at helping your spouse. I fell into a routine of once a week, rain or shine, jumping in the car and driving to the di Rosa Preserve, one of the most electric and innovative collections of modern art I've ever seen. It's located on the former di Rosa estate in the rolling green hills just outside of the town of Napa. I would go out there on my own and over the course of a couple of hours feel my soul get re-fueled among works of art that were thought-provoking, jarring, gorgeous, sexual, and playful.

Most of the works at the di Rosa had been produced in my lifetime from roughly the 1950s through the present. In ways I can't quite put into words, the color-saturated photographs, the pop-culture-inspired sculpture, the arch nudes, seemed to connect to pieces inside of me. Where my parents had come to be known as part of "The Greatest Generation" I'd been part of a pretty amazing generation myself – and I'd known many of its leading lights. Wandering among this collection of artwork, with its LSD color palettes and experimental shapes and textures, was like seeing the music of those days when Hollywood had seemed to me like a college dorm.

Everywhere I went I met people who were very considerate and for the most part found my acting background, when it came up, interesting if not a bit of a curiosity. I got the sense that when people ran into an actor, they had the feeling that you're only there because you've wandered out of your cage and really someone needs to pick you up and take you back to Los Angeles. Occasionally I ran into a person here or there in Napa who was a bit sniffy as though they assumed I was going to be some kind of diva. Hopefully I proved them wrong.

In conversations the question always came up, "So what are you doing now?"

It was a natural, normal thing to ask but a question that increasingly I dreaded.

I didn't want to say, "Nothing – because I'm my husband's caregiver." First of all, it wasn't nothing. It was a tough, demanding job. But it also wouldn't be fair to David. He hadn't asked to become ill. He didn't want to be lying in bed while the world moved on without him.

If our situations were reversed I knew he would take the "in sickness or in health" part of our wedding vows as seriously as I did. That's what you do when you love someone.

I didn't want people to think that I wasn't working because I wasn't good enough to get parts any longer. Or because of my age. Or worse because I was lazy.

And still the question came, "What are you doing now?"

The answer finally came to me.

"I'm retired."

Ugh. How I hated saying those words. Being retired meant "I quit," "I've walked away," "I'm done with all that." And there was no part of me that wanted my career to be over. I was dying to work. I would kill to get a script in my hands, to have a character to tackle, to step into the lights and ugliness of a sound stage, to have a great scene partner like Peter Falk, Jimmy Stewart, Kevin Bacon, Melissa Gilbert, Karen Grassle, Kyle MacLachlan or Michael Landon. Hell, I'd have been happy with Dennis Weaver or Jack Lord.

I missed the cast parties. I missed watching dailies and the crew – those great guys who were like my dad's old friends, guys who liked to tell jokes, work their butts off, and drink beer from a can. I missed hitting my mark and that feeling of my heart beating in my throat just before the director said, "Action."

It all seemed so distant now, as though it had all happened to some other Charlotte whom I had only vaguely known. As time had moved on there were fewer and fewer reminders of the life I'd once lived.

So many people I'd known, loved, and worked with were gone. Victor French, Dabbs Greer, Kevin Hagen, and Mike Landon from *Little House*, Mory Schoolhouse from *Damaged Goods*. Jim Morrison, Jack Nance, David Blue and Mickey Fox from *Human Highway*. Mickey who thought I had a knack for walking away from life's hard knocks unscathed. She once said to me, "Charlotte, I swear, you could fall down a manhole and come up with a set of dishes."

You should see me now, Mickey, I thought. I'm not sure I've got that set of dishes any longer.

Saying the words "I'm retired" filled me with such emptiness and yet it proved a convenient response. It was short and believable even if I didn't want to believe it.

Of course if you're retired, now you're put in the position of looking back on your lifetime of work. I'm not one for looking back, there's something about that that feels so … old. But there was I was faced with "my legacy."

Nothing worse than having legacy pushed in your face.

I was proud of the work I'd done. Well, most of it. If you force me to watch my scenes in *Damaged Goods* or with Elvis in *Speedway*, you will see me go into a full-on cringe. And, okay, it is hard to watch myself in general as I always see ways of improving the performance. Was my voice right in that moment? Could I have given more in that scene? Should I have pulled back in that one? But the question that tore at me was, had I done anything lasting? Anything memorable? If I had, wouldn't I know it? Wouldn't it be obvious?

Well, it wasn't. And I hadn't. And there it was.

I just needed to dive into this quiet life and forget about the past. It was gone. Half the people I'd known were dead.

I needed to be content with hundreds of wonderful photos and lots of good memories. I had been lucky and that needed to be good enough.

It was good enough.

I would sit by David's bed holding his hand as he slept, listening to the sounds of his tortured breathing, and seeing all the pills and the medical apparatus keeping him with me from day to day.

Being forgotten isn't so bad, I told myself. There are far worse things.

***

About this time I started hearing from Alison Arngrim, who'd of course played Nellie Oleson all those years ago. After *Little House* she'd continued to bump around with a great part here and there – including an episode of

The Love Boat. What she had not done – as had so many other actors her age – was to wander around the Hollywood party circuit cashing in her celebrity on endless rounds of free drinks and a million lines of cocaine. All of which are readily available.

Instead since about the late 1980s she'd traveled around the U.S. with various AIDS charities raising awareness of the disease – putting her celebrity to use helping people at churches and meeting halls around the country come to understand what AIDS was and just as importantly was not.

Recently though she'd started emailing me about an entirely different sort of undertaking – a *Little House* reunion event.

"You mean a TV show?" I asked.

"No, it's not a TV show. It's a fan event."

"What's that?"

"It's where a bunch of fans show up and you sign autographs and answer questions, stuff like that," she said.

"Who would do that?"

Meaning who would take time out of their day to show up for something like this? I could picture a large high school gymnasium somewhere with about three people parked in a sea of folding chairs.

Alison made an exasperated noise. "You have no idea do you?"

Apparently not.

Once, a few years prior, a handful of the *Little House* cast had been invited to an event in Sonora, California, where the show had occasionally filmed. It was some kind of cowboy days event – featuring actors and stunt people from various old western movies and TV shows. Alison was there along with Melissa Gilbert and several others. It was a lot of fun but the *Little House* portion of things was pretty small, kind of off to one side of the main proceedings.

Beyond the question of what sort of event Alison was trying to drag me to was the fact that it was in Nebraska.

Beatrice, Nebraska.

I'd never heard of this place and wasn't even sure if a person could get there from here.

But Alison was on a mission. She was after me, after Karen Grassle, Matthew Labyorteaux, Dean Butler, Radames Pera, and others.

When Alison won't let something go eventually everyone just has to freaking give in, which is what happened in this case. After finding someone to look after David for a couple of days, I was on a plane, my first ever trip to Nebraska for Homestead Days, which was sponsored by the U.S. Parks Service. All the cast members in attendance were given a stipend for our time, which Alison said made us all U.S. Parks Service employees. Like Smokey the Bear.

The day of the event a small group of cast members gathered in some kind of small anteroom in the park office outside of the town of Beatrice. God it was fun to see those guys again. Dean Butler was able to make it and was as good-humored and good-natured as always. Karen looked great and as she lived only about a half hour from me now, in Berkeley, we made promises to get together once we both got home. Alison looked so full of vitality and energy and as always turned the moment into a party. Radames – who you may recall was the one member of the Edwards family who did not survive the Mike Landon/Victor French break-up incident – looked handsome and was a pleasure as always to see. The twins who had played baby Carrie – Lindsay and Sidney Greenbush – are both so much fun. Matthew Labyorteaux showed up after we all thought he wouldn't. So there we were hugging, laughing, eating pizza and catching up.

I was kind of disappointed when one of the guys from the Parks Service stuck his head in, said it was time to go. We were having a great time.

As I filed out of the room with Alison, Karen, and the others into the outdoors it occurred to me that I had no idea what came next.

In all likelihood this was when we'd be walking into that big, empty, echoing school gym.

They led us out a side door and down a trail, a wooded and very pretty walkway with trees on either side. Then we stepped into a very large open area, a field really, and it took a moment to process what I was looking at. The hard, clean Nebraska sunlight was really bright and I put my hand to my eyes. It didn't seem possible that the sight before me was real.

For a second, I just stopped.

There were people as far as the eye could see. Seated on the ground looking expectant.

And then as we came into view they went completely nuts – applauding, cheering, standing up, whistling, and shouting.

For us.

The noise was deafening, the emotion coming from them was overwhelming. It was like we were astronauts returned from a lunar landing.

I turned to Alison and said over the thunder, "What's going on?"

"I tried to tell you," she said.

From the stage, where we were headed, came the sounds of the *Little House on the Prairie* theme song. Beginning with those first four hopeful notes of the French horn and then the rest coming in – music filled with faith, energy, and optimism. I've never loved that theme song more.

People were shouting, "We love you!"

As I stepped onto the stage, I felt shaky and stunned. Then came a convulsion of tears. An absolute wall of emotion I didn't know was inside me. After all these years … feeling so forgotten … like the work I'd done, we'd all done, hadn't mattered to anyone …

I looked over at Karen Grassle and she was crying too. Alison was beaming at me with tears glittering in her eyes.

"They love you," Alison said, giving my hand a squeeze.

***

And so as life has always done, it gave me something beautiful and good while at the same time handing me something unbearably difficult and sad.

Every few months of taking care of my beloved David, with his cartons of pills morning, noon and night, with the oxygen canisters and pain meds, was broken up with a visit with my new family – the fans.

The *Little House* fans, known affectionately as Bonnet Heads, gave those of us in the cast a gift – they let us know what the show had meant. And continued to mean.

As I said earlier, back in the '70s when we were filming the episodes we would sometimes see the Nielsen ratings – tiny numbers on a big spread sheet – but that didn't give any indication about how people felt about the show, the impact it was having, or why they watched. Speaking for myself, at the time between staying on top of my lines and the schedule, along with running The Liquid Butterfly and my social life, I had no clue about what the show meant.

Now, by contrast, in too many cases to count I would meet women my age who today watched the show with their grandchildren – it was something that knitted their family generations together. I was meeting hundreds of men and women who came to me, many with tears in their eyes, who said, "I'm a teacher because of you." That's big. That's so big. I still don't know what to do with that except to feel such gratitude. If nothing else, I'm thankful that I was able to take the shame I felt as a girl about my grades in school and turn it into kindness and empathy in the role of Miss Beadle. Which in turn inspired others to want to become the teachers they had never had.

Just as pain and darkness can be a spiral, so too can hope and joy – a spiral motivating people to become their very best.

I felt at the fan events such an outpouring of love for the character and for the show; it seemed like fans wanted something more. Something they could hold on to and keep that somehow connected them to Miss Beadle and to *Little House*.

Back at home in my sewing room, I began eyeing some scraps of cloth and then I looked over at my pile of feed bags that I'd been recycling as re-suable shopping bags and thought, "Hmmmm." The wheels began turning.

I started designing a bag, using squares of fabric – with a quilt-like approach – and when I'd finished I printed an image of Miss Beadle onto a cloth square and glued it on one side held in place with colorful trim. After

I'd made and sold quite a few of these little creations, I dubbed them "Beadle Bags" and over time they've grown larger and more complex in design. This little bag project that I started as a creative outlet became popular. People who attended the *Little House* conventions bought them like crazy and I've always had trouble keeping up with demand. I keep track of proceeds as they come in as I set aside a healthy percentage to help support the Wellness Center and their work with those with cancer.

***

In 2009 I drove David the 40-minute trip north to St. Helena Hospital for a visit with his pain management physician. It was always a bit eerie going there as this was the hospital where my dad had died. And it was a reminder that he had passed out of this life in such an appalling way without any friends or family with him. Somebody to hold his hand. To say 'I love you' one last time.

David's pain had continued to intensify, made worse by his physical deterioration, the result of being now almost entirely bedridden. What an awful downward cycle, one health issue feeding into another. David's doctor said we had reached the limit of what he could legally prescribe and the next best step would be for us to get David into the local hospice program. Once approved for hospice, they'd have the ability to give him morphine, which would be the last frontier in terms of managing his pain.

This shook us both and understandably David was resistant to the idea. We all know what hospice means – it's the start of the closing credits. The acknowledgement that you're not going to get better. This bout of sickness, unlike every other throughout your life, will not end with one day getting out of bed and saying, "Whew, glad that's over." And off you go. And life continues.

Hospice means this is your final illness.

Ultimately, though, as much as he wanted to, it was impossible for David to hold out against the pain and we did get him signed up for hospice. And it was a good thing. They surgically implanted a pain pump in his right side below his ribs. It created a strange lump under his skin, which was the downside. The upside was that the device allowed him to self-administer morphine throughout the day. Now, mind you, it's not like a free-flowing fountain. I had to manually re-activate it, using a remote control, several times a day so that he could give himself doses every few hours but still, it provided a level of pain relief that made him a lot more comfortable.

Besides the medication, hospice came with the help of some truly stellar people including the nurses who visited throughout the week along with the volunteers. One guy, who was one of my favorites – and David's – would come a couple of times a week, bring his guitar, and he and David would talk, joke around, and even sing together. These folks were truly amazing.

A sad part of this level of pain medication was that more and more David was detached from the world around him. He rarely left the house and increasingly he seemed less interested in doing so.

To keep things as lively as possible I set up a television in our bedroom and together we started following the San Francisco Giants. When games came on, we wore team hats and sweatshirts as we ate together and cheered on our guys.

His ability to engage came and went but I did everything I could to bring the world to his bedside. David's son Jason visited as often as possible as well as his sister Paula, making the trip from her home in San Diego. I tried to make sure he had visitors though his interest in socializing became less and less.

One year when his birthday was coming up I contacted all his old friends, all the people he'd worked with that I could find and asked them to send some memory of working with David along with photos, drawings, anything that would cheer him up. I got a huge response, lots of fun memories from old Pasadena Playhouse friends, crew who'd worked with him on Broadway and in Los Angeles. I collected all the materials into a huge, fat binder, created a nice cover, and gave it to him for his birthday. Another time I arranged for him to take a helicopter ride over Napa Valley with a friend of ours.

Nothing I could do though would make him better. It was all a matter of doing our best to manage the slow inevitable.

By early 2012 David's color wasn't good and I could tell something bad was going to happen. I asked the hospice nurse who came three times a week, "How will we know when he fails?"

"There will be signs," she said, with what I can only guess was intentional vagueness.

In the first weeks of that year we had a quiet, personal celebration of our 20th anniversary and we laughed about bootlegging our wedding and about how we'd gotten engaged – he'd hidden my ring in a box of Cracker Jacks. At times like this I was able to take his hand and tell him things like, "I'm going to miss you so much." He didn't react a lot at that point but he indicated that he understood and that he loved me, that he had loved our life together.

We celebrated my birthday on February 27 and almost as a rare gift, his eyes looked good and he was able to sit up. My niece, Mary, brought over a special dinner for us and David ate – he actually had an appetite, which was unusual. I saw that infectious smile of his again, even if it looked a little weary. It was a rare moment of feeling like maybe things weren't so bad.

On the afternoon of the following day something within him abruptly changed. David started to pant, hard, like a dog. The ins and outs coming quickly, like hearts beats, like the ticking of a stopwatch. I will never forget the look on his face, such panic and fear in his eyes as if to say "Is this it?"

I called the hospice nurse and she came over.

"What do I do?" I asked.

Nothing in my life – nothing – had prepared me for this moment.

She said with calm assurance that the thing to do was to increase his dose of morphine; it would relax him.

I now had liquid morphine in a small brown glass bottle, which I could administer with a dropper. Measuring out a small dose, I managed to get some through his chapped lips as he gasped hard for air.

I waited, hoping, praying, pleading silently for the panting to slow down, but nothing changed.

The nurse gathered her things to go, telling me to give him more as needed and reassuring me that it would help. With those instructions and nothing more – what was happening, what to expect – she was gone.

The panting went on and on and on. And on. I gave him more dribbles of liquid morphine but still there was no effect and I didn't want to give him too much for fear I would overdose him.

I made a pot of coffee, preparing to stay up all night with him if that's what it took. I remained there with my dear David as day turned to night, just focused on his breathing, the rapid, shallow intake and output of breath. For all his effort it was crushingly clear he wasn't getting oxygen. He was working 100 times harder for almost nothing in return. I don't remember what I said to him in those hours. I don't remember if I held his hand or stroked his hair or whispered I love you, though I'm sure I must have done all of those things. Somehow my memories are just of darkness and panting and trying somehow to make him hold on. Reaching out with my mind, with every ounce of energy in my own body to hold him here. To keep him here. To make him stay.

At some point around 5 a.m., I went into the kitchen to refill my coffee mug and when I came back, everything was quiet. Quiet in a wrong, excessive way. I moved closer to David. He was unmoving. The panting had stopped. Everything had stopped.

His mouth hung open unmoving.

His chest unmoving.

His eyes staring.

Catastrophic silence.

In a state of shattering fear I ran to the phone and called a neighbor, Judy, who was a crisis nurse. She came right over with a stethoscope and put it to his chest and then his neck.

I knew her words before she spoke them.

"Charlotte, I'm so sorry," she said. "He's gone."

More of that appalling silence.

I had the sickening sense that the floor was about to vanish. I was seconds away, moments away, from an emotional free fall that I must fight because what that crash looked like I didn't want to know. I needed to keep moving.

I pushed tears from my eyes and went to work on the checklist of things that was already forming in my mind. First I called hospice and they sent over the night nurse. She arrived quickly and said, "I'll take care of everything."

She repeated the same procedure with the stethoscope that Judy had gone through and possibly more. I don't know. I didn't want to be in the bedroom any longer. The nurse came out and gently asked what I would like him to be wearing. I told her which zippered jacket and which pair of pants to put him in. She got busy and before I knew it someone from the funeral home had come to take the body.

The body.

Already it didn't feel like David anymore.

That smile that had comforted me. Those arms that had made me feel safe. I was alone again. In a world without him.

The thought sent an arctic numbness through me that was unshakable.

There was so much to do.

I probably picked up the phone ten times before I was physically capable of making the two calls I knew I had to make – heartrending, gut-destroying phone calls to Jason, David and Lydia's son, and to David's sister Paula. Both were obliterated by the news. Both had hoped to see him one more time but the events of the past few hours had come so suddenly there'd been no time.

Paula just sobbed hopelessly and I said to her, "Paula, I need your help. I have to write an obituary and I need you to do it."

I knew that at this moment she would need a job just as badly as I did. Something that would require her to focus and to pull her mind and soul into one piece. Do something for David.

Of course her first draft was 12 pages long. I loved her for that. How can you take a life like his and distill it down to 600 words? How can you begin to do it justice?

Jason was able to get to Napa that afternoon and he was a great help and comfort. Thank God because over the next few days there was so much to do.

The following morning I realized there was an urgent errand that I needed to run and didn't want to do it alone. Jason and I took David's straw Panama hat to the mortuary where his body lay ready for the crematorium. I wasn't sure if I'd made it in time or not. When we arrived I went to the woman at the front desk and suddenly words left me. Without realizing I'd been rehearsing my words once I got there. Oh hell, I'd just say what I needed to say.

"I know this is a strange request," I said, my voice breaking, putting David's hat on the reception counter. "But my husband is here, David Banks, and he never went anywhere without his hat."

I couldn't continue.

The woman asked, just to be certain, if he was being cremated and I nodded. It's all I could do in response. She checked and there was still time for this last gesture.

It seemed like there were many moments like that, saying goodbye in a thousand small ways – getting rid of all the pills, cleaning out the room, giving away this or that memento to family members. Biggest of all though was that it became clear we needed not one but three memorial services, one in Napa, one in Los Angeles, and one in San Diego. I have wonderful memories of each. There was music, laughter, tears, and great, great memories. It was exactly what David would have wished for. And in fact I was so glad that to his dying breath he'd had that fat binder of stories and photos from all those friends and family members. He'd known how much, how widely, how deeply he was loved.

We scattered David's ashes – most of them – in San Diego Bay. But I kept a small amount for one final spot – his spiritual home in New Orleans. A friend was flying there on business and I told him where to go and what to do.

He told me that he got to the corner of St. Peter and Royal, waited for a moment, and reverently let David's remains spill to the street. And when he did so, he heard music. A moment later a brass band appeared from around the corner and marched right through David's ashes.

It happened right on cue.

Once a stage manager, always a stage manager.

***

And then I was home. And home was quiet. Home was David-less. I tried to do all the right things. For a time I went to a grief recovery group and learned that others like me suffered from atrocious guilt that they had overdosed their dying loved ones on morphine. I went to my alcohol recovery meetings and found comfort there too.

But there I was at home one night in the weeks after the memorials, after the friends and family had gone home, and I started crying.

And I couldn't stop.

I cried so hard and for so long I thought I would injure myself. But the sadness inside of me was so big there was no way for it to escape. It didn't want to seep out in teaspoons. This was the kind of sorrow that seemed to want to break out of me all at once like a tank through a chain link fence and if it did, it felt like it would physically tear me apart.

Finally after a few days of this, I didn't know what else to do. I went to a neighbor's house and said, through tears and hiccups, "I don't know what to do. I can't stop crying."

They gave me tight, warm hugs and took me out to dinner. What else can you do?

Within the next couple of days I tried to talk myself into feeling better. I made valiant attempts to tap into my mother's stoicism. I tried to come to terms with the raw hole, like a suppurating wound, in my world left by David's absence.

At times like this, when the stress and bigness of tragedy is so overwhelming, I think that unknowingly we fall into the oldest habits within us, the ones etched into our deepest architecture.

I stopped by a drug store in Napa to pick up a few things for the house and I found myself staring at a display at the end of an aisle. This was a colorful, friendly arrangement of little wine bottles in four-packs. Just sitting there being bright and cheerful.

Didn't I deserve a little brightness and cheerfulness? said an old voice inside me. Not my voice exactly but a voice that was familiar.

Hadn't I been good for the past 27 years?

Could it possibly hurt to dip into a little comfort?

I picked up a bottle and took a long look.

It's not like it was vodka. The alcohol level was like 12 or 13 percent. It was more like pain medication than wine.

And really what's the difference anyway? One you get from a pharmacist in an amber bottle and the other you get from a cheery display next to the sunglasses and pool toys.

I knew that no one would know. Not my alcohol recovery group. Not my family. Not my friends.

I needed this. I had earned this. After everything I'd been through.

Anyone who didn't understand how much I deserved this had no idea what I'd endured.

Said the voice.

And I gently lifted a four-pack from the display and went to the register.

When I got home, the house was silent. That same silence that had come to fill every corner like sand.

I sat down in my living room in front of the television with my little wine bottles, which felt so unfamiliar in my hands, and cracked the screw tops and for the first time since August 16, 1984, felt the sweetness and sting of alcohol cascade like liquid morphine down the back of my throat.

***

Drinking again came with some surprises. A few months later I was in New York City for a few days prior to a *Little House* fan event and I took a stroll down to the Times Square area and decided to help myself to a martini. My first since the Reagan Administration. I seated myself at a bar, ordered the drink and later when I was presented with my bill I nearly spewed. It was

$24! The price of drinks had really gone up in the past 20 years. I felt like Rip Van Winkle.

More than anything though I was surprised by how easy it all was. I was drinking and wasn't falling apart. I wasn't sliding around town drunk. I wasn't grasping for a giant bottle of vodka the moment I opened my eyes in the morning. I wasn't parking my car and finding the doors open and my purse on the sidewalk in the morning. I was totally in control. Of course I had to keep it strictly to myself. Half the people I knew, half the people in my family, including my sister, were in alcohol recovery.

They would all of course tell me this was the wrong thing to do. But I was fine. I just had to keep it to myself and not make a big deal about it. I stopped going to my alcohol recovery meetings three times a week and started just going once. I was quieter than I'd been in the past. But I was going. Everything about my life was working as it should.

I just needed a drink every now and then to get me through this stage, I told myself. I was in grief. My husband had died and I needed some time. I needed a little extra something. Then I'd quit again.

The truth is the best thing I had going for me through all of this were the fans and the support of old friends like Alison Arngrim. She and I would sit beside each other at fan events and autograph shows and she was such a friend and so relentlessly cheerful. It was with her encouragement that I began to think about writing this memoir.

Around this time I'd gotten to know a writer, Andy Demsky, who said to me back in 2009, "Charlotte, I think you have a book in you." And I said, "No, I don't think I do." I truly didn't see a story. Maybe a magazine article or a radio interview – I'd done lots of those. But a book? A book with hundreds of pages? With plot twists? That made you want to read the next page? No.

He was convinced otherwise and we went back and forth like this for several years until finally we met for coffee in 2012 and he gave me a copy of a memoir he'd collaborated on. He said, "See what you think. And if you ever change your mind, let me know."

I took the book home and read it and liked the voice, the style, and the tone and began to think maybe the idea was at the very least worth exploring. We started getting together once a week to map out how my story might take shape. And one theme that kept coming up again and again was alcoholism and alcohol recovery. Hmmm. What was I going to do with that?

Maybe we could write my story without talking about it. Just focus on the career stuff – the *Little House* stories, *Eraserhead*, *Twin Peaks* – keep things light and fun and leave out the addiction part.

I proposed the idea and Andy's eyes went a little vague and he said he'd think it over. What that really meant was that he didn't believe it would work and was too courteous to say so right off the bat. Those of us born and bred on the West Coast often like to take our time saying 'no.' My friend Jeanne, from the East Coast, would've just said, "Charlotte, you're fucking nuts, that'll never work."

Instead he came back a few days later with, "Well let's just keep working and see how all the pieces fit together."

Smooth. He wasn't letting me off the hook nor was he pushing me too hard. Not yet anyway.

In the meantime I was doing a lot of traveling and loving it. I'd gone to England, for the first time since my honeymoon with Tim, for two *Twin Peaks* festivals in London. While in the UK I spent time with friend Barnaby Marriott, a British *Little House* fan who always makes me laugh. We became close friends when he'd visit me in California over the years. Barnaby was with me in the South of France where I got that legendary bear hug I talked of in the opening paragraphs of this book.

In 2014, I went to the 40th anniversary of *Little House* on the Prairie held in the actual Walnut Grove, Minnesota, where the real events of Laura Ingalls Wilder's life had taken place. It was so thrilling to be there with nearly a dozen other cast members and to meet fans who stood in line – in the rain – to meet favorite actors and get autographs and take photos together.

And besides my *Little House* family, thanks to my work on *Gunsmoke*, *Bonanza*, and *The Virginian*, I was now being invited to weekends at Cowboy

Events, where I got to hang out with old actors and stuntmen from those beloved shows. I was even being invited to spend the weekend with Elvis impersonators at an annual event celebrating Elvis Presley because of my scenes in the film *Speedway*.

Beyond all of that I had my other crazy family – the fans of *Twin Peaks*. For something like 10 years now, I'd made the yearly trip to Washington State to do meet-and-greets with fans in North Bend, watch *Twin Peaks* episodes and David Lynch films at the Seattle Art Museum, or just to relax, talk, and laugh at the Salish Lodge with fans and cast members. This is where, over the years, I made so many friends including Brad Dukes, who went on to write the definitive guide to the filming and production of the show called, *Reflections: An Oral History of Twin Peaks*, featuring interviews with nearly all the cast and crew.

In between all of these shows and events I would come home to Napa and I found that I was drinking more. Not because I needed to any longer to staunch my grief but because it's just what I did now. I'd been busy—therefore, I deserved it. I'd worked hard on the book—I deserved it. I'd made a lot of Beadle Bags that day—I deserved it.

Some mornings now I would wake up and could not remember the night before.

One night I was vaguely aware that something bad had happened. There had been thrashing. And pain and then I fell back to sleep. In the morning I woke on the floor with horrible bruises all up and down my arm, the result of falling out of bed drunk in the night.

I stumbled to the bathroom and in harsh morning light examined the damage in the mirror. With a rising sense of horror I realized that this was just the beginning. I wasn't 25 anymore. I was in my 70s and next time I fell, I could break my arm. Break a hip. Snap my neck.

It hadn't taken long to get right back where I was in 1984.

That's how addiction works. It's never over. It never goes away. It never gives up.

I knew I needed help. And I would always need help.

My first call was to someone in my alcohol recovery group in Napa whom I'd come to rely on. I told her everything. Absolutely everything.

She wasn't shocked or sickened and she didn't judge. She'd been through this too. Her response was that I needed to first to make things right – to tell people who I'd been lying to that I'd been lying.

So. That's never easy. Looking people in the eye who've trusted you and saying you've been a lying sack of crap.

The thought of it is humiliating and crushing.

Still, I knew I had to do it if I was going to have any shot at getting healthy.

I called my sister Barbara Jean, who'd been sober almost as long as I had. She too was supportive and full of strength and optimism.

At my next coffee meeting with Andy I took his hand and said with tears in my eyes, "I've been lying to you."

When he heard me out he gave me a hug and said how much he admired my courage and that now maybe we could move forward with the book in a totally honest, authentic, nothing-held-back way – in other words to tell the truth. About everything.

And that's what I've tried to do here.

My goal has not been to shock or to be salacious or to name-drop. This is simply my life in all its many parts. Good, bad, and in between. I wish I had done some things differently. I wish to God that I'd stayed sober! Damn it! I was alcohol-free for 27 years and then I completely blew it. I am so grateful to my alcohol recovery group here in Napa. I went back to my next meeting and frankly I was scared. I thought they'd be scandalized, sickened, and judge-y. But there was nothing else I could do other than to face up to it. I did the only thing I knew how to do – just spill everything. And they were great. If anything I think a few of them were shaken up. If this could happen to someone with nearly 30 years of sobriety, it could happen to anyone in that room. If anything the strength and support we give each other grew in importance.

The result, for me, was total relief.

Alcohol is a weight in my case. And both times that I've let it go, it's like a sack of cannonballs has fallen off my shoulders.

I committed to going to 90 group meetings in 90 days, just as I had the first time after getting out of the program at New Beginnings. Only this time at 73 years of age I had come to a new-new beginning.

Does it ever end?

***

In late-ish 2014 I started to hear exciting rumblings and whisperings and gossip from friends in the entertainment business and from online news sources that David Lynch and the network Showtime were talking about filming a 9-episode reboot of *Twin Peaks*. Well that was unexpected. Then I heard about possible reboots of the shows *Full House* and *Coach*. All this combined with the fact that a Clinton and a Bush were both now vying for the White House and I thought, "Whoa – here come the '90s again."

On Tuesday, November 11 my phone rang. It was an assistant of David's who asked me to hold the line, which I did, rather too aware of the pulse beginning to roar in my neck and wrists.

"Charlotte!" came his brassy, joyful voice.

"Hi David."

"Are you ready to go back to work?" he fairly shouted.

Always.

Always.

Always.

Epilogue

It's October 2015 and I'm packing for a few days. Tomorrow I'll fly to Seattle, and then will drive out to Snoqualmie to do some filming for the new version of *Twin Peaks*, now slated for a 2017 debut. I've signed a nondisclosure agreement so I can't discuss anything with anyone.

After that phone call with David things fell apart between him and Showtime – sounded like a money issue. David tweeted that he was disappointed that he wouldn't get the chance to return to the world of *Twin Peaks*. So those of us in the cast banded together and started a Facebook page to save *Twin Peaks*.

We hoped that if enough fans showed their support, it might change things for the better.

There was some talk of Showtime producing *Twin Peaks* without David, which was beyond unthinkable and spurred the creation of a video in which members of the original cast all weighed in on the idea of what *Twin Peaks* without David would be like. In the video, which got nearly half a million views on YouTube, cast members such as Sheryl Lee, who was Laura Palmer said, "Twin Peaks without David Lynch ... is like a girl without a secret." Mädchen Amick said, "Twin Peaks without David Lynch ... is like a waitress without her uniform." Catherine Coulson, in a grainy phone video, was filmed saying, "Twin Peaks without David Lynch ... is like a log without its bark." I was quoted as saying, "Twin Peaks without David Lynch ... is like Abbott without Costello."

Maybe it was the surge in fan support that helped, who knows, but not long after, whatever differences had been in play were patched up. And now the reboot is back on and the original nine episodes are extended to even more.

And so, as Shakespeare wrote 500 years ago, once more into the breach.

I'm going back to *Twin Peaks* and cannot wait to see everyone again. Dana Ashbrook and I have been emailing again and I've been in touch with Kimmy Roberts and others.

When I am under those lights again, with the camera pointed at me, and David giving me his usual look of focus and patience, I will likely be petrified.

And yet, there's nowhere else in the universe I would rather be.

So. On the personal-life front, don't be shocked and judge-y, okay? But I have reconnected with an old friend. Michael Santos is a sweet, loving, patient, kind, good-looking guy whose entire life has been spent outside of entertainment. He's far more interested in meteorites and astronomy than in residuals and scripts and Hollywood gossip. But he loves the Giants, so he gets it. And we have a great time together.

Remember the name of that show from the '90s in which I played a total bitch? *Life Goes On*? That's what happens if you're lucky.

And I've been lucky. I should have died in the 1950s when as a careless teenager I flew over a highway embankment and through a billboard.

Then I should have bit the big one again in the 1960s when I swallowed God-knows-how-many tablets of Miltown when I wanted to escape all my crimes against Tim and our marriage.

I should by any account have expired of liver failure in 1984 when I was living with – and drinking with – Jack Nance in Los Angeles. Cancer could have taken me. Hells Bells, Walt Disney himself should have personally drowned me for smoking on the Jungle Ride.

Yet here I am staring down my 75th birthday with nearly everyone on the planet – who remembers such things – remembering me as Miss Beadle from *Little House on the Prairie*.

I'm happy to say that I'm still good friends with my two former husbands, Tim Considine and Jordan Hahn, and with nearly every guy I've had some type of fling with. I'm proud of that. It's a lot of bridges that didn't get burned. To me it represents friendship, conviviality, cutting some slack, and in some cases full-on forgiveness – the best parts of being human.

Every day I am blessed by my many families. My *Little House* family, who are so kind, thoughtful, and loyal and who've passed their love of the show onto their children and grandchildren. My *Twin Peaks* family who are full of friendship, laughter, and a dark and beautiful love for all things David Lynchian. My Pasadena Playhouse family including Liz Barron, Lydia DiVincenzo, Stuart Margolin, Sig Haig, Josh Bryant and many others who are now scattered all over the world and will always have a place in my heart. My alcohol recovery family, fellow soldiers in this fight, who are there everywhere I go and support me, listen to me, and help me pull through. And of course there's my actual family – my brother Lewis and sister Barbara Jean and my ten nieces and nephews who are like my kids too. I'm blessed by everyone who came into my life through David Banks, such as Jason, and now with Michael Santos and his children.

At the beginning of this book I said that after all this I hoped you would find some portion of what you loved in the Miss Beadle character somewhere in me. That's a tall order – I get that.

But in both Eva Beadle and Charlotte Stewart I believe there is hope, tenacity, empathy, patience, and love.

I don't have Eva Beadle's wide-eyed innocence. There's been way too much sex, drugs, and rock-n-roll in my life to pretend any of that. But after everything I've seen and been through, I still have her sense of wonder in the universe and belief in the goodness of people.

If you don't see a lot of Miss Beadle in me, I'd love for you to see some of Betty Briggs: the eternal optimist in spite of everything.

And as for Mary X in *Eraserhead*. You'll have to ask David Lynch what happened with her. But in her defense Mary X did try to hang in there under some pretty horrible circumstances. And we've all been there.

As for any other characters, we'll see. David Lynch is still kicking around. Neil Young could still pull another movie out of his battered hat. Or some as yet unknown writer-director could come along and dazzle us all with a film or a TV show we'll never forget.

I think I still have a few characters left in me.

Acknowledgments

I COULD NOT HAVE ATTEMPTED such an undertaking without the ass kicking of my writing partner, Andy Demsky, who nudged, pushed, pulled, and otherwise rattled my brain for tidbits of the adventures that made up my life. I probably wouldn't have survived at all without the support of friends like Alison Arngrim, Jeanne Field, John Binder, Ken Rose, David Lynch, Jack Nance, Elayne Lieberman, Josh Bryant, Joel Bernstien, Liz Baron, Shirley Dubin, Maggi Kelley, Lydia DiVincenzo, Karen Grassle, Maxine Jacobs, Aleah Koury, Rob and D'Ann Lindley, Barnaby Marriott, Neil Young, Elliot Roberts, Trip Friendly, Rebecca Friendly, Dalana Bettoli, Paul Valenti, Brandon Kjar, Jan and George Blevins, my dear Michael Santos, and my entire family of siblings, nieces, nephews, cousins and in-laws.

May God bless you all.

—Charlotte Stewart

This memoir is Charlotte's story from her perspective. If you happened to be around for any of it, A) I'm extremely jealous because you were likely having a great time and B) you may have an interpretation of events at variance from hers as to how things went. That's how memory works. Especially after the passage of 30, 40, or 50 years memory can become the dance-remix version of reality. In the case of this memoir, fortunately, we were kept pretty well plugged into actual history by Charlotte's daily calendar books which we have going all the way back to the early 1960s. In addition we were aided by archival newspaper and magazine stories both online and in Charlotte's records, her freakishly good memory, and various sources such as IMDB.com (the pro version, because we're spendy like that). We also owe a debt to several people who offered up a lot of time to help stir the memory cauldron. Jeanne Field met with me – once I found her house way up an L.A. canyon – and talked for several hours about her long friendship with Charlotte and their many escapades together. Then she and her husband, John Binder, fed me dinner. A classy move. Catherine Coulson told me she only had 10 minutes when I called in July of 2015 and then went on to talk for more than an hour. She met with me the next day in Ashland, Oregon, following her afternoon performance in *Guys and Dolls* at the Oregon Shakespeare Festival, and spoke for another hour or so. I adored her and was crushed when she died just a few months later. Delana Bettoli called and emailed with some engaging and thoughtful insights and details about rooming with Charlotte during the days of The Liquid Butterfly era. Alison Arngrim agreed to a phone call and talked for three of the most entertaining hours of my life about Little House, Hollywood, child actors, sex addiction (not hers), France, fan events, and quite a few other things that deserve to be edited into a podcast. Then she called several more times after reading the manuscript and offered writing tips, edits, ideas for book promotion, and more solid-gold help. A big thank you goes to my Napa posse who read the manuscript and offered thoughtful and thought-provoking questions, comments, and analysis: Mechele Small Haggard, Kate Scudero, Dan Scudero, Shelley Surh, Mike Dearborn, and Ann Dearborn. A massive thank-you goes to three people who meticulously reviewed a penultimate draft and helped us get the grammar, spelling, and wording cleaned up – Jeanne Field, Robert Schoonover, and Katy Howard (whom I am fortunate to call the love of my life). Finally, I enjoyed a delightful lunch on a rainy day in Napa with Charlotte and her sister, Barbara Jean, talking about great Stewart family stories. All of this – plus the countless joyful hours I spent with Charlotte herself – have shaped, enriched, and enlivened both my life and the story that exists within these pages. If you ever get the chance to write a book with Charlotte Stewart, do so; it comes with my highest recommendation.

—Andy Demsky

Index

CPSIA information can be obtained at www.ICGtesting.com
Printed in the USA
LVOW10s1740280716

498174LV00020B/862/P